Carl Engel

Musica Myths and Facts

Vol. I

Carl Engel

Musica Myths and Facts
Vol. I

ISBN/EAN: 9783337084752

Printed in Europe, USA, Canada, Australia, Japan

Cover: Foto ©Thomas Meinert / pixelio.de

More available books at **www.hansebooks.com**

MUSICAL MYTHS AND FACTS

BY

CARL ENGEL.

IN TWO VOLUMES.—VOL. I.

LONDON:
NOVELLO, EWER & CO.,
1, BERNERS STREET (W.), AND 80 & 81, QUEEN STREET, CHEAPSIDE (E.C.)
NEW YORK: J. L. PETERS, 843, BROADWAY.

MDCCCLXXVI.

[*All rights reserved.*

FACULTY OF MUSIC

UNIVERSITY OF TORONTO

NOVELLO, EWER AND CO.,
TYPOGRAPHICAL MUSIC AND GENERAL PRINTERS,
1, BERNERS STREET, LONDON.

PREFACE.

An idealized portrait of Beethoven, representing him as, in the opinion of many of his admirers, he must have looked in his moments of inspiration, would undoubtedly have made a handsomer frontispiece to this little work, than his figure roughly sketched by an artist who happened to see the composer rambling through the fields in the vicinity of Vienna.

The faithful sketch from life, however, indicates precisely the chief object of the present contribution to musical literature, which is simply to set forth the truth.

Whatever may be the short-comings of the essays, they will be of some use should they impress upon musical pedants the truth of Göthe's dictum:

"Grau, theurer Freund, ist alle Theorie,
Und grün des Lebens goldner Baum."

For the sake of correctness, one or two statements occurring in this volume require a word of explanation.

On page 5, the comprehensive 'Encyclopædia of Music, by J. W. Moore, Boston, United States, 1854, should perhaps not have been left unnoticed; it is, however, too superficial a compilation to be of essential use for reference. Dr. Stainer's 'Dictionary of Musical Terms' was not published until the sheet containing page 5 had gone through the press.

The poem, on page 175, ascribed to Shakespeare, "If music and sweet poetry agree," is by some recent inquirers claimed for Richard Barnfield, a contemporary of Shakespeare.

On page 218, *Sovter Liedekens*, the title of a Dutch book published in the year 1556, is incorrectly translated. *Sovter*, an obsolete Dutch word, means "Psalter," just like the English *Sauter* mentioned in Halliwell's 'Dictionary of Archaic and Provincial Words.' *Liedekens* should have been rendered "Little Songs."

In Volume II., the compositions of Henry Purcell noticed on page 202 form only a small portion of the works of this distinguished English musician. The Prospectus issued by the 'Purcell Society,' which has recently been founded for the purpose of publishing all his works, enumerates forty-five Operas and Dramas, besides many Odes, Hymns, Anthems, and other sacred music, instrumental pieces, &c., most of which exist only in manuscript, and which ought long since to have been in the hands of the lovers of music.

Should the reader disapprove of the easy tone in which the Myths are told, he will perhaps derive some satisfaction from the carefulness with which I have endeavoured to state the Facts.

CARL ENGEL.

Kensington.

CONTENTS OF VOLUME I.

	PAGE
A MUSICAL LIBRARY ...	1
ELSASS-LOTHRINGEN ...	8
MUSIC AND ETHNOLOGY ...	23
COLLECTIONS OF MUSICAL INSTRUMENTS ...	32
MUSICAL MYTHS AND FOLK-LORE ...	74

	PAGE		PAGE
Curious Coincidences ...	77	The Wild Huntsman ...	85
Hindu Traditions ...	79	The Bold German Baron	87
Celestial Quarrels ...	80	Prophetic Calls of Birds	89
Al-Farabi ...	82	Whistling ...	91
Trusty Ferdinand ...	84		

	PAGE
THE STUDIES OF OUR GREAT COMPOSERS ...	94
SUPERSTITIONS CONCERNING BELLS ...	129

	PAGE		PAGE
Protective Bell-ringing	130	The Church Bells banishing the Mountain Dwarfs ...	137
Significant Sounds of Bells ...	131		
Baptised Bells ...	134	The Expulsion of Paganism in Sweden ...	139
Inscriptions on Church Bells ...	136		

	PAGE
CURIOSITIES IN MUSICAL LITERATURE ...	141
THE ENGLISH INSTRUMENTALISTS ...	166

Sacred Songs of Christian ...

A MUSICAL LIBRARY.

IF we cast a retrospective glance at the cultivation of music in England during the last twenty or thirty years, we cannot but be struck with the extraordinary progress which, during this short period, has been made in the diffusion of musical knowledge. The prosperity of England facilitates grand and expensive performances of the best musical works, and is continually drawing the most accomplished artists from all parts of the world to this country. The foreign musicians, in combination with some distinguished native talent, have achieved so much, that there are now, perhaps, more excellent performances of excellent music to be heard in England than in any other country.

Taking these facts into consideration, it appears surprising that England does not yet possess a musical library adequate to the wealth and love for music of the nation. True, there is in the British Museum a musical library, the catalogue of which comprises above one hundred thick folio volumes; but anyone expecting to find in this library the necessary aids to the study of some particular branch of music is almost sure to be disappointed. The plan observed in the construction of the catalogue is the same as that of the new General Catalogue of the Library in the British Museum. The titles of the works are written on slips of thin paper, and fastened, at a considerable distance from each other, down the pages, so that space is reserved for future entries. The musical catalogue contains only two entries upon the one side of a leaf and three upon the other. Each volume has about one hundred and ten leaves. The whole catalogue contains about 60,000 titles of musical compositions and literary works on the subject of music. The British Museum possesses, besides, a collection of musical compositions and treatises in manuscript, of which a small catalogue was printed in the year 1842. It contains about 250 different works, some of which are valuable.

Even a hasty inspection of the written catalogue must convince the student that it contains principally entries of compositions possessing no value whatever. Every quadrille, ballad, and polka which has been published in England during the last fifty years appears to have a place here, and occupies just as ample space as Gluck's 'Alceste,' or Burney's 'History of Music.' This is perhaps unavoidable. If works of merit only were to find admission, who would be competent to draw the line between these and such as ought to be rejected? In no other art, perhaps, do the opinions of connoisseurs respecting the merit of any work differ so much as in music. Since music appeals more directly and more exclusively to the heart than other arts, its beauties are less capable of demonstration, and, in fact, do not exist for those who have no feeling for them. There are even at the present day musicians who cannot appreciate the compositions of J. Sebastian Bach. Forkel, the well-known musical historian, has written a long dissertation, in which he endeavours to prove that Gluck's operas are execrable.* Again, among the adherents of a certain modern school despising distinctness of form and melody may be found men who speak with enthusiasm of the works of Handel, Gluck, Mozart, and other classical composers, although these works are especially characterised by clearness of form and melodious expression. Besides, it must be borne in mind that even our classical composers have now and then produced works of inferior merit, which are nevertheless interesting, inasmuch as they afford us an insight into the gradual development of their powers.

In short, in a musical library for the use of a nation, every musical composition which has been published ought necessarily to be included. In the Musical Library of the British Museum it unfortunately happens, however, that many of those works are wanting which are almost univer-

---

* *Vide* 'Musikalisch-Kritische Bibliothek,' Band I., Gotha, 1778.

sally acknowledged to be of importance. Indeed, it would require far less space to enumerate the works of this kind which it contains than those which it does not, but ought to, contain.

Again, the student must be prepared for disappointment, should he have to consult any of our scientific treatises on music. However, there may be more works relating to the science of music in the Library of the British Museum than would appear from the catalogue of music. Several have evidently been entered in the new General Catalogue. Would it not be advisable to have all the books relating to music entered in the musical catalogue? Even the most important dissertations on musical subjects which are found in various scientific works might with advantage be noticed in this catalogue. Take, for instance, the essays in the 'Asiatic Researches,' in the works of Sir W. Jones and Sir W. Ouseley, in 'Description de l'Egypte,' in the 'Philosophical Transactions.'

Thus much respecting the Musical Library in the British Museum. Let us now consider how a national musical library ought to be constituted. Premising that it is intended as much for the use of musical people who resort to it for reference, as for those who are engaged in a continued study of some particular branch of the art, the following kinds of works ought to form, it would appear, the basis of its constitution.

1. *The Scores of the Classical Operas, Oratorios, and similar Vocal Compositions, with Orchestral Accompaniments.*—Many of these scores have not appeared in print, but are obtainable in carefully revised manuscript copies.

2. *The Scores of Symphonies, Overtures, and similar Orchestral Compositions.*—The editions which have been revised by the composers themselves are the most desirable. The same remark applies to the scores of operas, oratorios, etc.

3. *Vocal Music in Score.*—The sacred compositions *Alla Cappella*, and the madrigals of the old Flemish, Italian, and other continental schools, as well as those of the celebrated old English composers. The choruses of the Greek Church in Russia, etc.

4. *Quartets, Quintets, and similar Compositions in Score.*—The study of these works of our great masters is so essential to the musician, that special care should be taken to secure the best editions. The classical trios for pianoforte, violin, and violoncello, and some other compositions of this kind, originally published in parts, have more recently been issued in score. The latter editions are greatly preferable to those in which the part for each instrument is only printed separately. The same remark applies to the concertos of Mozart, Beethoven, and other masters, which have been published with the orchestral accompaniment in score, as well as with the orchestral accompaniment arranged for the pianoforte or for some other instruments.

5. *Sonatas, Fantasias, Fugues, etc.*—Of all the classical works composed for a single instrument, the original editions, generally revised by the composers themselves, are indispensable. Besides these, the most important subsequent editions of the same works would be required. Beethoven's pianoforte sonatas, for instance, have been re-edited by several eminent pianists. It is instructive to examine the readings of these musicians, which differ in many points from each other.

6. *Arrangements.*—Those of operas, oratorios, masses, and other elaborate compositions with orchestral accompaniment, must necessarily be confined to the instrumental portion, otherwise they are useless either for study or reference. Those arrangements are greatly preferable which have been made by the composers themselves, or under their superintendence.

7. *National Music.*—All the collections of national songs and dances which have been published in different countries. The advantage which the musician might derive from a careful study of them is not yet so fully appreciated as it deserves; but it would probably soon be better understood, if these treasures were made more easily accessible.

8. *Books of Instruction for Vocal and Instrumental Practice.*—The best books for every instrument, as well as for the voice, which have been published in different countries and languages.

9. *Works on the Theory and History of Music.*—All the standard works ought to be found in the library, not only in the languages in which they were originally written, but also in translations, if any such exist. Many of the latter are valuable, on account of the explanations and other additions by the translators. This is, for instance, the case with some English books which have been translated into German; as Brown's 'Dissertation on the Rise, Union, and Power of Music,' translated by Eschenburg; 'Handel's Life,' by Mainwaring, translated by Mattheson, etc. It need scarcely be added that the biographies of celebrated musicians ought also to be included among the desirable requisites.

10. *Works on Sciences intimately connected with the Theory of Music.*—Treatises on acoustics, on the construction of musical instruments, on æsthetics, etc.

11. *Musical Journals.*—All the principal ones published in different countries and languages. To these might advantageously be added the most important literary journals containing critical and other dissertations on music.

12. *Dictionaries, Catalogues, etc.*—The English language possesses no musical dictionary, technical, biographical, or bibliographical, similar to the French and German works by Fétis, Schilling, Gerber, Koch, Rousseau, and others, which are indispensable for the library. With these may be classed the useful works on the Literature of Music compiled by Forkel, Lichtenthal, and Becker, as well as Hofmeister's comprehensive 'Handbuch der musikalischen Literatur.' The collection of catalogues should comprise all those of the principal public musical libraries on the Continent and in England; those of large and valuable private libraries, several of which have appeared in print,—as, for instance, Kiesewetter's 'Sammlung alter Musik,' Becker's 'Tonwerke des XVI. und XVII. Jahrhunderts,' and others; those of the principal music-publishers, and those of important musical libraries which have been disposed of at public auctions.

There is no necessity for extending this list any further, as it will suffice to indicate the plan which, in my opinion, ought to be pursued in the formation of a national musical library. I shall therefore only observe further that there are, besides the above mentioned, several kinds of works which can scarcely be considered as of secondary importance, such as musical travels, novels, and entertaining as well as instructive musical essays; librettos of operas, and the poetry of other elaborate vocal compositions; drawings illustrating the construction of musical instruments,—as, for instance, of the most celebrated organs, of the various improvements in the pianoforte, etc; engravings from the best portraits of celebrated musicians; faithful sketches from sculptures and paintings of nations of antiquity in which musical instruments and performances are represented, etc.

There remains yet another point which requires a moment's consideration,—namely, the daily increasing difficulty of forming such a library as has just been planned. The interest in the study of classical works relating to music is no longer confined to the professional musician, but is spreading among amateurs and men of science. Their libraries now absorb many of the old and scarce works which formerly were almost exclusively in the hands of musicians. Moreover, the English colonies have already drawn upon our limited supply of the old standard works, and there is every reason to suppose that the demand for them will continue to increase. Many of these works have evidently been published in an edition of only a small number of copies. Still it is not likely that they will be republished. In a few instances where a new edition has been made, it has not apparently affected the price of the original edition, because the latter is justly considered preferable. To note one instance: the new edition of Hawkins' 'History of Music' has not lessened the value of the first edition, the price of which is still, as formerly, on a par with the price of Burney's 'History of Music' of which no new edition has been published. About ten years ago it was possible to procure the original scores of our old classical operas, and other works of the kind, at half the price which they fetch now, and there is a probability that they will become every year more expensive. Indeed, whatever may be the intrinsic value of any such work, the circumstance of its being old and scarce seems sufficient, at least in England, to ensure it a high price.

If, therefore, the acquisition of such a national musical library as I have endeavoured to sketch is thought desirable, no time ought to be lost in commencing its formation.

ELSASS-LOTHRINGEN.

WHATEVER may be thought of the value of the well-known aphorism, *"Let me make a nation's Ballads; who will may make their Laws"*—it can hardly be denied that through the popular songs of a country we ascertain to a great extent the characteristic views and sentiments of the inhabitants.

The villagers of Alsace recently may not have been in the mood for singing their old cherished songs; otherwise the German soldiers must have been struck by recognizing among the ditties old familiar friends slightly disguised by the peculiar dialect of the district. Take, for instance, the cradle songs, or initiatory lessons as they might be called. Here is one as sung by the countrywomen of Alsace:—

"Schlof, Kindele, schlof!
Dien Vadder hied die Schof,
Dien Muedder hied die Lämmele,
Drum schlof du guldi's Engele;
Schlof, Kindele, schlof!"

(Sleep, darling, sleep!
Thy father tends the sheep,
Thy mother tends the lambkins dear,
Sleep then, my precious angel, here;
Sleep, darling, sleep!)

And another:—

"Aie Bubbaie was rasselt im Stroh?
D'Gänsle gehn baarfuesz, sie han keen Schueh;
Der Schuester het's Leder, keen Leiste derzue."

(Hush-a-bye baby, what rustles the straw?
Poor goslings go barefoot, they have not a shoe;
The souter has leather, no last that will do.)

Making allowance for the pronunciation of the words, which sounds odd to the North-German ear, these are the identical lullabies with which the mothers in the villages near Hanover sing their babies to sleep. Some of the old ballads, legends, fairy-tales, and proverbs, popular in Alsace, are current throughout almost the whole of Germany. Then we have the old-fashioned invitation to the wedding feast, stiff and formal, as it is observed especially in Lower Alsace, and likewise in the villages of Hanover and other districts of North Germany. In Alsace the weddings take place on a Tuesday, because, they say, we read in the Bible: "And the third day there was a marriage in Cana of Galilee." In sacred poetry Alsace can pride herself upon having produced some of the most distinguished German writers. The oldest known of these is Ottfried von Weissenburg, who lived about the middle of the ninth century. Gottfried von Strassburg, in the beginning of the thirteenth century, was renowned as a writer of hymns as well as of *Minnelieder*. The first sacred songs of a popular character recorded in Alsace date from about the middle of the fourteenth century. But it is especially since the time of the Reformation that this branch of sacred poetry has been much cultivated here as in other parts of Germany. The authors of sacred poetry were generally either theologians or musicians. The latter often composed the words as well as the airs. Music and poetry were not cultivated so separately as is the case in our day. Of the musicians, deserves to be mentioned Wolfgang Dachstein, who, in the beginning of the sixteenth century, was organist in Strassburg, first at the Cathedral, and afterwards, when he become a Protestant, at the Thomas Church. His hymn *An Wasserflüssen Babylon* is still to be found in most chorale books of the German Protestants.

The secular songs of the villagers are not all in the peculiar dialect of the province. Some are in High German, and there are several in which High German is mixed with the dialect. Occasionally we meet with a word which has become obsolete in other German districts; for instance, *Pfiffholder* for "Schmetterling," Low German "Buttervogel," English "butterfly;" *Irten* (Old German *Urt, Uirthe*) for "Zeche," English "score." Of the lyric poets of the present century, Hebel is, perhaps, the most popular in Alsace.

His "Allemannische Gedichte" used to be sung especially in the southern district, which, until recently, formed the French department of Haut-Rhin. The people of this district have a less soft pronunciation than those of Bas-Rhin.

As regards the popular songs of Lorraine, those which have been collected and published are, almost all of them, from the French districts of the province.

The Société d'Archéologie Lorraine has published a collection, entitled 'Poésies populaires de la Lorraine, Nancy, 1854;' and R. Grosjean, organist of the Cathedral of Saint-Dié-des-Vosges, has edited a number of old Christmas Carols, arranged for the organ or harmonium, and published under the title of 'Air des Noëls Lorrains, Saint-Dié, 1862.' In the German villages we meet with songs in a peculiar dialect, not unfrequently interspersed with French words. The following example is from the neighbourhood of Saarlouis:—

"Of de Bam senge de Viglen bei Daa ond Naat,
D'Männtcher peife hibsch on rufe: ti-ti-pi-pi,
On d'Weibcher saan: pi-pi-zi-zi.
Se senge luschtig on peife *du haut en bas.*
Berjer, Buwe on Baure d'iwrall her,
Die *plassire* sich recht *à leur aise.*
Se senge *ensemble* hibsch on fein.
D'gröscht *Pläsirn* hot mer van de Welt
Dat mer saan kann am grine Bam;
Dat esch wohr, dat esch keen Dram."

(On the tree sing the birds by day and night,
They pipe and call, ti-ti-pi-pi;
Their mates reply, pi-pi-zi-zi.
They cheerfully chirp *du haut en bas,*
High life and low life, from all around,
Placent themselves quite *à leur aise.*
They sing *ensemble* sweet and fine.
No greater *plaisir* earth can give
Than the sight of a greenwood tree;
That's truth, no idle dream.)

Thus much about the words of the popular songs. As regards the airs, those which have been traditionally preserved by the villagers of Alsace exhibit the characteristics of the German national music. That the construction of the airs has not altered much in the course of a century is evident from the specimens of songs and dance-tunes which Laborde gives in his 'Essai sur la Musique,' published in the year 1780. Still earlier, about two hundred years ago, the French composers adopted from Alsace a German tune of a peculiar construction, the *Allemande*. This happened at the time of the invention of the *Suite*, a composition which consists of a series of short pieces written in the style of popular tunes of various countries. The Allemande, which generally formed the introductory movement to the series, is more dignified than the sprightly Courante, Gavotte, and Bourrée, originally obtained from different provinces of France.

Particularly interesting is the music of the peasant of Kochersberg. The mountain called Kochersberg is situated in the vicinity of the town of Zabern in Upper Alsace. The district immediately surrounding the mountain is also called Kochersberg. The villagers of this district are considered by the French as rather rude in manner, but as honest, straightforward, and trustworthy. They have several old favourite dances, as for instance, *Der Scharrer* ("The Scraper"), *Der Zäuner* ("The Fence Dance"), *Der Morisken* (evidently the "Morrice" or Moorish Dance, formerly also popular in England, and originally derived from the Moors in Spain), *Der Hahnentanz* ("The Cock Dance"). The last-named dance, which is also popular in other districts of Alsace, and, with some modifications, in the Black Forest of Germany, is generally performed in a large barn. On a cross-beam is affixed a dish, in which is placed a fine large cock (called *Guller*). The cock is ornamented with ribands of various colours. Near the dish hangs a tallow-candle, through which a string is drawn horizontally. To one end of the string is attached a leaden ball. The dancers arrange themselves in pairs, one behind the other. As soon as the musicians strike up, the candle is lighted, and the first pair receive a nosegay, which they have to hold as long as they continue dancing. When they are tired, and stop to rest, they must give the nosegay to the next following pair, and so on. The pair which have possession of the nosegay at the moment when the candle burns the string, and the ball falls into the dish, win the cock. The *Hammeltanz* of the Kochersberg peasants is likewise known in Baden. In this dance a fat wether is the prize of the lucky pair who happen to be dancing when a glass suspended by a burning match-cord becomes detached and falls to the ground. Some of the dancers are accompanied with singing; for instance, the *Bloue Storken*, in which the song begins with the words:—

"Hon err de bloue Storken nit g'sähn?"
(Have you not seen the blue storks?)

The *Bloue Storken* is one of the oldest national dances of the Alsatian peasants. It is danced by one person only. At the commencement his performance resembles that of the slow and grave minuet; after awhile it becomes more animated.

However, in a musical point of view, the most interesting of these dances is the *Kochersberger Tanz*, which is mentioned by Reicha and other musical theorists on account of its peculiar rhythm. According to Reicha's notation it is in $\frac{5}{8}$ time. Perhaps it would have been as correctly written in $\frac{3}{8}$ and $\frac{2}{8}$ alternately, like *Der Zwiefache*, or *Gerad und Ungerad* ("Even and Uneven"), of the villagers in the Upper Palatinate of Bavaria, to which it bears altogether a strong resemblance. The musical bands attending the villagers at dances and other rural pastimes are, as might be expected, very simple—a clarionet and one or two brass instruments generally constituting the whole orchestra.

In Alsace a certain musical instrument is still to be found which, about three centuries ago, was popular in Germany. Some of the works on music published in the beginning of the seventeenth century contain drawings of it. Its German name is *Scheidholt*, and its French name is *bûche*. It consists of an oblong square box of wood, upon which are stretched about half-a-dozen wire-strings. Some of the strings run over a finger-board provided with iron frets. These strings are used for playing the melody. The others are at the side of the finger-board, and serve for the accompaniment. The strings are twanged with a plectrum. The *Scheidholt* may be considered as the prototype of the horizontal cither which, in the present century, has come much in vogue in Bavaria and Austria, and which has recently been introduced also into England.

Formerly, the professional musicians of Alsace formed a guild, the origin of which dates from the time of the *Minnesänger*, when players on musical instruments wandered from castle to castle to entertain the knights with their minstrelsy. In the year 1400 a Roman imperial diploma was granted to Count Rappoltstein constituting him protector of the guild. The musicians were called *Pfeiffer*, and Count Rappoltstein and his successors had the title of *Pfeiffer-König* (" King of the Pipers "). In the seventeenth century the *Pfeiffer* held annually a musical festival at Bischweiler, a small town near Strassburg. Having gradually fallen into decay, this old guild died out in the year 1789.

Considering the influence which the principal town of a country usually exercises upon the taste of the rural population, a few remarks relating to the cultivation of music in Strassburg may find here a place. Strassburg possesses, indeed, valuable relics illustrative of the history of music as well as of the other fine arts. Unfortunately, several of these treasures were injured at the recent bombardment. The town library, which was burnt, contained some valuable musical manuscripts; for instance, the *Gesellschaftsbuch der Meistersänger* from the year 1490 to 1768, and an historic treatise on the music and the *Meistersänger* of Strassburg written in the year 1598, by M. Cyriacus Spangenberg. To antiquarians who deplore the loss of these relics it may afford consolation to know that the town library of Colmar, in Alsace, possesses a manuscript collection of more than 1,000 old Minne-songs and Meister-songs, which originally belonged to the guild of shoemakers of Colmar. It must be remembered that in the beginning of the fourteenth century, after the *Minnesänger* of the Middle Ages, like the old chivalry with which they were associated, had become obsolete, there sprang up in Germany a corporation of poets and singers constituted of citizens, and known as the Meistersänger. Strassburg was one of the first among the German towns in which the Meistersänger flourished. An old sculpture of a Meistersänger, life-size, placed under the celebrated organ of the cathedral, testifies to the popular esteem enjoyed by this corporation. The town library possessed two curious oil-paintings on panel, dating from about the year 1600, which belonged to the Meistersänger of Strassburg, who used to place them one at each side of the entrance to their hall of assembly. A collection of antiquated musical instruments, which, probably, originally belonged to the Meistersänger, was formerly in a public building called Pfenningthurm, from which, in the year 1745, it was removed to the town library, where it was reduced to ashes.

However, the most interesting musical instrument in Strassburg is the organ of the cathedral made by Andreas Silbermann. Notwithstanding the care exercised by the beleaguerers to prevent damage to the cathedral, a shell found its way right through the centre of the organ, and must have greatly injured this work of art. Andreas Silbermann was no mere handicraftman, but an artist like Amati or Stradivari. He was born in Saxony, settled in Strassburg in the year 1701, and built the organ of the cathedral in 1715. His brother, Gottfried Silbermann of Saxony, was likewise a distinguished maker, not only of organs, but also of clavichords, and an improver of the pianoforte soon after its invention, in the beginning of the eighteenth century. Almost all the organs built during the eighteenth century for the churches of Strassburg are by Andreas Silbermann and his sons. Among the latter, Johann Andreas is noteworthy on account of his antiquarian pursuits. He wrote, besides other works, a 'History of the Town of Strassburg,' which was published in folio, with engravings, in the year 1775. His collection of sketches drawn by himself of the most remarkable scenery, and of old castles and other interesting buildings of Alsace, and likewise his collection of the old coins of Strassburg, were preserved in the town library, and are, it is to be feared, now lost. As even the catalogue of the library has, it is said, been burnt, it may be worth while to notice some of the losses. With the irreparable ones must be recorded a copy of the first hymn book of the Protestant Church, of which no other copy is known to be extant. It was published at Erfurt in the year 1524, and contains twenty-five songs, eighteen of which are by Luther. Its title is *Enchiridion, oder eyn Handbuchlein eynem yetzlichen Christen fast nutzlich bey sich zu haben, zur stetter vbung vnd trachtung geystlicher gesenge vnd Psalmen, Rechtschaffen vnd Kunstlich vertheutscht*. ("Enchiridion, or a little Hand-book, very useful for a Christian at the present time to have by him for the constant practice and contemplation of spiritual songs and psalms, judiciously and carefully put into German.") The musical notation is given with the words. It is believed that Luther gave the manuscript of his own songs, and most likely also of the other songs, and of the musical notation, into the hands of the publisher;—that, in fact, the "Enchiridion" emanated directly from Luther. A *fac-simile* of this book was published in Erfurt in the year 1848. Only three chorales are known with certainty to be of Luther's composition.

With the musical relics of the olden time preserved in Strassburg must be classed the so-called Astronomic Clock. This curious piece of mechanism, which is in the cathedral, was, in the year 1570, substituted for one which dated from the year 1354. Having been out of repair since the year 1789, it was restored about thirty years ago. The cylinders of the old mechanism of 1354, which act upon a carillon of ten bells, have been retained. The old tonal system exhibited in the arrangement of the cylinders, which produce hymn tunes, cannot but be interesting to musical antiquarians. Also, the wonderful mechanical cock, which, at the end of a tune, flapped its wings, stretched out its neck, and crowed twice—a relic of the work of 1354—is still extant; but whether it continues to perform its functions, I cannot say.

Let us now refer for a moment to the theatrical performances patronised by the burghers. Some interesting records relating to the history of the opera in Strassburg have been published by G. F. Lobstein, in his 'Beiträge zur

Geschichte der Musik im Elsass, Strassburg, 1840.' The oldest theatrical representations in Strassburg are of the sixteenth century. They consisted of sacred and historical pieces, and likewise of dramas of the Greek and Latin classics. The actors were scholars, or academicians, and the performances were called *Dramata theatralia, Actiones comicae* or *tragicae, Comoediae academicae*. About the year 1600 also the Meistersänger occasionally engaged in dramatic performances, or, as they called it, in *Comödien von Glück und Unglück* ("Comedies treating of Happiness and Unhappiness") and they continued to act such pieces in public until towards the end of the seventeenth century. In the year 1601 we find, the first time, mention made of the English comedians who, like the Meistersänger, evidently introduced music into their dramatic performances. Respecting the companies of English comedians who visited Germany at the time of Shakespeare, much has been written by Shakespearean scholars; but little attention has, however, been given by them to the musical accomplishments of these strollers. The old records which have recently been brought to light in Germany relating to the history of the theatres of the principal German towns, contain some interesting notices of "English instrumentalists" who formed part of the companies of English comedians. Indeed, most of the so-called English comedians appear to have been musicians and dancers (or rather tumblers) as well as actors. Probably it was more the novelty of their performances than any superiority of skill which rendered these odd foreigners temporarily attractive in Germany. Howbeit, to the musical historian they are interesting.

The invention of the opera, it must be remembered, dates from the year 1580, when, at Florence, the Count of Vernio formed at his palace a society for the revival of the ancient Greek musical declamation in the drama. This endeavour resulted in the production of the operas 'Dafne' and 'Orfeo ed Euridice,' composed by Peri and Caccini. The first German opera was performed in Dresden, in the year 1627. It was the libretto of 'Dafne,' just mentioned, written by Rinuccini, which was translated into German, and anew set to music by Heinrich von Schütz, Kapellmeister of the Elector of Saxony. In France the first composer of an opera was Robert Cambert, in the year 1647. He called his production 'La Pastorale, première comédie française en musique.' This composition was, however, performed only at Court. The first public performance of an opera in France occurred not earlier than the year 1671.* However, before the invention of the opera, strolling actors, such as the English comedians, and the Italian companies, which were popular in Strassburg, used to intersperse their performances with songs, accompanied by musical instruments such as the lute, theorbo, viol, etc. The first operatic representations, properly so called, in Strassburg, took place in the year 1701, and the operas were German, performed by German companies. Later, Italian companies made their appearance, and still later, French ones. In the year 1750 the French comic opera 'Le Devin du Village,' by J. J. Rousseau, was much admired. However, even during the eighteenth century the German operas and dramas enjoyed greater popularity in Strassburg than the French, notwithstanding the protection which the French companies received from the Government officials of the town. Indeed, the theatrical taste of the burghers has never become thoroughly French, if we may rely on G. F. Lobstein, who says, "The diminished interest evinced by the inhabitants of Strassburg at the present day" [about the year 1840] " in theatrical performances dates from the time when the French melodramas and vaudevilles made their appearance. The hideous melodramatic exhibitions, and the frivolous subjects, unsuitable for our town, and often incomprehensible to us—depicting Parisian daily occurrences and habits not unfrequently highly indecent—have, since their introduction on our stage, scared away those families which formerly visited the theatre regularly. They now come only occasionally, when something better is offered."

As regards the musical institutions and periodical concerts of Strassburg, suffice it to state that the local government

---

*The opera was introduced into England from Italy about the year 1660.

has always encouraged the cultivation of music; it is, therefore, not surprising, considering the love for music evinced by the Alsatians, that Strassburg has been during the last three centuries one of the chief nurseries of this art on the Continent. Until the year 1681, when Strassburg was ceded to France, it possessed an institution called Collegium Musicum, which enjoyed the special patronage of the local government. An Académie de Musique, instituted in the year 1731 by the French Governor of the town, was dissolved, after twenty years' existence, in 1751. At the present day the musical societies are not less numerous in Strassburg than in most large towns of Germany. An enumeration of the various kinds of concerts would perhaps only interest some musicians.

But Pleyel's Republican Hymn of the year 1792 is too characteristic of French taste at the time of the great events which it was intended to celebrate to be left unnoticed. Ignaz Pleyel, the well-known musician, was born in a village near Vienna, in the year 1757. On visiting Strassburg, after a sojourn in Italy, in the year 1789, he was made Kapellmeister of the cathedral. Unfortunately for him, soon his political opinions were regarded with suspicion by the National Assembly, especially from his being a native of Austria. He found himself in peril of losing his liberty, if not his life. Anxious to save himself, he conceived the happy idea of writing a brilliant musical composition in glorification of the Revolution. He communicated his intention to the National Assembly; it found approval, and he was ordered to write, under the surveillance of a gendarme, a grand vocal and orchestral piece, entitled 'La Révolution du 10 Août (1792) ou le Tocsin allégorique.' The manuscript score of this singular composition was, until recently, preserved in Strassburg, but has now probably perished. A short analysis of its construction will convince the reader that the monster orchestra which Hector Berlioz has planned for the music of the future, and of which he says in prophetic raptures: "Its repose would be majestic as the slumber of the ocean; its agitation would recall the tempest of the tropics; its explosions, the outbursts of volcanoes," was already anticipated by Pleyel nearly a hundred years ago. Pleyel required for his orchestra not only a number of large field-guns, but also several alarm-bells. The financial condition of France at that period, and the abolition of divine worship, induced the National Assembly to decree the delivering up of all the church-bells in Alsace. About 900 bells were consequently sent to Strassburg. Pleyel selected from them seven for the performance of his work; and all the others were either converted into cannon, or coined into money—mostly one-sol and two-sol pieces.

The *Introduzione* of Pleyel's composition is intended to depict the rising of the people. The stringed instruments begin *piano*. After a little while a low murmuring noise mingles with the soft strains, sounding at first as if from a great distance, and approaching gradually nearer and nearer. Now the wind-instruments fall in, and soon the blowing is as furious as if it were intended to represent the most terrific storm. It is, however, meant to represent the storming of the Tuileries. Fortunately the awful noise soon passes over, and only some sharp skirmishes are occasionally heard. After about a hundred bars of this descriptive fiddling and blowing, the alarm-bells begin—first one, then another, and now all in rapid succession. Suddenly they are silenced by a loud trumpet signal, responded to by a number of drums and fifes. The fanfare leads to a new confusion, through which the melody of some old French military march is faintly discernible. The excitement gradually subsides, and after awhile the stringed instruments alone are engaged, softly expressing the sighs of the wounded and dying. Presently the Royalists make themselves heard with the song, "*O Richard, ô mon roi*" (from 'Richard Cœur de Lion') which, after some more confusion, is followed by the air, "*Où peut-on être mieux?*" at the end of which discharges of cannon commence. Another general confusion, depicted by the whole orchestra with the addition of cannon and alarm-bells. Suddenly a flourish of trumpets, with kettle-drums, announces victory, and forms the introduction to a jubilant chorus with full orchestral accompaniment: "*La victoire est* à nous, le peuple est sauvé!" This again, after some more instrumental interluding, is followed by a chorus with orchestral accompaniment founded on the tune "Ça ira, ça ira," a patriotic song which was, during the time of the Revolution, very popular with the French soldiers. The remaining portion of the composition consists of a few songs for single voices alternating with choruses. As the words are not only musically but also historically interesting, they may find a place here.

"*Chorus.*

"Nous t'offrons les débris d'un trône,
Sur ces autels, ô Sainte Liberté!
De l'éternelle vérité.
Ce jour enfin, qui nous environne,
Rend tout ce peuple à la félicité;
Par sa vertu, par sa fierté,
Il conquiert l'égalité.
Parmis nos héros la foudre qui tonne
L'annonce au loin à l'humanité.

"*A Woman.* (*Solo.*)

"Mon fils vient d'expirer,
Mais je n'ai plus de rois!

"*Romance.*

"Il fut à son pays avant que d'être à moi,
Et j'étais citoyenne avant que d'être mère.
Mon fils! par tes vertus j'honore ta poussière.

"*Chorus.*

"Nous t'offrons les débris d'un trône, etc., etc.

"*Solo.* (*Soprano.*)

"Ah! périsse l'idolatrie
Qu'on voue à la royauté.
Terre ne sois qu'une patrie,
Qu'un seul temple à l'humanité,
Que l'homme venge son injure
Brise, en bravant, le faux devoir,
Et le piédestal du pouvoir   } *Repeated by*
Et les autels de l'imposture,   } *the Chorus.*
Rois, pontifs! ô ligue impure
Dans ton impuissant désespoir
Contemple aux pieds de la nature
Le diadème et l'encensoir!

Versailles et la fourbe Rome
Ont perdu leurs adulateurs.
Les vertus seront les grandeurs,   } *Repeated by*
Les palais sont les toits de chaume. } *the Chorus.*

"*Solo. (Tenore.)*
" Les Français qu'on forme à la guerre
Appellent contre les tyrans
Les représailles de la terre,
Du haut des palais fumans.
Des bords du Gange à ceux du Tibre
Dieu! rends bientôt selon nos vœux
Tout homme un citoyen heureux,   } *Repeated by*
Le genre humain un peuple libre. } *the Chorus.*

"*Solo Recit. (Basso.)*
" Nous finirons son esclavage
Ce grand jour en est le présage!
  "*Chorus (concluding with a brilliant orchestral Coda).*
" Nous t'offrons les débris d'un trône," etc., etc.

This curious composition was performed in the Cathedral of Strassburg, and created great sensation. Everyone declared that only an ardent patriot could have produced such a stirring work. Nevertheless Pleyel, after having been set free, thought it advisable to leave Strassburg for London as soon as possible.

Besides those already mentioned, several other distinguished musicians could be named who were born or who lived in Strassburg. Ottomarus Luscinius, a priest, whose proper German name was Nachtigall, published in the year 1536, in Strassburg, his 'Musurgia, seu Praxis Musicae,' a work much coveted by musical antiquarians. Sebastian Brossard, who, about the year 1700, was Kapellmeister at the Strassburg Cathedral, is the author of a well-known musical dictionary. Sebastian Erard, the inventor of the repetition-action and other improvements in the pianoforte, as well as of the double-action in the harp, was born at Strassburg in the year 1752.

In short, Elsass-Lothringen has been the cradle of many men distinguished in arts and sciences. The prominent feature of the national character of the inhabitants, revealed in their popular songs and usages, is a staidness which is not conspicuous among the pleasant qualities of the French. This innate staidness accounts for the reluctance recently shown by them to being separated from France, just as it accounts for their former disinclination to become French subjects. Moreover it will probably, now that they are reunited to their kinsmen, gradually make them as patriotic Germans as they originally were. That they require time to transfer their attachment redounds to their honour.

MUSIC AND ETHNOLOGY.

THE following scheme devised for obtaining accurate information respecting the music of different nations is probably without precedent.

In the year 1874 the British Association for the Advancement of Science resolved to issue a book of instructions for the guidance of travellers and residents in uncivilized countries, to enable them to collect such information as might be of use to those who make special study of the various subjects enumerated in the book.* The subjects relate to manners and customs, arts, sciences, religion, war, social life,—in fact, to everything which throws light upon the stage of civilization attained by the people, and which the ethnologist may desire to ascertain. The book is for this purpose divided into a number of sections, each on a certain subject, on which it contains a number of questions. These are preceded by a short note explanatory of the subject. In order to render the questions as effective as possible, especial care has been taken that they should enter into all necessary details.†

---

* 'Notes and Queries on Anthropology, for the Use of Travellers and Residents in Uncivilized Lands. Drawn up by a Committee appointed by the British Association for the Advancement of Science. London, 1874.'

† The book contains the note: "The Council of the Anthropological Institute of Great Britain and Ireland will be glad to receive any communications relating to the queries contained in this volume. Communications to be addressed to the Secretary, 4, St. Martin's Place, Trafalgar Square, London." It is understood that a certain number of copies of the book will be gratuitously distributed by the committee to English consular agents, naval officers, missionaries, and others who are likely to turn them to good account.

Having been requested to undertake the section headed "Music," and to draw up a list of numbered questions in accordance with the plan adopted by the committee, I have endeavoured to direct the attention of those for whom the book is intended to the musical investigations which, in my opinion, are especially desirable; and I have occasionally interspersed among the questions a hint which may assist the investigator. It appeared to me unnecessary to give definitions of musical terms made use of in the questions—such as *interval, melody, harmony*, etc.—which are to be found in every dictionary of the English language. Some terms, however, required an explanation to render them fully intelligible to those travellers who are but little acquainted with music. Of this kind are, for instance, the names of the different musical scales. The English missionaries, traders, merchants, consuls, and other residents in foreign countries, seldom possess any available knowledge of music. Still, among the questions here submitted to them are many which they may be able to answer satisfactorily; while, on the other hand, it must be admitted, not a few can be properly replied to only by men of musical education and experience. However, what one person is unable to investigate another may do; and thus, perhaps, we may hope, in the course of time, to be supplied with reliable and instructive answers to most of the questions from different parts of the world.

Some of the questions may appear, at a first glance, to be of but little importance; it is, however, just those facts to which they refer which ought to be clearly ascertained before we can expect to discern exactly the characteristics of the music of a nation or tribe.

It will be observed that certain questions pre-suppose a somewhat advanced state of civilization—as, for instance, those referring to musical notation, instruction, literature, etc. There are several extra-European nations—as the Japanese, Chinese, Hindus, etc.—which have advanced so far in the cultivation of music as to render these questions necessary; and it would be very desirable to possess more detailed information concerning the method pursued by these nations in the cultivation of the art than is at present available.

The present scheme is quite as interesting to the musician, or even more so, than it is to the ethnologist. Professional musicians in general are, however, not likely to become acquainted with the instructions for musical researches published together with various other scientific inquiries by the British Association. It is for this reason that they are here inserted, since the present work has a better chance of coming into the hands of professional musicians than the anthropological publication. Howbeit, years must elapse before it leads to a practical result. The originator of the questions may never enjoy the advantage of receiving the answers; but he has, at least, the pleasure of preparing the way for an accumulation of well-ascertained facts which intelligent musicians of a future generation will know how to turn to good account.

" (Section LXVIII.) Music.

"The music of every nation has certain characteristics of its own. The progressions of intervals, the modulations, embellishments, rhythmical effects, etc., occurring in the music of extra-European nations, are not unfrequently too peculiar to be accurately indicated by means of our musical notation. Some additional explanation is, therefore, required with the notation. In writing down the popular tunes of foreign countries, on hearing them sung or played by the natives, no attempt should be made to rectify anything which may appear incorrect to the European ear. The more faithfully the apparent defects are preserved the more valuable is the notation. Collections of popular tunes (with the words of the airs) are very desirable. Likewise, drawings of musical instruments with explanations respecting the construction, dimensions, capabilities, and employment of the instruments represented.

" *Vocal Music* :—

" 1. Are the people fond of music?

"2. Is their ear acute for discerning small musical intervals?

"3. Can they easily hit a tone which is sung or played to them?

"4. Is their voice flexible?

"5. What is the quality of the voice? is it loud or soft, clear or rough, steady or tremulous?

"6. What is the usual compass of the voice?

"7. Which is the prevailing male voice—tenor, baritone or bass?

"8. Which is the prevailing female voice—soprano or alto?

"9. Do the people generally sing without instrumental accompaniment?

"10. Have they songs performed in chorus by men only, or by women only, or by both sexes together?

"11. When they sing together, do they sing in unison, or in harmony, or with the occasional introduction of some drone accompaniment of the voice?

"12. Is their singing in regular time, or does it partake of the character of the recitative?

"13. Have they songs for solo and chorus,—or, with an air for a single voice, and a burden (or refrain) for a number of voices?

"14. Describe the different kinds of songs which they have (such as sacred songs, war-songs, love-songs, nursery-songs, etc.), with remarks on the poetry.

"*Instruments* :—

"15. What are their instruments of percussion (such as drums, castanets, rattles, cymbals, gongs, bells, etc.)?

"16. Have they instruments of percussion containing sonorous plates of wood, glass, stone, metal, etc., upon which tunes can be played? and if so, write down in notation, or in letters, the tones emitted by the slabs.

"17. Have they drums with cords, or some other contrivance by means of which the parchment can be tightened or slackened at pleasure?

"18. Have they drums with definite tones (like our kettle-drums)? and, if so, what are the tones in which they are tuned when two or more are played together?

"19. Any open hand-drums with one parchment only (like our tambourine)?

"20. Are the drums beaten with sticks or with the hands?

"21. What wind-instruments (trumpets, flutes, etc.) have they?

"22. Any trumpets with sliding tubes (like the trombone)?

"23. How are the flutes sounded? is there a plug in the mouth-hole?

"24. Any nose-flutes?

"25. What is the number and the position of the finger-holes on the flutes?

"26. What tones do the flutes yield if the finger-holes are closed in regular succession upwards or downwards?

"27. If the people have the syrinx (or Pandean pipe), ascertain the series of musical intervals yielded by its tubes.

"28. Do the people construct wind-instruments with a vibrating reed, or some similar contrivance, inserted in the mouth-hole?

"29. If they have a reed wind-instrument, observe whether the reed is *single* (like that of the clarionet) or *double* (like that of the oboe.)

"30. Have they a kind of bagpipe?

"31. What musical instruments have they which are not used by them in musical performances, but merely for conveying signals and for such like purposes?

"32. Have they stringed instruments the strings of which are sounded by being twanged with the fingers?

"33. Any stringed instruments twanged with a plectrum?

"34. Any stringed instruments beaten with sticks or hammers (like the dulcimer)?

"35. Any stringed instruments played with a bow?

"36. If there are stringed instruments with frets on the neck (as is the case with our guitar), note down the intervals produced by the frets in regular succession.

"37. What are the substances of which the strings are made?

"38. Is there any peculiar contrivance on some of the instruments in the arrangement and situation of the strings?

"39. Are there stringed instruments with sympathetic strings (*i.e.*, strings placed under those strings which are played upon. The sympathetic strings merely serve to increase the sonorousness)?

"40. What are the musical intervals in which the stringed instruments are tuned?

"41. Do the people possess any musical instrument of a very peculiar construction? If so, describe it minutely.

"42. Give the name of each instrument in the language of the country.

"43. Describe each instrument, and give illustrations, if possible.

"44. Give some account of the makers of musical instruments; of the woods, metals, hide, gut, hair, and other materials they use; of their tools, etc.

"45. What are the usual adornments and appendages of the musical instruments?

"*Compositions:*—

"46. On what order of intervals is the music of the people founded? Is it the Diatonic Major Scale (like c, d, e, f, g, a, b, c)? Or the Diatonic Minor Scale (in which the third is flat; like c, d, e flat, f, g, a, b, c)? Or the Pentatonic Scale (in which the fourth and the seventh are omitted, thus c, d, e, g, a, c)? Or some other order of intervals?

"47. Is the seventh used sharp (c-b), or flat (c-b flat)?

"48. Does the superfluous second occur in the scale? (In the example c, d, e flat, f sharp, g, a flat, b, c, the steps from the third to the fourth, and from the sixth to the seventh, are superfluous seconds.)

"49. Does the music contain progressions in semitones, or chromatic intervals?

"50. Are there smaller intervals than semitones, such as ½ tones, ¼ tones?

"51. Are there peculiar progressions in certain intervals

which are of frequent occurrence in the tunes? If so, what are they?

"52. Do the tunes usually conclude on the tonic (the keynote, or the first interval of the scale), or, if not, on what other interval?

"53. Do the tunes contain modulations from one key into another? If so, describe the usual modulations.

"54. Are there certain rhythmical peculiarities predominant in the music? If so, what are they?

"55. Is the time of the music generally common time, triple time, or irregular?

"56. Are there phrases or passages in the melodies which are of frequent re-occurrence?

"57. Have the airs of the songs re-occurrences of musical phrases which are traceable to the form of the poetry?

"58. Have the people musical compositions which they regard as very old? and do these compositions exhibit the same characteristics which are found in the modern ones?

"59. Are the compositions generally lively or grave?

"60. Describe the form of the various kinds of musical compositions.

"*Performances:*—

"61. Have the people musical bands or orchestras?

"62. Which are the instruments generally used in combination?

"63. Which are the instruments commonly used singly?

"64. What is the number of performers in a properly constituted band?

"65. Is there a leader of the band? How does he direct the performers?

"66. Does the band play in unison or in harmony?

"67. If vocal music is combined with instrumental music performed by the band, is the instrumental accompaniment in unison (or in octaves) with the voice, or has it something of its own?

"68. Is the *tempo* generally fast or slow?

"69. Are there sudden or gradual changes in the *tempo*?

"70. Are there changes in the degree of loudness?

"71. Do the musicians, on repeating a piece, introduce alterations, or variations of the theme?

"72. Do they introduce embellishments *ad libitum?*

"73. Mention the occasions (religious ceremonies, social and public amusements, celebrations, processions, etc.) on which musical performances take place.

"74. Are there military bands? and how are they constituted?

"75. Is music employed to facilitate manual labour?

"76. Are there songs or instrumental compositions appertaining to particular occupations or trades?

"77. Have the people a national hymn or an instrumental composition which they perform in honour of their sovereign or in commemoration of some political event?

"78. Describe minutely the musical performances in religious worship, if there are any.

"79. Have they sacred dances performed in religious ceremonies, at funerals, etc.?

"80. Any war-dances, dances of defiance, etc.?

"81. Any dances in which they imitate the peculiar movements and habits of certain animals?

"82. Are there dances accompanied by musical instruments, by singing, or merely by rhythmical sounds such as clapping of hands, snapping of fingers, reiterated vociferation, etc.?

"83. Give a list of all the dances.

"84. Endeavour to ascertain whether the rhythm of the music accompanying the dance is suggested by the steps of the dancers, or *vice versâ.*

"*Cultivation :*—

"85. Do the people easily learn a melody by ear?

"86. Have they a good musical memory?

"87. Are the children taught music? and if so, how is it done?

"88. Are there professional musicians?

"89. Any performers who evince much talent?

"90. Any minstrels, bards, reciters of old ballads?

"91. Any professional improvisators?

"92. Are there professional musicians of different grades?

"93. Who composes the music?

"94. Do the musicians follow other professions besides music?

"95. Are the ministers of religion also musicians and medical men?

"96. Have the people some kind of musical notation?

"97. Have they written signs for raising or lowering the voice in singing, for giving emphasis to certain words or phrases, or for similar purposes? If so, describe the signs.

"98. Do they possess treatises on the history, theory, etc., of music; instruction books for singing, and for playing musical instruments, etc.? If so, give a detailed account of their musical literature.

"99. Have they musical institutions? Give an account of them.

"100. How do the people appreciate their own music?

"101. What impression does the music of foreign nations produce upon them?

"*Traditions:*—

"102. Are there popular traditions respecting the origin of music?

"103. Any myths about a musical deity, or some superhuman musician?

"104. Any legends or fairy-tales in which allusion to music is made? If so, what are they?

"105. Any tradition about the invention of certain favourite musical instruments?

"106. Any tradition or historical record respecting the antiquity of stringed instruments played with a bow?

"107. Any records respecting their sacred music?

"108. Is music believed to possess the power of curing certain illnesses?

"109. The power of enticing and taming wild animals?

"110. Are there popular tunes, or certain rhythmical figures in the tunes, which, according to tradition, have been suggested by the songs of birds?

"111. If there is anything noteworthy about music which has not been alluded to in the preceding questions, notice it."

COLLECTIONS OF MUSICAL INSTRUMENTS.

IN Thibet, and other Asiatic countries in which the Buddhist religion is established, variously-constructed musical instruments are generally deposited in a certain part of the temple, to be at hand for the priests when required in ceremonies and processions. In examining the Assyrian bas-reliefs in the British Museum, we are led to surmise that a similar custom prevailed in Western Asia before the Christian era. At any rate, it appears probable that the various instruments represented in the hands of musicians who assisted in religious rites observed by the king were usually deposited in a room appropriated to their reception. The same appears to have been the case in the Temple of Jerusalem. King David had, it is recorded, musical instruments made of a wood called *berosh*, which afterwards, under the reign of Solomon, were made of *algum*, or *almug*, a more precious wood imported from foreign districts. King Solomon, being in possession of superior instruments, probably preserved the inferior ones of his father as venerated memorials; and the *kinnor* upon which David played before Saul may have been as carefully guarded by King Solomon as the Emperor of Germany guards in his cabinet of curiosities the flute of Frederick the Great.

Howbeit, Josephus records that Solomon had made for the musical performances at the dedication of the Temple a large number of stringed instruments and trumpets, all of which were kept together in the Temple with the treasures. It is not likely that at so early a period collections of antiquated instruments were formed for any scientific purpose; the art of music was too much in its infancy to suggest the preservation of evidences elucidating its gradual development.

The collections of ancient and scarce musical instruments which, in modern time, have been made in several European countries are very interesting to the lover of music, although they have, in most instances, evidently been formed less with the object of illustrating the history of the art of music than for the purpose of preserving curious and tasteful relics of bygone time, or of exhibiting characteristic contrivances of foreign nations.

In Italy some of the Conservatories of Music possess antiquated instruments of great rarity. Curious old spinets, lutes, mandolines, and guitars, are said to be found dispersed among private families and in convents, especially in Naples and its vicinity. In the Liceo Comunale di Musica, at Bologna, are deposited above fifty instruments, among which are an Italian cither (*cetera*) of the beginning of the sixteenth century; an arch-lute by "Hieronymus Brensius, Bonon" (Bologna); a chitarrone, by "Matteo Selles, alla Corona in Venetia, 1639;" a chitarrone inscribed "In Padova Uvendelio Veneto, 1609;" a theorbo by "Hans Frei in Bologna, 1597;" a lute by "Magno Stegher in Venetia." A lute, "Magno Dieffopruchar a Venetia, 1612." This lute has fourteen strings arranged in seven pairs, each pair being tuned in unison. Several marine trumpets, one of which bears the inscription, "Pieter Rombouts, Amsterdam, 17 ." A viola da gamba, inscribed "Antonius Bononiensis." A sordino, or pochette, by "Baptista Bressano," supposed to date from the end of the fifteenth century. Its shape is peculiar, somewhat resembling that of the Portuguese *machête*, representing a fish. A viola d'amore, with the inscription "Mattias Grieser, Lauten und Geigenmacher in Insbrugg, Anno 1727;" two curious old harps; an old tenor flute, measuring in length about three feet; some curious double flutes; cornetti, or zinken, of different dimensions. An archicembalo. This is a kind of harpsichord with four rows of keys, made after the invention of Nicolo Vicentino, and described in his work "L'Antica Musica ridotta alla moderna prattica. Rome, 1555." The compass of this archicembalo comprises only four octaves; but each octave is divided into thirty-one intervals, forming in all one hundred and twenty-five keys. It was made by Vito Trasuntino, a Venetian, who lived towards the end of the sixteenth century, and who added a *tetracordo* to it, to facilitate the tuning of its minute intervals. However, the archicembalo was probably not the first instrument of the harpsichord kind which contained an enharmonic arrangement of intervals. The clavicymbalum perfectum, or Universal-clavicymbel, which Prætorius states he saw in Prague, and which was likewise made in the sixteenth century, was of a similar construction. One of the most singular instruments in the collection of the Liceo Comunale de Musica at Bologna is the *cornamusa*, which consists of five pipes inserted into a cross-tube, through which they are sounded. Four of the pipes serve as drones; and the fifth, which is the largest, is provided with finger-holes, like the chanter of a bagpipe. The instrument has, however, no bag, although it is probably the predecessor of the species of bagpipe called *cornamusa*.

Instruments played with a bow of the celebrated Cremona makers are at the present day more likely to be met with in England than in Italy. In the beginning of the present century Luigi Tarisio, an Italian by birth, and a great connoisseur and collector of old violins, hunted over all Italy and other European countries for old fiddles. To avoid the high custom dues which he would have had to pay on the old instruments, he took them all to pieces, as small as possible, and carried the bits about him in his pockets and in a bag under his arm. So thoroughly was he acquainted with his acquisitions that, having arrived at the place of his destination, he soon restored them to their former condition, assigning to each fragment its original position. Tarisio made his first appearance in Paris, in the year 1827, with a bag full of valuable *débris* from Italy; and he continued his searches for nearly thirty years. During this time he imported into France most of the beautiful violins by Antonius Stradiuarius, Joseph Guarnerius, Bergonzi, Montagnana, and Ruggeri, which are of highest repute, and the greater number of which have afterwards found their way into England.

In Germany we meet with several collections of interest. The Museum of Antiquities, at Berlin, contains, among other musical curiosities, well-preserved lyres which have been found in tombs of the ancient Egyptians. The Gesellschaft der Musikfreunde ("Society of Lovers of Music"), at Vienna, possesses a collection of antiquated instruments, among which are noteworthy: a viola di bardone by Jacobus Stainer, 1660; a viola di bardone by Magnus Feldlen, Vienna, 1556; a viola di bardone by H. Kramer, Vienna, 1717; a viola d'amore by Weigert, Linz, 1721; a viola d'amore by Joannes Schorn, Salzburg, 1699; a tromba marina (marine trumpet) by J. Fischer, Landshut, 1722; a lute by Leonardo Tieffenbrucker, Padua, 1587; a theorbo by Wenger, Padua, 1622; a theorbo by Bassiano, Rome, 1666; a Polish cither by J. Schorn, Salzburg, 1696; a large flute made in the year 1501; an old German schalmey (English *shalm* or *shawm*) by Sebastian Koch; an old German trumpet by Schnitzer, Nürnberg, 1598; an oboe d'amore, made about the year 1770, etc.

A curious assemblage of scarce relics of this kind is also to be found in the Museum of the Germanic Society at Nürnberg. The most noteworthy specimens in this collection are: two marine trumpets, fifteenth century; a German cither with a double neck (bijuga-cither) sixteenth century; a German dulcimer (*hackbret*), sixteenth century; a lute by Michael Harton, Padua, 1602; a viola da gamba by Paul Hiltz, Nürnberg, 1656; a viola d'amore, with five cat-gut strings, and eight sympathetic wire strings, seventeenth century; an arpanetta (*harpanetta*, German *spitzharfe*) mounted on one side with brass wire, and on the opposite side with steel wire, sixteenth century; a clavecin with finely painted cover, by Martinus van der Biest, Antwerp, 1580; two German zinken (*cornetti*) sixteenth century; two specimens of the bombardo, viz., a German alt-pommer and tenor-pommer, by J. C. Denner, seventeenth century; some specimens of the cormorne (German *krummhorn*) of the sixteenth and seventeenth centuries; a trumpet made by J. C. Kodisch, Nürnberg, anno 1690; a splendid brass trombone (German bass-posaune) ornamented with the

German eagle and imperial crown, made by Friedrich Ehe, in Nürnberg, anno 1612; a Polish bagpipe, seventeenth century; a syrinx of reeds covered with black leather, sixteenth century; eight military pipes, made by H. F. Kynsker, in Nürnberg, seventeenth century; a small portable organ (*regal*) with two rows of keys, sixteenth century. The regal has become very scarce. There are only a few specimens known to be in existence; one, of the sixteenth century, is in the possession of the Chanoinesses de Berlaimont, at Brussels; another, made about the middle of the seventeenth century, belongs to the Duke of Athol, and is at Blair Athol, in Scotland; another, which belongs to Mr. Wyndham S. Portal, Malshanger, Basingstoke, is in the shape of a book, and its pipes have reeds, or vibrating tongues of metal. This regal, which probably dates from the sixteenth century, is of the kind which was called in German *Bibelregal*, because it resembles a Bible in appearance.

Old musical instruments are generally so fragile, and were formerly thought so little of when they came out of use, that it is perhaps not surprising to find of those dating from a period earlier than the sixteenth century very few specimens, and these have generally been altered, and it is seldom that they have been properly restored to their original condition. As an instance how valuable specimens are gradually becoming more and more scarce, may be mentioned the interesting collection of obsolete German harps, pipes, and trumpets, dating from a period anterior to the year 1600, which was preserved in the Town Library of Strassburg, and which, at the recent bombardment of the town, was reduced to ashes. It contained, among other curiosities: a cornetto curvo; some specimens of the cornetto dritto; a flauto dolce. Several specimens of the bombardone, the predecessor of the bassoon; a dulcinum fagotto; two specimens of the cormorne, an oddly-shaped wind instrument belonging to the shalm or oboe family. An arpanetta. This instrument, called in German *spitzharfe* or *drathharfe*, is especially interesting, inasmuch as it resembles the old Irish harp called *keirnine*, which was of a similar form, and which was also strung with wire instead of catgut. There is such a harp extant in the museum of the Society of Lovers of Music, at Vienna, before-mentioned.

If the lumber-rooms of old castles and mansions in Germany were ransacked for the purpose, some interesting relics of the kind would probably be brought to light. In the year 1872 Dr. E. Schebeck, of Prague, was requested by Prince Moriz Lobkowitz to examine the musical instruments preserved in Eisenberg, a castle of the Prince, situated at the foot of the Erzgebirge, in Bohemia. Most of them had formerly been used in the private orchestra kept by Prince Josef Franz Maximilian Lobkowitz, the well-known patron of Beethoven, to whom the composer has dedicated some of his great works. The present Prince Lobkowitz, who seems to have inherited his parent's love for music, wished to have an examination of the instruments, with the object of making a selection of the most interesting ones for the great Vienna Exhibition in 1873. Dr. Schebeck found, among other rarities, violins by Gaspar di Salo, Amati, Grancino, Techler, Stainer, and Albani; a violoncello by Andreas Guarnerius; a scarce specimen of a double-bass by Jacobus Stainer; two precious old lutes by Laux Maler, who lived at Bologna during the first half of the fifteenth century; a lute, highly finished, and apparently as old as those of Laux Maler, with the inscription in the inside "Marx Unverdorben a Venetia;" a lute, with the inscription "Magno Dieffoprukhar a Venetia, 1607." There can be no doubt that we have here the Italianised name of the German Magnus Tieffenbrucker, who lived in Italy.*

Fortunately for musical antiquarians the collection of rare instruments in the Conservatoire de Musique at Paris has been preserved uninjured during the recent disasters in that city. Among the instruments may be noticed, a small and beautiful musette with drones of ivory and gold, which belonged to Louis XIII.; a German regal, or portable organ, sixteenth century; a pochette by Stradiuarius; a *courtaud*, an early kind of bassoon, dating from the fifteenth

* Some account of the instruments in Eisenberg appeared in the Vienna paper, "Die Presse," of November 27th, 1872.

century; several bass-flutes, and other rare old wind instruments; Boïeldieu's pianoforte; Grétry's clavichord; a "Trumpet of Honour," which was made by order of Napoleon I., and which has the name of "T. Harper" engraven on its silver rim. M. Victor Schœlcher has presented to the Conservatoire de Musique about twenty rather primitive instruments of uncivilised nations obtained by him during his travels in Western Africa and South America, among which may be noted several Negro contrivances of the harp and guitar kind.

An interesting catalogue of the instruments in the Musée du Conservatoire National de Musique has recently been published by Gustave Chouquet, the curator of the museum. It comprises 630 instruments, or portions of instruments, each fiddle-bow, mute, etc., being separately numbered. On the whole, the Paris collection, though large, is far less valuable than that of the South Kensington Museum.

One of the most valuable private collections ever formed of ancient musical instruments was that of M. Louis Clapisson in Paris. During a course of more than twenty years M. Louis Clapisson succeeded in procuring a considerable number of scarce and highly decorated specimens of instruments of the Middle Ages and the Renaissance. The collection has been dispersed since the death of its owner; a large portion of it is now incorporated with the collection of the Conservatoire de Musique at Paris, and some of its most valuable specimens were secured for the South Kensington Museum. It was, however, so unique that the following short survey of its contents will probably be welcome to the archæological musician.

Clapisson's collection comprised (according to the catalogue of its contents which was published in French, and which is now scarce) 167 instruments. Among them are especially noteworthy:—A clavecin (or harpsichord) with two rows of keys, dated 1612; embellished with paintings which date from the time of Louis XIV. In front is a painting by Teniers, and in the inside are some fine paintings by Paul Brill. An Italian spinet of the time of Louis XIV., embellished with paintings of garlands of flowers, cupids, etc., attributed to Poussin. The fine carving and the ornamentation of engraved amber on this spinet give it a stamp of originality. An Italian spinet, bearing the inscription " Francisci di Portalvpis Veronen opus, 1523," of ebony inlaid with ivory. An Italian spinet of the sixteenth century, ornamented with marquetry of various coloured woods. The corners of the key-board are adorned with caryatides finely carved in box-wood. A travelling spinet made in the shape of a mail-trunk dating from the time of Henri II. It is signed "Marins," which is the name of a celebrated manufacturer of that period. A clavecin made in France in the year 1657, ornamented with paintings and with marquetry of ivory, with the arms of the family of Pierre di Dreux (called Mauclere), Duke of Bretagne, who lived about the year 1250. An Italian dulcimer of wood carved and gilt, dating from the seventeenth century. It is tastefully inlaid with slips of silvered glass. A French dulcimer of the time of Louis XIV., with twisted columns of wood carved and gilt, and with paintings of flowers and birds. A French dulcimer, or timpanon, of the time of Louis XIII., ornamented with roses neatly carved in wood. The instrument is in a case, which is ornamented with paintings and inlaid slips of silvered glass. A French dulcimer of carved wood, ornamented with slips of engraved Venetian glass, with turquoises, and with paintings on *Vernis Martin*. A sonorous stone from China, in the form of a fish. A French harp, of the time of Louis XV., gilt and carved with flowers and paintings in relief. A harp of the time of Louis XVI., having belonged to the Princesse de Lamballe, whose name is engraven on it. It is finely painted with medallions on *Vernis Martin*. A theorbo of the time of Louis XIII., inlaid with designs in ivory. Engraven on it is the coat of arms of the House of Austria; also a portrait, and the device *Non omnes*. A French guitar made, according to an inscription, by Voboam, a celebrated lute-maker at the court of Louis XIV. It is made in the figure of a tortoise, the body being of tortoise-shell, and the head, feet and tail of coloured enamel. A French guitar of the time of Louis XIII., inlaid with ivory, on which are engraven subjects of the chase. A French guitar of the time of Louis XIII., inlaid with ivory engraved with mythological subjects. An Italian mandoline of citron-wood inlaid with mother-of-pearl, engraven with figures. An Italian mandoline, ornamented with marquetry, mother-of-pearl, and carving; assigned to Stradiuarius. A French mandoline of the time of Louis XVI., with the arms of the Dauphin inlaid with mother-of-pearl. A small Italian mandoline with three strings. A mandora of the time of Henri II., inlaid with broad strips of ivory, and with *fleurs de lys* in ebony. A French hurdygurdy (or *vielle*) of the time of Louis XIV., made of box-wood and citron-wood, carved, and ornamented with medallions of mother-of-pearl and with turquoises; formerly the property of Madame Adelaïde. A French hurdygurdy by Louvet, dated 1750; tastefully ornamented. A small hurdygurdy for the use of ladies, made in France during the period of Louis XVI. This *vielle*, elegant in form and tastefully inlaid with ivory, bears the inscription " Delaunay." A Hungarian violin, made in Presburg, inlaid with marquetry of various coloured woods. A small violin by Jacobus Stainer, inlaid with ornaments in silver, including the coat of arms of France; with a finely-carved head of a faun. A French *quinton*, or five-stringed viol, made by Guersan, in 1755. A viola da gamba, with a finely-carved head representing an angel bandaging the eyes of a female. A small viola da gamba of the kind on which the French ladies used to play at the time of Louis XIII. A pochette by Stradiuarius, known to be genuine. A pochette of the sixteenth century, of engraved ivory and ebony, inlaid with precious stones. A pochette of ivory and coloured woods, dating from the period of Louis XIII., and bearing the inscription "Marins." A crystal flute, the invention of Laurent; silver keys enriched with amethysts. A small Italian double-flute of ivory, made by Anciuti in Milan, anno 1722. An oboe of ivory, carved by Anciuti in Milan, beginning of the eighteenth century. A French oboe of ebony, inlaid with ivory, tortoise-shell, and enriched with gold and precious stones; of the time of Louis XIII. A small French oboe of the time of Louis XIV., made of ivory, with three silver keys. A French *musette* (a species of bagpipe with bellows); the pipes of ivory; twenty-one silver keys; the bag ornamented with embroidery in gold. This fine *musette* dates from the period of Louis XV. A small French *musette* of ivory, with silver keys, having belonged to the painter Vanloo. A *cornemuse bretonne* (bagpipe of Brittany) of the time of Louis XIII. A trumpet of the time of Henri IV., ornamented with embossed *fleurs de lys* and with the portrait of Henri IV., surrounded by butterflies. A serpent of the sixteenth century, made of wood, with the carved head of a demon finely executed.

Turning to Belgium, we again meet with some interesting collections. M. Fétis, the well-known musician, had a number of Eastern instruments procured from Egypt, to enable him to familiarise himself with the Arabic tonal system, which essentially differs from our own, but which undoubtedly is of much higher antiquity, and therefore of particular interest to the musical historian. After the death of Fétis, his collection was purchased by the Belgian Government. Dr. Burney, who visited Antwerp in the year 1772, records in his journal that he saw in a public edifice of the town, called Oosters Huys, a large number of wind instruments of a peculiar construction. "There are," he says, "between thirty and forty of the common flute kind, but different in some particulars—having, as they increase in length, keys and crooks, like hautbois and bassoons. They were made at Hamburg, and all of one sort of wood, and by one maker, 'Casper Ravchs Scratenbach,' was engraved on a brass ring or plate, which encircled most of these instruments. The large ones have brass plates pierced, and some with human figures well engraved on them. These last are longer than a bassoon would be if unfolded. The inhabitants say that it is more than a hundred years since these instruments were used, and that there is no musician at present in the town who knows how to play on any one of them, as they are quite different from those now [in the year 1772] in common use. In times when commerce flourished in this city these instruments used to be played on every day by a band of musicians, who attended the merchants trading to the Hanse Towns in procession to the Exchange."

No doubt there are some curious old harpsichords and lutes still to be found in Belgium and in the Netherlands—countries in former times distinguished for the cultivation of the art of music. Besides, the connection of the Netherlands with Asia has facilitated the acquisition of curious instruments from the East, a number of which may be seen deposited in the Museum at the Hague.

A glance at a collection made by a musical amateur, during the seventeenth century, is sure to interest the musical antiquarian. The collector, Jean-Baptiste Dandeleu, a man of position and property in Brussels, died in the year 1667. Among his effects were the following instruments, the list of which is here literally transcribed as it was written at the time of his decease:—"Une orgue, que l'on dit avoir appertenu à feu l'archiduq (de glorieuse mémoire), et couste trois milles florins.—Une espinette organisée.—Un coffre dans lequel y a neuf violes de gambes d'accord.—Encor une vieille viole de gambes.—Six corps de luths ou thiorbes dans des vieilles caisses.—Une mandore aussy dans sa caisse.—Une autre petit instrument en forme de poire avec le col rompu, ou decollé.—Une caisse doublée de baye rouge, dans la quelle y a six fluttes rares d'accord, qui sont de bouys, avec leurs escorces et noeuds.—Une cornette noire de musique.—Encore une flûte de bouys de la longueur d'environ un pied dans une caisse noire.—Trois caisses avec diverses flûtes de bouys grandes et petites d'accord, entre les quelles aucunes manquent.—Encor six flûtes semblables, que l'on croid estre celles qui manquent cy-dessus.—Encor une grande flûte, ou pippe noire.—Un violon dans sa caisse. —Un cistre aussy dans sa caisse.—Un instrument rare pour sa structure à mètre les livres des musiciens dessus pour un concert de musique.—Cincq petits lesseniers.

Most of the instruments in this collection were undoubtedly manufactured about the period in which they are mentioned. However, as regards lutes and viols, preference was given already as early as the seventeenth century to old ones, if they were the work of good makers. Thus, the lutes of Laux Maler, dating from the beginning of the fifteenth century—"pittifull old, batter'd, crack'd things," as Thomas Mace calls them in his 'Musick's Monument,' London, 1676—fetched as much as a hundred pounds apiece. "I have often seen," Mace remarks, "lutes of three or four pounds price far more illustrious and taking to a common eye. . . . . First know that an old lute is better than a new one." Thus also with viols: "We chiefly value old instruments before new; for by experience they are found to be far the best." The improvement by age he reasonably attributes to the circumstance that "the pores of the wood have a more and free liberty to move, stir, or secretly vibrate; by which means the air—which is the life of all things, both animate and inanimate—has a more free and easie recourse to pass and repass."

An interesting collection of antiquated musical instruments has been made by M. César Snoeck, of Renaix, in Belgium. It comprises among other rarities:—A small virginal bearing the inscription: "Paulus Steinicke me fecit, Anno 1657." A harpanetta, seventeenth century. A *cetera* or Italian cither, seventeenth century. The top terminates in a finely-carved figure, and the body is flattened towards the lower end. This interesting instrument is of the kind which the Italian *improvisatori* used for accompanying the voice. An assemblage of specimens, varying in size, of the German, or perhaps Dutch, zinken. These quaint-looking flute-trumpets, although blown through a mouth-tube somewhat similar to that of the trumpet, have finger-holes like a flute. They probably were made about the year 1700. A tenor-flute and three bass-flutes, probably of the seventeenth century.

The municipality of Ghent, in Belgium, possesses silver trumpets which were made in the fifteenth century. It will be remembered from the biblical records (Numbers, x., 2) that Moses constructed two trumpets entirely of silver. Neither was the use of the trumpet for strategical purposes unknown to the Hebrews, as is evidenced by Gideon's employment of the instrument (Judges, vii.). There is an old German treatise, quaintly entitled 'Versuch einer Anleitung zur heroisch-musikalischen Trompeter-und Pauker-Kunst' ("An Attempt at a Guide to the heroic-musical Art of the Trumpeter and the Kettle-Drummer "), written by Johann Ernst Altenburg, Halle, 1795, which contains some interesting accounts concerning the various occasions on which the trumpet was formerly used in different European countries, at Court ceremonies and public festivities, as well as in war. Altenburg, who himself was a distinguished military trumpeter, and, no doubt, also a brave warrior, remarks: "Awful and terrible is the sound of the trumpet when it announces the near approach of the enemy; or when the enemy demands by trumpet-signal the surrender of a beleagured town; or when he storms and enters the town with the blare of the trumpet of war! Likewise, the signal of alarm produces an uneasy impression upon a weaker corps when surprised and surrounded by a stronger corps. However, by means of this uncommon music, which has been made use of by many as a stratagem in olden time and at the present day, often important conquests have also resulted. During the Seven Years' War, in which I took part, it happened during a dark night that a large body of the enemy's troops nearly succeeded in surprising and cutting off one of our corps which was much smaller and weaker; but we, modifying the signals of our trumpets so as to make them appear to come from different quarters and from long distances, succeeded in intimidating the enemy, so that he suddenly turned and fled, believing that we were receiving succour."

This may be the place to notice a fine collection of old trumpets in the possession of Prince Charles of Hohenzollern-Sigmaringen. They were made by Johann Leonard Ehe, in Nürnberg; Hieronymus Stark, in Nürnberg, anno 1669; Christopher Frank, Magnus Wolf, Wilhelm Haas, anno 1688.

Passing over the Royal Museum of Northern Antiquities at Copenhagen, which contains highly curious specimens of the old Scandinavian brass trumpet called *lure*—especially interesting if compared with the bronze trumpets of mediæval time excavated from bogs or mosses in Ireland, and now preserved in the Museum of the Royal Irish Academy at Dublin—we now proceed to a cursory survey of the musical antiquities in the museums of London.

The British Museum possesses several instruments, or fragments of instruments, of the ancient Egyptians, Greeks, and Romans, and old Celtic trumpets which have been found in Ireland. In the ethnological department of the British Museum are particularly noteworthy :—The specimens of Chinese instruments brought over to England by Mr. Tradescant Lay; those from Siam, obtained by Sir John Bowring; those from Java, obtained by Sir Stamford Raffles; a considerable number of flutes, including nose-flutes, and of trumpets, from Otaheite, Tongataboo, and New Zealand; well-preserved drums from the Polynesian Islands; serpent-headed drums of the natives of New Guinea; Negro instruments from Western Africa, etc.

The Museum of the East India House, in London, contains upwards of 120 musical instruments, mostly from Hindustan and Burmah, some of which are very fine, but many are out of repair. An assemblage of curious pipes, trumpets, and drums of the Polynesians, as well as fiddles of the Hottentots and Kafirs in Southern Africa, may be seen in the Museum of the London Missionary Society. Furthermore, the Botanical Museum at Kew possesses several interesting contrivances of this kind, made of peculiar species of wood by Indian tribes in South America.

The collection of musical instruments belonging to the South Kensington Museum is now, as far as is known, the most comprehensive in existence. The latest edition of its catalogue, published in the year 1874, describes 353 instruments, of which 246 belong to the Museum, and 107 are on loan. The catalogue contains 143 wood-engravings and six photographs of instruments, and is preceded by an essay on the history of musical instruments. A glance at its comprehensive index will perhaps convey to the reader the impression that it takes cognizance of almost every musical instrument in the world. This is, however, by no means the case. Even an account of all our own instruments in use at the present day would fill a large volume. But, endeavour has been made to render the catalogue as comprehensive as is consistent with its object, and the reader will find in it illustrations and descriptions of most of the instruments mentioned in the present essay.

There have been some curious lists preserved of musical instruments which belonged to English amateur musicians, and which were sold, after the death of the owner, at public auctions.

The collection of musical instruments which belonged to King Henry VIII. appears to have been remarkably comprehensive and valuable. An inventory of its contents was compiled by Philip van Wilder, a Dutch lute-player in the service of the king. The manuscript of this inventory is preserved in the British Museum. Among the instruments entered are :—Two paier of clavicordes.—A payre of new long virginalls made harp-fashion, of Cipres, with keys of ivory, having the King's arms crowned and supported by His Grace's beastes within a garter gilt, standing over the keys.—Gitterons which are called Spanish vialles.—Flutes called Pilgrims' staves.—A great base recorder. Two base recorders of walnut. Pipes of ivory or wood, called cornets.

In 'The History and Antiquities of Hengrave, Suffolk, by John Gage, London, 1822,' are recorded among the effects of Sir Thomas Kytson of Hengrave Hall, about the year 1600 :—Six viols in a chest. Six violins in a chest. Lutes. Citterns. Bandoras. Seven recorders in a case. Hautboys. A curtall. Cornets. A lezarden. A pair of little virginals. A pair of double virginals. A wind-instrument like a virginal. A pair of double organs.

The "curtall" was probably the French *courtaud* mentioned previously, page 37; and the "lezarden" was probably similar to the *serpent*, an old wind-instrument mentioned in page 41.

Among the English private collections about two centuries ago deserves to be noticed one which was formed by Thomas Britton, the small-coal man. This extraordinary musical amateur, born in the year 1656 of poor parents in Northamptonshire, set out for London while still a lad to gain his living. After various vicissitudes he succeeded in

his project by becoming a seller of small-coal. During the
day he wandered through the streets carrying a sack of
coals on his back, and crying them for sale. In the evening
he practised his viol, and studied the theory of music.
Moreover, he was as fond of studying chemistry as he was
of making music. The library of books and musical compositions which he collected from second-hand book-stalls,
in his peregrinations through the streets during a period of
thirty-six years, was extensive, considering his position. A
list of his music-books is given in Hawkins's 'History of
Music.' Thomas Britton lived in Aylesbury Street, Clerkenwell, in a hired stable converted into a dwelling-house. The
ground-floor he used for the repository of his small-coal;
and the room above—a long and narrow space, with a ceiling
so low that a tall man could but just stand upright in it—
was his concert-room. Here the best musicians in London
—among them Dr. Pepusch, Matthew Dubourg, the violinist,
who at that time was a little boy, and Handel, during the
last four years of Thomas Britton's life—were glad to perform. The fine concerts and the estimable character of
Thomas Britton became soon more generally appreciated;
his concerts, given gratuitously, attracted a genteel audience,
among whom might be seen dukes, lords, and other persons
of rank and wealth. The musical instruments of this great
small-coal man, which were sold by public auction after his
death in 1714, are entered in the catalogue of the sale as
follows:—" A fine guitar in a case. A good dulcimer.
Five instruments in the shape of fish. A curious ivory Kitt
and bow in case. A good violin by Ditton. Another very
good one. One said to be a Cremona. An extraordinary
Rayman. Three others ditto. One very beautiful one by
Claud Pieray of Paris, as good as a Cremona. One ditto.
Another very good one. Another ditto. A very good one
for a high violin. Another ditto. An excellent tenor.
Another ditto by Mr. Lewis. A fine viol by Baker of
Oxford. Another excellent one, bellied by Mr. Norman.
Another, said to be the neatest and best that Jay ever made.
A fine bass violin, new-neck'd and bellied by Mr. Norman.
Another rare good one by Mr. Lewis. A good harpsichord

by Philip Jones. A Rucker's virginal, thought to be the best in Europe. An organ of five stops, exactly consort pitch, fit for a room, and with some adornments may serve for any chapel, being a very good one."

The "five instruments in the shape of fish" were, probably, specimens of the *machête*, a small kind of guitar made in Portugal and Madeira, and occasionally brought to England as a curiosity. However, the *pochette* also was sometimes made in the shape of a fish. As regards the instrument-makers mentioned in Britton's list, suffice it to state that Jacob Rayman, who lived in Southwark about the year 1640, enjoyed a reputation especially as a maker of fine violas, and that Edward Lewis, who lived in London about the year 1700, was a distinguished violin-maker. Barak Norman in London, Henry Jay in Southwark, and John Baker in Oxford, were distinguished viol-makers of the seventeenth century.

Some fine collections made in the present century by English gentlemen consisted almost entirely of Italian violins, violas and violoncellos. It is but natural that the possessor of real or supposed works of art should feel particularly gratified when he finds them admired by persons whose judgment he has reason to esteem. Louis Spohr, in his 'Autobiography,' describes a visit which he paid to an enthusiastic musical *dilettante* and collector of violins, in London, in the year 1820. Spohr had come over from Germany to England to give concerts, and was unacquainted with the English language. He relates: " One morning a livery-servant brought me a note containing the words: ' Mr. Spohr is requested to call upon the undersigned to-day at four o'clock precisely.' As the name of the writer was unknown to me, I answered in the same laconic manner: ' I am engaged about that time, and cannot come.' On the following morning the servant in livery brought another note, much more politely written: ' Mr. Spohr is requested to favour the undersigned with the honour of a visit, and to fix himself the time when it will be convenient for him to come.' The servant had also been desired to offer me the use of his master's carriage, and as I had meanwhile ascertained that the gentleman was a celebrated physician who habitually frequented concerts, and who took special interest in violin performances, I no longer hesitated to accept his invitation. At the time fixed by me the carriage arrived, and I drove to his house. A courteous old man, with gray hair, met me already on the stairs; but now we discovered that we could not talk together, as he spoke neither French nor German. We stood for a moment embarrassed face to face, till he took me by the arm and led me into a large room, on the walls of which were hung a great number of violins. Other violins had been taken out of their cases and were placed on the tables. The Doctor gave me a violin-bow and pointed to the instruments. I now perceived that he desired to have my opinion as to the value of his fiddles. I, therefore, began at once to try one after the other, and to arrange them in a certain order, according to their merit. This was no easy task; for, there were so many, and the old gentleman brought all of them to me without missing one. When, after the lapse of an hour, I had selected the six most valuable ones, and was playing upon these alternately, to ascertain which was the best, I perceived that the Doctor cast upon one of them glances especially tender, and that whenever I touched the strings of this one with the bow his face quite brightened up. I, therefore, gladly afforded the good old man pleasure by declaring this instrument to be the most superior one of the whole collection. Highly delighted with this decision, he fetched a viola d'amore and extemporised a fantasia upon this instrument, which has long since gone out of use. I listened with pleasure, because the viola d'amore was at that time unknown to me, and the Doctor proved a by no means bad player. Thus ended the visit to our mutual satisfaction. When I took my hat to leave, the old gentleman, with a kind smile and a deep bow, slipped a five-pound note into my hand. Surprised, I looked at the money and at the giver, not understanding at first what he meant by it; but suddenly it occurred to me that it was intended as a fee for having examined his violins. I smilingly shook my head, laid the paper on the table, pressed the Doctor's hand, and descended the stairs. He followed me to the street-door. . . . Some months later, when I gave my benefit-concert, the Doctor procured a ticket, for which he sent me a ten-pound note."

One of the largest private collections of this kind, more recently formed by an English musical amateur, was sold in London by auction in the year 1872, after the death of its owner, Mr. Joseph Gillott of Birmingham. It contained above 150 instruments played with a bow. Among them were two viola da gambas, by Gaspar di Salo and Barak Norman; a viola d'amore, by Bertrand, Paris, 1614; violins, violas, and violoncellos assigned to Gaspar di Salo, Stradiuarius, Amati, Guarnerius, Testore, Guadagnini, Bergonzi, and other famous makers.

If, as occasionally happens, an amateur who considers himself a good judge of old violins is overreached by a dealer who professes to have but little knowledge on the subject, the transaction is simple enough. However, the purchaser of a "splendid Amati," or an "incomparable Stradiuarius," obtained by him at a bargain, might remember that the number of violins manufactured by the famous Cremona makers is limited, and that the history of the specimens still extant is almost as traceable as the pedigree of a prince or of a racehorse. As regards the various lutes, cithems, wind instruments with reeds, etc., which were popular during the last three centuries, many of them are now so scarce as to be unknown, even to professional musicians, except to a few with an archæological turn of mind.

It may easily be understood, that a reference to books alone does not ensure so thorough an acquaintance with the instruments as is obtainable from a careful examination of the actual specimens which are therein described. Should it interest the musician to restore to its original condition some dilapidated lute or cithern which he may happen to pick up, and to learn to play upon it according to the old method taught in some old book, he will become acquainted with niceties in the construction of the instrument, such as the peculiar arrangement of its pegs, frets, bridge, pins, and other contrivances, which are not to be learnt from books. Such knowledge of details gathered from practical experience, which at a first glance may appear unimportant, is often of great use, since it tends to throw light upon questions of more general interest relating to the history of music. Indeed, in a search after truth, every well-ascertained fact is of importance, since it serves as a solid step for progress.

Again, in playing on the lute, harpsichord, or other antiquated instrument the compositions written for it by our old masters, the performer is sure to discover certain charms in the music which cannot be expressed on any modern instrument, and which reveal faithfully the original conceptions of the composer. Take, for instance, Handel's 'Suites de Pièces,' conceived by him for the harpsichord, with its different stops and qualities of sound. In playing them on the pianoforte, the strictly musical beauties can be expressed, and these, it must be granted, constitute the greater charm of the compositions; but many additional beauties, calculated upon the characteristics of the harpsichord, are entirely lost. It does not, of course, therefore follow that musicians ought to learn the harpsichord, lute, or any other antiquated instrument, for which good music has been written. Enough, if these observations convince them that there have been charming musical instruments, as well as charming compositions, in former times, from which valuable hints may be derived for further progress in the inexhaustible art of music.

At all events, it appeared to me advisable to save from oblivion and decay any such antiquities as I happened to meet with, in England. When I began to form my collection, in the year 1868, scarcely any musician in London took interest in the matter; and it was perhaps this circumstance which enabled me soon to lay a good foundation for my collection by searches in the old curiosity shops in Wardour Street, and in similar places. Although the chief object was to obtain specimens of the various musical instruments used by our forefathers, which are alluded to by Shakspeare and other classical authors, it appeared to me desirable, as illustrative of the history of music, to incorporate into the collection the most interesting of the extra-European contrivances of the kind, and among these principally such instruments of Asiatic nations as are the prototypes of certain ones of our own. Moreover, some of the extra-European acquisitions may be regarded as being antiquated, since the introduction of Christianity and European civilisation into some distant islands caused the natives to discontinue the construction of such instruments as they formerly used in their pagan ceremonies. About forty Hindu and Burmese instruments were selected from the comprehensive collection which was sent from Hindustan to the International Exhibition, London, 1872. They represent the most characteristic inventions of the kind popular in Hindustan and Burmah, and are, moreover, in an unimpaired condition, which is seldom the case with such brittle manufactures tossed about on the sea from distant lands.

As regards the European curiosities in the collection, their number was perhaps most advantageously increased by some treasures which formed part of the museum of Signor Mario in Florence, and which were sold in London some years ago. Thus the collection has grown so as to comprise now about two hundred and fifty instruments, some of which are of great scarcity, and several are of great beauty. I gladly take this opportunity to supply the musician with a survey of the collection, since I know from experience how interesting and instructive such a list is to the archæological student. About a hundred instruments of the collection, which are at present exhibited in the South Kensington Museum, shall be noticed but briefly, since they are described in the musical catalogue of the Museum, which is easily accessible. Omitting some unimportant specimens, the collection contains:—

Sancho, a stringed instrument from Senegambia, Western Africa. Valga, a stringed instrument from Congo, Western Africa. Its five strings are made of vegetable fibre, and are tuned by being wound round five canes inserted in the body. Length, 3 feet. The brass-headed buttons with which the instrument is ornamented may have been derived from England. It is not unfrequently the case that savages or semi-civilised people in remote parts of the world adorn their rude works of art with some acquisitions of European manufacture scarce with them, and therefore much prized. In fact, European nations often evince a similar predilection in the ornamentation of their articles of luxury. Five is the usual number of canes in the valga; but there are also specimens with ten canes, and consequently with ten strings. The canes are generally stuck in holes under the body of the valga, and as they can be inserted more deeply or drawn out at pleasure, this is probably the method most commonly resorted to for tuning the strings. The valga is made of different shapes. Some of these are precisely like the river-boats of the Negroes, of which illustrations are given in Speke's 'Journal of the Discovery of the Source of the Nile.' The valga is, however, most popular in Western Africa, where it is known by different names in different districts. Near the Gaboon river it is called *wambee;* and in Benguela, *kissumba.* Kasso, a species of Negro harp from Senegambia. Ingomba, a Negro drum from Lower Guinea, made of the stem of a palm-tree, 6 feet 6 inches in length; covered at both ends with the skin of an elephant's ear. Negro trumpet from Eastern-central Africa. Made of the tusk of an animal. With two holes for blowing and for modulating the sound, perforated towards the thinner end. This trumpet was brought to England by the African traveller Petherick. Abyssinian fiddle with bow. The whole instrument is cut out of one block of wood. The belly is of parchment. Seven catgut strings. The thinnest string is shorter than the others, and the peg by means of which it is tuned is placed at the side of the neck close to the body. The instrument in shape bears some resemblance to the *chikarah* of the Hindus. There are some musical instruments to be found on the Eastern coast of Africa which probably were derived originally from Hindustan. The present fiddle, which was brought to England by a soldier engaged in the Abyssinian war, confutes the statement of Bruce and some other travellers that the Abyssinians possess no instrument of the violin class. Fiddle of the Zulu Kafirs, South-eastern Africa. A very primitive contrivance, consisting of an iron basin, over which a skin is stretched, and of a rudely-made bow. It has three gut-strings. The back is open, the bottom of the basin having purposely been knocked out. This instrument was sent by Mr. Alfred J. Topham, from Pieter-Maritzburg, to the Manchester Exhibition. Marouvané, a bamboo instrument from Madagascar. Length, 21 inches. Its seven strings are cut out of the bark of the bamboo and are raised by bridges consisting of little plugs of wood. The tones produced are

but as the position of some of the bridges may have been slightly altered since the instrument came into the hands of Europeans, not much reliance is to be placed on the odd arrangement of intervals here exhibited.

Five nose-flutes, called *vivo* and *fango-fango*, of the Polynesian Islanders. Four of these instruments were brought to England by Vice-Admiral Sir Henry Denham. Two are from the Tonga Islands, and two from the Fiji Islands. Among the latter is especially noteworthy a large and fine one, profusely ornamented with designs burnt into the surface, which was obtained by Sir H. Denham at Angras, one of the Fiji Islands. The fifth specimen is from Otaheite. Jew's harp, brought by Vice-Admiral Sir Henry Denham from the Fiji Islands. It is neatly made of a sort of cane. Three Pandean pipes (one with nine tubes, and two with eleven tubes) brought by Vice-Admiral Sir Henry Denham from the Fiji Islands. These neatly-constructed specimens of the syrinx yield the following tones :—

Bone flute of the Caribi Indians, in Guiana, South America. Two rattles of the Indians of Vancouver Island, brought from Nootka Sound. Of wood, formed in imitation of a bird and of a fish, and painted with different colours. These rattles, called *belapella*, contain pebbles, and are used by the Medicine Men in their incantations. Dancing rattles of the Indians in the vicinity of the River Amazon, Brazil. Made of a species of nut, a large number of which are hollowed, and suspended to a cord, to be hung over the shoulders. By way of embellishment, some bright feathers and the tail of a quadruped are interspersed between the nuts. The sound produced by this rattle, when shaken, is soothing and pleasant, somewhat like the sound caused by the waves over the shingle on the sea-shore when heard at a distance. At any rate, it is preferable to some more pretentious musical performances of the present day. Sakasaka, a rattle of the Negroes of St. Lucia, West Indies. Ornamented with some rude designs cut on the surface. It contains a number of small red berries of an oval shape, known as jamboo berries.

Samsien, a Japanese stringed instrument. With a large plectrum of a white wood. Its three strings are of silk. The body is square, and is covered in front and at the back with parchment. Koto, a kind of dulcimer, from Japan, with silken strings and movable bridges. The present specimen is one of the smallest. Pepa, a Chinese kind of lute, with four silken strings. Two specimens. Yue-kin, or "Moon-guitar," a Chinese instrument, with four silken strings. Two specimens. San-heen, a Chinese stringed instrument. Ur-heen, Chinese fiddle. Two specimens. Tche, a Chinese stringed instrument, mounted with sixteen thin wire-strings. Kin, a Chinese instrument, the favourite of the great Confucius, and called, somewhat inappropriately, "Scholar's Lute." With its case lacquered and gilt. Yang-kin, Chinese dulcimer, with two little sticks or wooden hammers of a rather peculiar shape. Ty, Chinese flute. Cheng, Chinese organ, with seventeen bamboo tubes, containing vibrating tongues of metal, like our harmonium. Two specimens. Hiuen-tchung, antique Chinese bell. Two specimens. Chinese kind of tambourine, with a wooden hammer. Used in Buddhist worship. Chinese wooden castanets called pan, made in the shape of two spoons combined.

Ranat, a kind of harmonicon from Siam. It has nineteen slabs of sonorous wood placed over a sound-board resembling a canoe, and tuned diatonically. Thro, three-stringed fiddle of the Burmese; two specimens. The top of the fingerboard of one of these fiddles is ornamented with carvings in wood, and with a figure in ivory of a little idol. The strings are of silk; the head of the other specimen is likewise elaborately carved. This fiddle probably dates from the eighteenth century, if not earlier, and is a fine specimen of Burmese art. It was formerly in Signor Mario's museum. Megyoung, a Burmese stringed instrument in the form of an alligator, with three silken strings and eleven small bridges. Osee, a Burmese drum of a very peculiar construction. Walet khot, Burmese castanets, consisting of a pair of large split bamboos, 33 inches in length. Keay zoot, a pair of diminutive castanets of metal, from Burmah; they are in the shape of a saucer, and measure only an inch in diameter. The silvery tinkling sound which they produce is pleasant.

Sitar, a Hindu stringed instrument from Nagpoor. Sitar, a fine specimen with movable brass frets, Hindustan. The strings are of thin wire. Vina, the principal national instrument of the Hindus, also known as the Bengalese vina, strung with wire. The present specimen, which is of the smaller kind, is also called *kinnari*. Been, or Anthara vinai, Hindustan. This species of vina, is called by some Europeans, "the Benares vina," while the old national instrument of the Hindus, which is somewhat different in shape, is called, as we have just seen, "the Bengalese vina," no doubt on account of their being most popular in the districts indicated by their names. Rudra vina, from Bombay, a kind of *been* with sympathetic wire-strings, placed under the wire-strings which are sounded by the player. Taûs and bow, Hindustan. The taûs is a kind of sitar, the thin wire strings of which are played with a bow. It is made in the shape of a peacock, hence its name *taûs*, which signifies "peacock." The present specimen, which was sent by the Rajah of Navha to the International Exhibition, London, 1872, is from the Punjab. It is richly coloured, and gilt. The crest and the tail of the bird represented are peacock's feathers, stuck into holes made for the purpose. Koka, a rude kind of Hindu fiddle, mounted with two wire strings, from Bombay. The body consists of a large nut. The instrument bears a strong resemblance to the *gunibry* of the Barbary States; the latter is, however, played with the fingers, instead of a bow. Chikarah, a Hindu instrument of the violin class, from Bombay. It is cut out of a single block of wood, which, when rubbed or damped, emits a peculiar aromatic scent. The belly is of parchment. The instrument has three catgut-strings, beneath which are placed seven thin strings of wire. The wire-strings are fastened to tuning-pegs situated at the side of the neck. They merely serve as sympathetic strings, to increase the sonorousness when the catgut-strings are played upon with the bow. Sarungi, a Hindu instrument of the violin class, from Bombay. It is constructed of the same kind of wood as the chikarah before mentioned, but its shape is different. The belly is of parchment. The four catgut-strings with which the sarungi is mounted are played with the bow, and thirteen strings of thin brass wire, which run through little holes in the ivory bridge, are placed under the catgut-strings to serve as sympathetic strings. The performer on the sarungi does not press the catgut-strings down upon the finger-board, but touches them at the side with his fingers to produce the tones which he desires. He places the instrument before his breast in a nearly perpendicular direction. Whatever may be thought of this method of playing, the sarungi is certainly considered a very effective instrument, not only by the Hindus, but even by some European listeners. For instance, Colonel Meadows Taylor (' Proceedings of the Royal Irish Academy, Dublin, 1865,' p. 115) remarks: "Its tones are nearer, perhaps, in quality to the human voice than any other instrument with which I am acquainted." However, he does not appear to be acquainted with many instruments. Sarinda, a Hindu violin, with three strings. It is made of a single block of wood, hollowed, and carved. The upper part of the body is left partially open, and is partially covered with skin resembling bladder, generally from a species of gazelle. Sarod, with bow; a Hindu instrument with four catgut-strings, and underneath them five thin strings of brass. On the neck are three catgut-frets. The instrument is painted with designs in various colours. It came from Gwalior. Rabab, a kind of guitar of the Hindus, played with a plectrum. It resembles the saruda. Toontoonee: this curious Hindu instrument, with one wire-string, is used by mendicants and ballad-singers in the Dekhan. Santir, a dulcimer, from Cashmere. Sarmundal, from Kattyawar, Hindustan; a kind of dulcimer in a case. This scarce instrument is tastefully ornamented with painted flowers and fanciful designs. Its wire-strings are twanged with a plectrum made of wood and glass. Murchang, Jew's harp; two specimens of a peculiar shape, from Cashmere. Shank, conch trumpet, from Kattyawar, Hindustan, beautifully ornamented with brasswork. The shank is a sacred instrument blown by the Brahmin priests. Tootooree, a horn of metal, from Hindustan. Kombu, a horn of the Hindus, resembling in its semicircular shape the tootooree, but being smaller and heavier; from Madras. Bhangull, a very thin and long metal trumpet, from Kattyawar, in Hindustan. Kurna, a metal trumpet, straight and large, from Hindustan. Seeng, a large brass trumpet, from Hindustan. Poongee (also called magoudi and toomeree), the snake-charmer's double pipe, from Hindustan. Each tube contains a single reed. There are three specimens of the poongee in the collection, one of which is painted with various designs. The tubes of the poongee are inserted in a gourd. Mukha, a kind of oboe, from Madras. Mukhavinai, a small kind of oboe, Hindustan. Ottu, a species of oboe, somewhat resembling the Arabic zourna, from Janpore, in Hindustan. Zourna, from Hindustan; made of a dark brown wood, with nine finger-holes. Buguri, a very peculiar reed wind-instrument, having finger-holes like a flute, and being at its lower end provided with a bell like a trumpet, from Madras. Bansee, flute, Hindustan. Double flageolet, from Hindustan. Nagarah, a drum, from Surat, Hindustan. The body is of red earthenware, and the parchment is affixed to it by means of a leathern network, which is tastefully adjusted over the back of the drum; diameter at the top, 16 inches; height, $6\frac{1}{2}$ inches. Banyan,

COLLECTIONS OF MUSICAL INSTRUMENTS. 59

a small hand-drum, Hindustan. Davandai, a kind of double drum, or rather a double darabouka, Hindustan. Kudu Kuduppai, a very diminutive double darabouka of brass and fish bladder, Hindustan. Ghunta, a small bell with a handle, used by the Brahmin priests of Hindustan in religious ceremonies. Jalar, a pair of large castanets of metal, resembling small cymbals, from Hindustan. The sound of them is remarkably pure and sustained.

Rebab; a three-stringed fiddle from Persia. The body, cut out of a single piece of wood, is rudely ornamented with a pattern which is burnt on it. The strings are of catgut. They run at the top of the neck through holes, and are fastened at the back to the tuning-pegs. This *rebab* is an exact counterpart of the *rebec* formerly popular in Western Europe. Kemângeh a'gouz, with bow; from Egypt; a species of Eastern violoncello, with two strings made of horsehair. The body consists of the shell of a cocoa-nut, covered at the top with a bladder and perforated at the back with a number of sound-holes. Tanbour Baghlama; the eastern mandoline, strung with four thin wire-strings. Two specimens from Egypt. Gunibry; a rather primitive two-stringed instrument of the guitar kind, from Morocco; two specimens. Kuitra, a kind of guitar from the Barbary States. The body is made of a tortoise. The *kuitra*, or *kitar*, an instrument of the Persians and Arabs, is evidently the prototype of our guitar. The present specimen is one of the small kinds of kuitra; the larger kind has eight strings of sheep's gut arranged in four pairs.

Three English flageolets, made in the beginning of the present century. An ivory flûte à bec, made by Stanesby, junior, London, 1740. An ivory flauto piccolo with a silver key; English, eighteenth century. An ivory flauto traverso with one silver key; English, eighteenth century. This ivory flute and the two preceding ones are handsome instruments. A flûte à bec; English, about 1700; of boxwood and ivory; length, 18 inches; eight finger-holes, and without any key. An English recorder, of wood stained black; length, 26 inches; it probably dates from the seventeenth century. Two tenor

E

flutes, German, made about the year 1600. Length, 2 ft. 9 in. Seven finger-holes and one key. These scarce instruments were formerly in Signor Mario's museum. An English bass flute, made about the year 1650. Wood and ivory; with a brass tube for blowing the instrument. Six finger-holes, and one brass key at the upper side, and one finger-hole for the thumb at the opposite side. Length, 3 ft. 8 in. Three double flageolets dating from the beginning of the present century, two of which are made by Bainbridge in London, and the third is inscribed "Simpson." A triple flageolet, on which harmony in three parts can be played; made by Bainbridge in London, in the beginning of the present century. An English horn (oboe da caccia) made of red cedar, by Thomas Stanesby, junior, in London, about 1740. An English horn (oboe da caccia), eighteenth century; probably made in England. Wood, stained black, and ivory. This is the kind of oboe which J. S. Bach has employed in his 'Passion of St. Matthew.' A dolciano, a small bassoon. Inscription: "Wood and Ivy, late Ger^d Wood, London." A basset horn (corno di bassetto), probably English. A border bagpipe, from Northumberland. With bellows, and four drones. A French bagpipe (cornemuse). An English trumpet in case; made probably in the eighteenth or in the beginning of the nineteenth century. A small trombone, English, made by Allen and Pace. A horn, of brass; the bell terminating in the head of a serpent; English, eighteenth century. A serpent, by "Gerrock Wolf, in London;" beginning of the present century. Two alphorns, made by M. von Euw in Bürgy, Rigi Kulm, Canton Swyz, Switzerland, of birchwood neatly covered with birch-bark. Length, 8 ft. 1 in. A cither, a specimen of the kind which was commonly found in England, some centuries ago, in barbers' shops; English, about 1700.* A German cither; end of the seventeenth century. Ornamented with marquetry. A small English cither, made about the year 1700. The open strings produce only five tones instead

---

* In England the cither was formerly called *cittern, cithern, cythorn, citharen*, etc.

of six. Specimens of this kind are very scarce. An English cither of the eighteenth century. An English cither made by Remerus Liessem, London, 1756. The body is of a very old-fashioned form, having several incurvations at the sides. A small English cither of the eighteenth century. The sound-hole is ornamented with a rose made of wood. The rose of the English cither is more usually made of bronze. Cetera; an Italian cither, made about the year 1680. This is the most beautiful cither in the collection. The entire instrument, except the belly, is inlaid with tasteful designs in ivory and ebony. Also the tone is remarkably fine. A Scotch cither neatly inlaid with wood ornamentation. At the back is a plate of mother-of-pearl with the inscription "Rudiman, ABD<u>N</u>, DG." Perhaps this cither belonged to the well-known Latin grammarian Rudiman, who, about the year 1700, was at King's College in Aberdeen. An Irish cither with an ivory finger-board and with ten tuning-screws of brass. A large specimen. Made by Perry in Dublin; eighteenth century. Cithara; a Portuguese cither with six pairs of wire-strings, inlaid with tortoise-shell and ivory. Made by Joan Vieira da Silva at Lisbon, about 1700. Cithara; a Portuguese cither, probably dating from the beginning of the eighteenth century. Mounted with twelve strings in pairs. A very fine-toned instrument. Inscription: "Cyprianio Antonio a fez em Lisboa, ao Largo da Esperança." A keyed cither; English, eighteenth century. It has six ivory keys. The idea of applying keys like those of the pianoforte to the cither, and thus striking the wire-strings with hammers instead of twanging them with a quill originated in Germany, but proved to be of no practical advantage. Bijuga cither (*i.e.* a cither with a double neck, like the theorbo). Two French specimens, dating from about the middle of the eighteenth century. Bijuga cither, made by Renault in Paris, anno 1779. This handsome species of cither, constructed like the theorbo, but having a flat back, was evidently often strung in France with catgut instead of wire, and played with the fingers like the theorbo. It is probably the instrument which in some old French books is called *pandore*. It has sixteen strings. A French bijuga cither of the eighteenth century, inlaid with mother-of-pearl, ivory and ebony. A fine specimen. An English bijuga cither, eighteenth century. A German bijuga cither (or Grosszither, as it used to be called in Germany), sixteenth century. With seventeen wire-strings. This old instrument is very beautiful in shape, and has a remarkably picturesque rose in the middle of the sound-board. Two Neapolitan mandolinos, inlaid with designs in mother-of-pearl tortoise-shell and ivory. One of these handsome instruments bears the inscription "Januarius Vinaccio fecit, Neapoli, in Rio Catalana, A. Domini 1776." A beautiful Neapolitan mandolino in its old Italian case. Inside the instrument is the inscription "Vincentius Vinaccio fecit, Neapoli, Sito Nella Calata de Spitalletto, A.D. 1785." A Milanese mandolino, dating from about the year 1700. Rosewood, inlaid with mother-of-pearl, tortoise-shell, and ivory. Silver frets. In front, a figure of Apollo under a canopy and other embellishments in mother-of-pearl. An ornamented sound-hole, the rose being covered with glass. A figure, made of mother-of-pearl, inlaid near the bridge, contains the engraved initials "A. G.," which may be those of the maker of this elegant instrument—possibly Andreas Guarnerius. This mandolino, the handsomest I ever saw, is of the kind called by some musicians "mandurina." It has twelve wire-strings which are arranged in pairs, and therefore produce six tones; while the more common Neapolitan mandolino has eight strings constituting four pairs. A French mandoline, made by Eulry-Clement, in Mirecourt, Vosges, beginning of the present century; the back inlaid with strips of different woods. Eight strings arranged in four pairs. A mandola; Italian, seventeenth century. This scarce instrument may be most briefly described as a huge Neapolitan mandolino. It has the shape of the mandolino, but the size of a large lute; sixteen wire-strings, placed in pairs, produce eight tones of the open strings. The sound is remarkably full and fine. A mandola, similar to the preceding one, inscribed "Gio. Battista, Neapoli, A.D. 1701." Length, 2 ft. 11 in.; depth of body, 10 in. The mandola was played with a quill like the mandolino and the cither. Pandura, two specimens, made in Italy about the year 1700. Bandurria; Spanish, eighteenth century; played with a plectrum usually made of tortoise-shell. Pandore; English, seventeenth century; played with a quill. It is also called chiterna. Pandurina; Italian, about 1700; its nine catgut and wire strings are arranged in pairs tuned in unison, except the lowest, which is single. The open strings, therefore, produce five tones. The neck is provided with catgut frets. The pandurina, which in shape resembles a diminutive lute, even smaller than the Neapolitan mandoline, was usually played with the fingers, but occasionally also with a quill. On the Continent, gentlemen used to carry it under their mantle when they went to musical parties, or for serenading. Pandurina, twelve-stringed. Inscription: "Carlo Steffani fece. L'Anno 1712, in Mantova." Pandurina, in its old Italian case, with brass ornamentation. The back made of strips of ebony and ivory; length, 20 in. Ivory frets; twelve metal strings. Inscription in the inside: "Joseph Molinari, Venetus, Anno, 1737." Quinterna, Italian, seventeenth century. A species of guitar somewhat resembling a violin in shape, with frets made of catgut. Mounted with eight catgut-strings which produce five tones, as they are arranged in three pairs and two single ones. A five-stringed guitar inlaid with mother-of-pearl and tortoise-shell. Italian, eighteenth century. A French guitar, made by Vobeam, a celebrated lute-maker of the time of Louis XIV. The strings are arranged in pairs tuned in unison. An English guitar, made in the beginning of the present century; the back and sides of the body are of rosewood; the sides have several indentations. Machine head. Portuguese guitar, made about the year 1600, with three sound-holes. The head is bent backwards somewhat like that of the lute; the frets are of catgut, as they used likewise to be on the lute. Not only the belly, but the entire body is made of thin pine-wood. The strings, twelve in number, are arranged so that the higher six are in sets of two, and the lower six in sets of three. As the strings of each set are tuned in unison, five tones are produced by the open strings. An inscription in the inside of this guitar, now greatly obliterated, runs as follows: "Manoel Correa de Alm^{da} Uileiro da Rainha, N.S., morador na Ruadireita la Esperança LX^a." It would, therefore, appear that the guitar was made by Manoel Correa of Almeida in the province of Beira, Portugal, and that the maker had the title of manufacturer of musical instruments to the Queen. The Portuguese musician, Manoel Correa, born in the year 1590, at Lisbon, and engaged about the year 1620 as chapelmaster at the Cathedral in Saragossa, was probably of the same family as the maker of this instrument. A guitar of the Portuguese peasants, made in Lisbon, eighteenth century; oval shape with indentations at the side; six strings. Inside is a label with the inscription: "Joze Terreira Coelho a fez em, Lisboa, ao Poco los Negros, a Cruz da Esperança." Machête, a small guitar with four strings; Portuguese, eighteenth century. Harp-guitar; English, about 1800. On the finger board is the inscription: "Clementi and Co., London;" painted with flowers, etc.; eight strings. The pianist and composer Clementi gave his name to a firm of music-sellers in the year 1800. Harp-guitar; English, about 1800; seven strings. The harp-guitar was manufactured with the intention of producing a sort of guitar with a superior quality of sound, by adopting the body of the harp. Lyre-guitare; French, period of Louis XV.; a guitar in the form of Apollo's lyre, with the addition of a finger-board in the middle. Lyre-guitare; French, said to have belonged to Queen Marie-Antoinette; carved and gilt. Guitar-lyre; English, made by R. Wornum, Wigmore Street, London, about 1770. The English guitar-lyre is in its construction almost identical with the French lyre-guitare. Harp-lute; English, about 1800; painted green, with gilt ornamentation of flowers, and other designs. Ditalharp; English. An improved harp-lute, recorded to have been invented by Edward Light, London, about the year 1800. Harp-ventura; English, invented at the beginning of the present century by Angelo Benedetto Ventura, in London. This gorgeously-ornamented instrument resembles the ditalharp and the harp-lute in construction. Harp-theorbo; English, made by Walker, about 1800. Lute, the back inlaid with ivory and various woods. From an inscription in the inside, now greatly obliterated, it would appear that this lute was made by Magnus Tieffenbruker, in Venice, about 1580. Lute, by Laux Maler, in Bologna, fifteenth century. Brass and ivory screws have been substituted for the original tuning-pegs. This contrivance, as well as a painting of flowers on the sound-board, is probably not older than a hundred years. The places where some of the ancient tuning-pegs were fixed are still discernible. The cracks on its pear-shaped body rather contribute to its dignity, and might be likened to the wrinkles of a venerable grandsire. The sound of this old lute is very fine. A German lute, made by Jacobus Heinrich Goldt, in Hamburg, anno 1712. According to an inscription in the inside, it was altered in the year 1753. A French lute of the seventeenth century. An Italian lute; inscription: "Vvendelio Venere in Padova, 1600;" with the head turned backwards; twenty strings. This lute is of one of the most celebrated Italian lute-makers, and is in a well-preserved and playable condition, notwithstanding its high age. An English lute with a double neck (Testudo theorbata) made about 1650. A theorbo, Italian, seventeenth century. It has twenty-four catgut strings, which are arranged in pairs tuned in unison, except the highest two which are single strings. It was the custom to have the highest string, called *chanterelle*, single; it principally served for playing the melody. Sometimes, as in the present instance, two *chanterelles* were used. The twenty-four open strings, therefore, produce thirteen different tones. The frets are of catgut. A French theorbo, made about the year 1700. An archlute; Italian, about 1700; a large instrument, with eighteen strings, ten of which are for the upper set of tuning-pegs, belonging to the bass strings which are at the side of the finger-board. The ten bass strings produce five tones with their octaves, each tone having two strings tuned in an octave. The archlute, or bass-theorbo, is the largest sized kind of the theorbo, or lute with a double neck. An Italian archlute, inscribed: "Matheus Bucchenberg, Roma, 1619." From Signor Mario's museum. Bucchenberg, or Bueckenberg as he was more generally called, was one of the most celebrated lute-makers in Italy, and a German by birth. The present archlute has three ornamented sound-holes. It is provided with a mechanism by means of which any one of the bass strings by the side of the finger-board can be raised a semitone in pitch at the pleasure of the performer. This ingenious contrivance, which renders the bass strings more useful in compositions having modulations into distant major or minor keys, occurs also on a French theorbo dating from about the year 1700, which is in my collection. But on this French theorbo, the mechanism acts upon all the strings beside the finger-board simultaneously, while on the archlute just noticed it is contrived so that any single string may be altered in pitch independently of others. As the mechanism is evidently not a later addition, but was made with the instrument in 1619, it is suggestive to musical antiquarians, inasmuch as it reveals a higher degree of progress in the construction of the lute than is generally supposed to have been attained about the beginning of the seventeenth century. An Italian theorbino, or the smallest kind of theorbo, seventeenth century; with sixteen strings, six of which run beside the finger-board. A chitarrone, or large Roman theorbo; Italian. Inscription: "Vitus de Angelis, Bonon, 1609." It is about six feet long, and has twenty-one strings. The chitarrone was formerly called Roman theorbo, because it was principally used at Rome. There was a similar instrument popular at Padua, somewhat smaller in size. The present specimen was made in Bologna. The chitarrone was used in the orchestra, assisting at dramatic performances as well as in church music. It was often strung with wire instead of catgut; the same was the case with the common theorbo of Germany and England. A chitarrone, with marquetry and three ornamented sound-holes; made by M. Bueckenberg, in Rome, anno 1614. From Signor Mario's collection. An Irish harp (clarseth), strung with wire; made by Egan, in Dublin, in the beginning of the present century. An arpanetta (German, Spitzharfe), English, seventeenth century; with one hundred steel wire-strings and thirty-five brass wire-strings. A bûche (German, Scheidholt), from Val d'Ajol, in the Vosges mountains, in France; made in the beginning of the present century. An English specimen of the *hummel*, probably made during the eighteenth century; with twelve wire strings. It resembles the bûche, and may be regarded as an antiquated species of our present horizontal cither. A bell-harp, made by John Simcock, in Bath, about the year 1700: length, 20 in. It has sixteen tones. Each tone is produced by three thin brass wire-strings tuned in unison. The strings are twanged with two little plectra, or quills, of which the performer fastens one to the thumb of each hand. The two wooden handles, one on each side of the instrument, are for holding while swinging it during the performance, to produce the effect of a distant bell. A bell-harp; English, about 1700. Inscribed: "Bath, John Simcock, inventor and maker." This instrument has twenty-four tones produced by thin brass wire-strings. The highest tones have each four strings tuned in unison, the others have three, except the deepest, which is produced by a single string covered with wire. The instrument is in its old case. Dulcimer; English, with movable bridges. Inscribed: "Old Weston, Huntingdonshire, 1846." Dulcimer; English, beginning of the present century; of mahogany, the soundboard of pine, being painted green, and gilt. Sixteen sets of wire-strings, each set consisting of three strings tuned in unison. Salterio, Italian dulcimer, made by Antonio Bertefice, at Florence, in the year 1745. Salterio; Italian dulcimer; a small specimen, inscribed at the back: "Antonius Berri fecit, Anno 1722." From Signor Mario's museum. Echelette; French, eighteenth century. It has twenty-two slabs of a hard and sonorous wood, which are sounded by being struck with two little mallets. A sordino, or boat-shaped pochette; English, seventeenth century. An Italian sordino, dating from about the year 1600. The body is of tortoise-shell, inlaid with silver; the tuning-pegs are of ivory; with a carved head of wood and ivory. The entire length of this sordino is only 14 inches. A kit, or pochette, in the shape of the violin; Italian, about 1600. Violetta piccola, the smallest kind of the old viol instruments, shaped with a slanting neck like the viola da gamba. This small species of treble viol was called by the French *haute-contre*. Italian, seventeenth century. A five-stringed viol, called by the French *quinton*. Inscription " Antonius Gragnani fecit, Anno 1741." A small six-stringed viol, called by the French *dessus-de-viole;* French, seventeenth century. A six-stringed viol, called by the French *pardessus;* French, seventeenth century. A treble viol, with a carved head; English, about 1700. Its neck has catgut frets, and its six strings were tuned like those of the bass-viol, or viola da gamba, but an octave higher. A counter-tenor-viol; English, seventeenth century. Inside is the inscription: " Henry Jay, in Southwarke, 1667." The scroll is finely carved. The belly has, besides the usual two sound-holes, an oval sound-hole in the middle, with an ornamental rose. The back has a peculiar curve towards the end; probably, the instrument was intended to rest on the left shoulder when played. Like the viola da gamba, it has six strings and catgut frets. It was tuned a fifth higher than the viola da gamba. A tenor-viol; English, about 1620. This small species of viola da gamba is now very scarce. It was tuned a fourth higher than the larger viola da gamba, or bass-viol. Viola da gamba, inlaid with mythological representations and other ornamentation in ivory, mother-of-pearl, tortoise-shell, and precious stones. Made about the year 1580, probably by Joachim Tielke in Hamburg; a splendid instrument. Viola da gamba; English, seventeenth century; with a finely-carved head representing the bust of a girl. Inside is the inscription: " Richard Meares, without Bishopsgate, near to Sir Paul Pinder's, London, Fecit 1677." In the *Post Boy* of the 9th of July, 1720, we find the following advertisement: " This is to give notice to all gentlemen and ladies, lovers of musick, that the most celebrated new opera of 'Radamistus,' composed by Mr. Handell, is now engraving finely upon copper-plates by Richard Meares, musical instrument maker and music printer, at the Golden Viol. To make this work more acceptable, the author has been prevailed upon to correct the whole." The Golden Viol was

the sign of a music-shop in St. Paul's Churchyard, where
Richard Meares, the publisher of Handel's opera, lived.
But, to judge from a notice of this publisher given in
Hawkins's 'History of Music' (Vol. V., p. 109), it appears
that he was the son of the maker of the present viola da
gamba. At any rate, when Handel came to England this
instrument was no longer a new one; for it was made before
Handel was born. The bow belonging to it is of the old-
fashioned kind known as the Corelli bow. And it may
be here mentioned that with most of the viols before
enumerated curious bows are placed which have long since
gone out of use. Viola da gamba; Italian, about 1600;
with a finely-carved head. The finger-board is inlaid with
designs of flowers, etc., in tortoise-shell and ivory. This
fine-toned bass-viol is supposed to have been made by
Gaspar di Salo. At all events, it is a valuable specimen by
some early Italian maker. Viola da gamba; English, about
1700. The instrument resembles a small violoncello, since
its body does not slant towards the neck. An illustration
of this kind of viola da gamba is given in 'The Division-
Violist, by Christopher Simpson, London, 1659.' Its body
is remarkably flat, and its quality of sound is consequently
very clear. Like the common viola da gamba, the instrument is six-stringed, and has catgut frets. A seven-stringed
viola da gamba; probably Italian; towards the end of the
seventeenth century. The addition of a seventh string to
the viola da gamba is said to have been first resorted to
by the French *virtuoso* Maria Marais, towards the end of
the seventeenth century. The string added is the lowest,
and is tuned a minor third lower than the C string on the
violoncello. The innovation evidently did not find much
favour with gamba players in general; and it is seldom that
one still meets with a seven-stringed gamba. A four-
stringed viola da gamba; made by John Baker in Oxford,
anno 1688. Four-stringed gambas met with at the
present day are almost invariably altered six-stringed
ones, on which the neck has been narrowed, and the
head shortened, so that the instrument may be used as
a small violoncello. This one was originally made with

only four strings, and has evidently never been tampered with. Viola d'amore; Italian, seventeenth century. A fine specimen, in a well-preserved condition. Viola d'amore; Italian, seventeenth century. Old-fashioned shape, having several incurvations at the sides, and a sound-hole with a rose in the middle of the belly. Seven catgut-strings, and underneath them seven sympathetic strings of thin steel-wire. Viola d'amore; German, eighteenth century. Probably made by Jacob Rauch, in Mannheim, about 1740. With only five catgut-strings, and with eight sympathetic wire-strings. An English viola d'amore strung entirely with wire, seventeenth century; with a curiously-constructed head, ornamented with a carved female bust. A so-called psaltery (also known as sultana and cither-viol). Mounted with six wire-strings, and played with a bow. Irish; eighteenth century. Made by Thomas Perry, in Dublin, anno 1767. A psaltery, made by Thomas Perry, in Dublin, second half of eighteenth century. The neck and the tail-piece are of ivory. Its ten strings are of steel and brass wire, the highest eight being arranged in four pairs producing four tones, and the others are single ones producing two tones. Hardangerfelen. A kind of viola d'amore of the Hardanger peasants in Norway, inlaid with mother-of-pearl and ivory. The top, carved and gilt, represents a dragon's head. This fiddle has four catgut-strings, and four thin steel-strings beneath them. Inside is the inscription "Fabrokert of Knudt Erikson, Helland, 1872." It was sent to me from Christiania. Violins of unusual shapes, three curious specimens, made during the eighteenth century. A violin made of iron. Probably English, beginning of the present century. If on no other account, this violin is certainly interesting in an acoustic point of view, since it proves that much sound is obtainable merely by the vibration of the strings acting upon the column of air in the violin, without any assisting vibration of the belly or sound-board. At all events, the substance of which this violin is made is not likely to contribute to the sonorousness. A tromba marina or marine trumpet, probably Dutch, seventeenth century. Besides one string of thick catgut upon the instrument, there are in the inside forty-one sympathetic strings of thin steel-wire. A nyckel-harpa, a curious instrument of the Swedish peasantry, which may be briefly described as a combination of a fiddle and a hurdy-gurdy. A crwth, an antiquated Welsh instrument of the fiddle class. The body is cut out of a single block of wood, the belly only being glued to it. Two specimens of the nail-violin, one of which has sympathetic strings of thin brass-wire running over the sound-board. These two curious instruments were probably made in France or Germany about the year 1800. The invention of the nail-violin is attributed to a German of the name of Wilde, who lived in St. Petersburg about the middle of the eighteenth century. A hurdy-gurdy (French, *vielle*), made by Pagot at Jenzat, a small town near Orleans, about the year 1840. Carved head. Six tuning-pegs at the top, and one at the tail-piece. This hurdy-gurdy is of the kind which the French call *vielle en luth*, because its body is shaped like that of the lute. The other kind, which has indentations at the sides resembling those of the guitar, is called *vielle en guitare.* Organ hurdy-gurdy, or *vielle organisée*, made by a Frenchman residing in London during the middle of the eighteenth century. This curious instrument, which was formerly also known in England, where it was called *flute-cymbal*, consists of a hurdy-gurdy combined with a small organ of two stops, and it is so contrived as to allow the hurdy-gurdy or the organ to be used each separately, or both combined, at the pleasure of the performer. Some portions of it have been restored in the present century. Clavichord, generally called in German *Clavier.* Made in Einbeck, near Hanover, about the year 1800. Clavichord, made in Thuringia. Clavichord, made by the celebrated manufacturer, Barthold Fritz, in Brunswick, in the year 1751 ; ornamented with painting and engraving. Harpsichord, inscribed " Jacobus Kirkman, Londini, fecit 1772." The case is of walnut, inlaid with tulip-wood. Carved legs representing eagle's claws grasping a ball. With two keyboards, constituting a "double harpsichord," as it used to be called in England. The woodwork about the keyboards is ornamented with designs in marquetry of various coloured woods. This harpsichord has six stops and two pedals, and is provided with a Venetian swell. Jacobus Kirkman, having obtained an order from King George III. to produce a fine harpsichord intended as a present for Queen Charlotte, made—as manufacturers under such circumstances not unfrequently do—two harpsichords exactly alike, viz., one for Queen Charlotte, and the present one, which was bought by John Bacon, the famous sculptor, after whose death it came into the possession of Dr. Sclatter, priest-vicar of Exeter Cathedral, who had it for nearly half-a-century, and after whose death it was sold at a sale of his effects. Harpsichord with two keyboards, six stops, and two pedals. Inscribed " Jacobus et Abraham Kirkman, fecerunt 1773." The case is of mahogany; the wood near the keyboards is walnut, inlaid with tulip-wood and a tesselated border of various coloured woods. Only the lute-stop has jacks with crow-quills; the jacks of the other stops are provided with small pieces of prepared leather instead of quills. The variety in the colour of sound thereby obtained is very effective. This instrument probably exhibits the highest degree of perfection which was ever attained in the construction of the harpsichord, in so far as quality and power of sound are concerned. As regards outward appearance, the beauty of some of the Dutch harpsichords, or *clavicembali*, ornamented with paintings by celebrated artists, is unsurpassed.

It now remains to draw attention to the fact that many of the Museums of Antiquities in different countries instituted by Government contain some curiosities of the kind in question which cannot fail to interest the musical antiquarian. This is the case even in America, where in the museums of Mexico, Lima, and other towns, may be found among the examples of workmanship and arts of the Aztecs and the Inca Peruvians various contrivances relating to music. That royal personages in their cabinets of curiosities obtained from distant lands should not unfrequently have scarce, or handsome, or grotesque-looking musical instruments is only what might be expected. There are, for instance, about forty acquisitions of this kind in Windsor Castle, which consist chiefly of Asiatic and African drums, pipes, and stringed instruments. Several of them, however, are spoiled by having been " improved," or Europeanized. Some have descriptive labels attached to them, as, for instance, an Ashanti war-trumpet made of a human bone, and ornamented with human jawbones; and an Ashanti war-drum, carved from the trunk of a tree, and likewise ornamented with human jawbones; which two curiosities, the labels inform us, belonged to the King of Ashanti, from whom they were taken "in the action in which he was defeated by Colonel Purden. Sent by Sir Herbert Taylor in 1827. Brought to England by Major-General Sir Neil Campbell, commanding on the Western Coast of Africa." There is also in this assemblage a fanciful contrivance, which is intended for a sort of guitar, and of which a label affixed informs us: "This instrument was made from the head of the Duke of Schomberg's horse, killed at the battle of the Boyne, 1690."

Of the special exhibition of ancient musical instruments held in the South Kensington Museum in the year 1872, an account has been given in the Descriptive Catalogue of the Musical Instruments in the South Kensington Museum, London, 1874. The present survey would, however, be imperfect if that remarkable exhibition were left entirely unnoticed, although the collection which it comprised had an existence of four months only. Suffice it here to record that it contained upwards of five hundred instruments, including a large number of violins, violas, and violoncellos of the celebrated Cremona makers. Should a similar exhibition be attempted, an equally successful result is not likely to be achieved for years, if ever. Old and scarce musical instruments have become of much more antiquarian interest than formerly was the case. The specimens still obtainable by purchase gradually find their way into public museums, not only in European countries, but also in America, and in the English colonies. Whenever they have been secured for a museum they generally are no longer obtainable on loan for other exhibitions. Private persons possessing such treasures set upon them a higher value than formerly, and are therefore less inclined to expose them to the risk of being injured. For these reasons it appears all the more desirable that there should be some record of the collections known to be still in existence.

MUSICAL MYTHS AND FOLK-LORE.

Music is so delightfully innocent and charming an art that we cannot wonder at finding it almost universally regarded as of divine origin. Pagan nations generally ascribe the invention of their musical instruments to their gods or to certain superhuman beings of a godlike nature. The Hebrews attributed it to man; but as Jubal is mentioned as "the father of all such as handle the harp and organ" only, and as instruments of percussion are almost invariably in use long before people are led to construct stringed and wind instruments, we may suppose that, in the biblical records, Jubal is not intended to be represented as the original inventor of all the Hebrew instruments, but rather as a great promoter of the art of music.

However this may be, thus much is certain: there are among Christians at the present day not a few sincere upholders of the literal meaning of those records who maintain that instrumental music was already practised in Heaven before the creation of the world. Elaborate treatises have been written on the nature and effect of that heavenly music, and passages from the Bible have been cited by the learned authors which are supposed by them to confirm indisputably the opinions advanced in their treatises.

It may, at a first glance, appear singular that nations have not generally such traditional records respecting the originators of their vocal music as they have respecting the invention of their musical instruments. The cause is however explicable; to sing is as natural to man as to speak, and uncivilised nations are not likely to speculate whether singing has ever been invented.

There is no need to recount here the well-known mythological traditions of the ancient Greeks and Romans referring to the origin of their favourite musical instruments. Suffice it to remind the reader that Mercury and Apollo were believed to be the inventors of the lyra and the kithara; that the invention of the flute was attributed to Minerva; and that Pan is said to have invented the syrinx. More worthy of our attention are some similar records of the Hindus, because they have hitherto scarcely been noticed in any work on music.

In the mythology of the Hindus the god Nareda is the inventor of the *vina*, the principal national musical instrument of Hindustan. Saraswati, the consort of Brahma, may be considered as the Minerva of the Hindus. She is the goddess of music as well as of speech. To her is attributed the invention of the systematic arrangement of the sounds into a musical scale. She is represented seated on a peacock and playing on a stringed instrument of the guitar kind. Brahma himself we find depicted as a vigorous man with four handsome heads, beating with his hands upon a small drum. And Vishnu, in his incarnation as Krishna, is represented as a beautiful youth playing upon a flute. The Hindus still possess a peculiar kind of flute which they consider as the favourite instrument of Krishna. Furthermore, they have the divinity of Genēsa, the god of wisdom, who is represented as a man with the head of an elephant holding in his hands a tamboura—a kind of lute with a long neck.

Among the Chinese we meet with a tradition according to which they obtained their musical scale from a miraculous bird called Foung-hoang, which appears to have been a sort of Phœnix. As regards the invention of musical instruments, the Chinese have various traditions. In one of these we are told that the origin of some of their most popular instruments dates from the period when China was under the dominion of heavenly spirits called Ki. Another assigns the invention of several of their stringed instruments to the great Fohi, called "the Son of Heaven," who was, it is said, the founder of the Chinese empire, and who is stated to have lived about B.C. 3000, which was long after the dominion of the Ki, or spirits. Again, another tradition holds that the most important Chinese musical instruments, and the systematic arrangement of the tones, are an invention of Niuva, a supernatural female, who lived at the time of Fohi, and who was a virgin-mother. When Confucius, the great Chinese philosopher, happened to hear on a certain occasion some divine music, he became so greatly enraptured that he could not take any food for three months afterwards. The music which produced this miraculous effect was that of Kouei, the Orpheus of the Chinese, whose performance on the *king*, a kind of harmonicon constructed of slabs of sonorous stone, would draw wild animals around him and make them subservient to his will.

The Japanese have a beautiful tradition according to which the Sun-goddess, in resentment of the violence of an evil-disposed brother, retired into a cave, leaving the universe in darkness and in anarchy; when the beneficent gods, in their concern for the welfare of mankind, devised music to lure her forth from the retreat, and their efforts soon proved successful.*

The Kalmuks, in the vicinity of the Caspian Sea, adore a beneficent divinity, called Maidari, who is represented as a rather jovial-looking man, with a moustache and an imperial, playing upon an instrument with three strings, somewhat resembling the Russian balalaika.

Almost all these ancient conceptions we meet with also among European nations, though more or less modified.

Odin, the principal deity of the ancient Scandinavians, was the inventor of magic songs and Runic writings.

In the Finnish mythology the divine Vainamoinen is said to have constructed the five-stringed harp, called kantele, the old national instrument of the Finns. The frame he made out of the bones of the pike, and the teeth of the pike he used for the tuning-pegs. The strings he made of hair from the tail of a spirited horse. When the harp fell into the sea, and was lost, he made another, the frame of which was of

---

* 'Notices of Japan.' The Chinese Repository, Vol. IX. Canton, 1840, p. 620.

birchwood, with pegs made out of the branch of an oak-tree. As strings for this harp he used the silky hair of a young girl. Vainamoinen took his harp, and sat down on a hill near a silvery brook. There he played with so irresistible an effect that he entranced whatever came within hearing of his music. Men and animals listened enraptured; the wildest beasts of the forest lost their ferocity; the birds of the air were drawn towards him; the fishes rose to the surface of the water, and remained immovable; the trees ceased to wave their branches; the brook retarded its course, and the wind its haste; even the mocking echo approached stealthily, and listened with the utmost attention to the heavenly sounds. Soon the women began to cry; then the old men and the children also began to cry; and the girls, and the young men—all cried for delight. At last Vainamoinen himself wept; and his big tears ran over his beard, and rolled into the water, and became beautiful pearls at the bottom of the sea.

Several other musical gods or godlike musicians could be cited, and, moreover, innumerable minor spirits, all bearing evidence that music is of divine origin.

True, people who think themselves more enlightened than their forefathers smile at these old traditions, and say that the original home of music is the human heart. Be it so. But do not the purest and most beautiful conceptions of man partake of a divine character? Is not the art of music generally acknowledged to be one of these? And is it not, therefore, even independently of myths and mysteries, entitled to be called the divine art?

CURIOUS COINCIDENCES.

It is a suggestive fact that several nations in different parts of the world possess an ancient tradition, according to which some harp-like instrument was originally derived from the water.

The Scandinavian god Odin, the originator of magic songs, is mentioned as the ruler of the sea; and as such he had the name of Nikarr. In the depth of the sea he played the harp with his subordinate spirits, who occasionally came up to the surface of the water to teach some favoured human being their wonderful instrument.

Vainamoinen, the divine player on the Finnish kantele, according to the Kalewala, the old national æpos of the Finns, constructed the first instrument of this kind of fish-bones.

Hermes, it will be remembered, made his lyre, the chelys, of a tortoise-shell.

In Hindu mythology the god Nareda invented the vina, a five-stringed instrument, considered as the principal national instrument of the Hindus, which has also the name *kach'-hapi*, signifying a tortoise. Moreover *nara* denotes in Sanskrit "water," and *Narada* or *Nareda* "the Giver of Water."

Like Nareda, so Nereus and his fifty daughters, the Nereides, mentioned in Greek mythology, were renowned for their musical accomplishments.

Again, there is an old tradition, preserved in Swedish and Scottish national ballads, of a skilful harper who constructs his instrument out of the bones of a young girl drowned by a wicked woman. Her fingers he uses for the tuning screws, and her golden hair for the strings. The harper plays, and his music kills the murderess.* A similar story is told in the old Icelandic national songs, and the same tradition has been found still preserved in the Faroe Islands, as well as in Norway and Denmark.†

May not the agreeable impression produced by the rhythmical flow of the waves and the soothing murmur of running water have led various nations, independently of each other, to the widespread conception that they obtained their favourite instrument of music originally from the water? Or is this notion traceable to a common source, dating from a pre-historic age—perhaps from the early period when the Aryan race is surmised to have diffused its

---

* 'Deutsche Mythologie, von Jacob Grimm. Göttingen, 1854.' P. 860.

† 'Alt-isländische Volks-Balladen, übersetzt von P. J. Willatzen. Bremen, 1865.' P. 83.

lore through various countries? Or did it originate in the old belief of the world with all its charms and delights having arisen from a chaos in which water constituted the predominant element?

Howbeit, Nareda, the Giver of Water, was evidently also the ruler of the clouds; and Odin had his throne in the skies. Indeed, many of the musical water-spirits appear to have been originally considered as rain-deities. Their music may, therefore, be regarded as derived from the clouds rather than from the sea. In short, the traditions respecting spirits and water are not in contradiction to, but rather confirmatory of the belief that music is of heavenly origin.

HINDU TRADITIONS.

MIA TONSINE, a wonderful musician in the time of the Emperor Akber, sang one of the *night-rags* at mid-day. The power of the music was such that it instantly became night, and the darkness extended in a circle round the palace as far as the sound of the voice could be heard. Rags are characteristic songs composed in certain modes or scales; and each Rag is appropriated to a distinct season, in which alone it must be sung or played at prescribed hours of the day or night; for, over each of the six Rags, or kinds of compositions, presides a certain god, who presides likewise over the six seasons. The six seasons are: *Seesar*, the dewy season; *Heemat*, the cold season; *Vasant*, the mild season, or spring; *Greesshma*, the hot season; *Varsa*, the rainy season; and *Sarat*, the breaking-up, or end of the rains.*

Whoever shall attempt to sing the Rag *Dheepuck* (or "Cupid the Inflamer") is to be destroyed by fire. The Emperor Akber ordered Naik Gopaul, a celebrated musician, to sing that Rag. Naik Gopaul endeavoured to excuse himself, but in vain; the Emperor insisted on obedience. The unhappy musician therefore requested permission to go home, and to bid farewell to his family and

---

* 'Sketches relating to the History, Religion, Learning, and Manners of the Hindoos,' [by Q. Craufurd.] London, 1790.' P. 153.

friends. It was winter when he returned, after an absence of six months. Before he began to sing he placed himself in the waters of the Jumna till they reached his neck. As soon as he had performed a strain or two the river gradually became hot; at length it began to boil, and the agonies of the unhappy musician were nearly insupportable. Suspending for a moment the melody thus cruelly extorted, he sued for mercy from the monarch, but sued in vain. Akber wished to prove more strongly the powers of the Rag *Dheepuck*. Naik Gopaul renewed the fatal song: flames burst with violence from his body, which, though immersed in the waters of the Jumna, was consumed to ashes.

The effect produced by the Rag called *Maig Mullaar* is immediate rain. It is told that a singing girl once, by exerting the powers of her voice in this Rag, drew from the clouds timely and refreshing showers on the parched rice-crops of Bengal, and thereby averted the horrors of famine from the "Paradise of Regions," as the province of Bengal is sometimes called.

Sir William Ouseley, who obtained these traditions, it would appear, from oral communication, states that they are related by many of the Hindus, and implicitly believed by some. However, on inquiring of the people whether there are still musical performers among them who can produce effects similar to those recorded, one is gravely told that the art is now almost lost, but that there are still musicians possessed of miraculous powers in the west of Hindustan; and if one inquires in the west, they say that should any such musicians remain, they must be found in Bengal.*

A reliable collection of Hindu traditions relating to music might, probably, be suggestive and valuable to the musical historian, especially if he examined them with reference to the myths of the ancient Egyptians and Greeks.

CELESTIAL QUARRELS.

THERE appears to be a notion universally prevailing among uncivilised people that, during an eclipse of the sun

---

* 'The Oriental Collections, Vol. I. London, 1797.' P. 70.

or moon, the two luminaries are quarrelling with each other, or that their conjugal happiness is being disturbed by some intruding monster.

The natives of the Polynesian Islands have an old tradition, according to which the moon (called *marama*) is the wife of the sun (called *ra*), and, during an eclipse, the moon is supposed to be bitten or pinched by some angry spirit.*

The Javanese, and the natives of the Indian Archipelago in general, when an eclipse takes place, shout and beat gongs to prevent the sun or moon from being devoured by the great dragon (called *nága*), which they suppose to be attacking the luminary.† This notion appears to have been adopted by the Malays from the Hindus, in whose mythology a god called Rahu—who is recorded to have been originally a giant, and who is painted black—at the time of an eclipse swallows up the sun and moon, and vomits them up again.

Of the Chinese we are told : " As soon as they perceive that the sun or moon begins to be darkened, they throw themselves on their knees and knock their foreheads against the earth. A noise of drums and cymbals is immediately heard throughout the whole city. This is the remains of an ancient opinion entertained in China, that by such a horrid din they assist the suffering luminary, and prevent it from being devoured by the celestial dragon."‡

The Greenlanders have, according to Crantz, a somewhat similar tradition; but, instead of musical instruments, the men carry kettles and boxes to the top of the house, and rattle and beat them, and the women pinch the dogs by the ears, to frighten away the moon, who, they suppose, is insulting his wife, the sun.§ In Greenland, the moon is the man, and the sun is the wife, as in Germany.

---

* ' Polynesian Researches, by William Ellis. London, 1829.' Vol. II., p. 415.
† ' History of the Indian Archipelago, by John Crawfurd. Edinburgh, 1820.' Vol. I., p. 304.
‡ ' A View of the History, Literature, and Religion of the Hindoos, by the Rev. W. Ward. Madras, 1863.' P. 62.
§ ' The History of Greenland, by David Crantz. London, 1767.' Vol. I., p. 233.

Again, the Negroes in Western Africa appear to have much the same notion. The traveller Lander, during his stay at Boussa in Soudan, witnessed the wild behaviour of the Negroes at the occurrence of an eclipse of the moon. Their principal exertions to avert the supposed impending calamity consisted in blowing trumpets, beating drums, singing and shouting.*

The Japanese legend of the sun-goddess, who, after having hidden herself in a cavern, is enticed from her dark abode by the power of music, is apparently likewise a poetical conception of an eclipse. Titsingh, in reciting the same tradition, says that Fensio-Daysin, the sun-goddess, fled to the cavern in consequence of a dispute she had with her brother, Sasanno-Ono-Mikotto, the god of the moon.†

From these examples it seems that musical performances, or, at least, the sounds of loud instruments, are considered the most effective agent for appeasing the anger of the quarrelling celestial bodies. But there is no reason to assume that this peculiar notion originally emanated from one people. Like several other popular traditions, it most likely owes its origin to impressions produced on the mind by a certain natural phenomenon; and it may, therefore, have suggested itself to different nations quite independently, instead of having been transmitted from one nation to another.

AL-FARABI.

Most of the popular legends and fairy tales which have been traditionally preserved are of high origin. Many of those which appear to have originated during the Christian era are only modifications of older ones dating from heathen times. Thus, we find the Virgin Mary in a legend substituted for a pagan goddess, and one or other Saint for a pagan god. Sometimes a remarkable incident, recorded in ancient history, is related as having occurred at a much

---

* 'Journal of an Expedition to explore the Course of the Niger, by Richard and John Lander. New York, 1844.' Vol. I., p. 366.

† 'Illustrations of Japan, by M. Titsingh. London, 1822.' P. 201.

more recent time. Perhaps it may have happened again, but in many cases the old tradition has, undoubtedly, been borrowed by one nation from another, and has been adapted to circumstances which favoured its adaptation.

In the musical records of the Arabs mention is made of the wonderful accomplishments of a celebrated musician, whose name was Al-Farabi, and who acquired his proficiency in Spain, in one of the schools at Cordova, which flourished as early as towards the end of the ninth century. The reputation of Al-Farabi became so great, that ultimately it extended to Asia. The mighty Caliph of Bagdad himself desired to hear the celebrated musician, and sent messengers to Spain with instructions to offer rich presents to Al-Farabi, and to convey him to the Caliph's court; but the musician feared that if he went he should be detained in Asia, and should never again see his home, to which he felt deeply attached. However, at last he resolved to disguise himself, and to undertake the journey, which promised him a rich harvest. Dressed in a mean costume he made, unrecognized, his appearance at the court just at the time when the mighty Caliph was being entertained with his daily concert. Al-Farabi, unknown to everyone present, was permitted to exhibit his skill. He sang, accompanying himself on the lute. Scarcely had he commenced his performance in a certain musical mode when he set all his audience laughing aloud, notwithstanding the efforts of the courtiers to suppress so unbecoming an exhibition of mirth in the presence of the mighty Caliph. In truth, even the mighty Caliph himself was compelled to burst out into a fit of laughter. Presently, Al-Farabi changed to another mode, and the effect was that immediately all his hearers began to sigh, and soon tears of sadness replaced the previous tears of mirth. Again he sang and played in another mode, which excited his audience to such a rage that they would have fought each other if he, seeing the danger, had not directly gone over to an appeasing mode. After this wonderful exhibition of his skill, he concluded in a mode which had the extraordinary effect of making his listeners fall into a profound sleep, during which Al-Farabi took his departure.

It will be seen that this incident is almost identical with one recorded as having happened about twelve hundred years earlier at the court of Alexander the Great, and which forms the subject of Dryden's fine poem, 'Alexander's Feast.' The distinguished flutist, Timotheus, playing before Alexander, successively aroused and subdued different passions by changing the musical modes during the performance, exactly in the same way as did Al-Farabi more than a thousand years later.

TRUSTY FERDINAND.

The Germans have a curious story in which an incident occurs calling to mind Arion's famous adventure. It will be remembered that Arion, after having gained by his musical talents great riches, was, during a voyage, in imminent danger of being murdered by the sailors, who coveted the treasures he was carrying with him. When he found that his death was decided upon, he asked permission to strike once more his beloved lyre. And so feelingly did he play, that the fishes surrounding the ship took compassion. He threw himself into the water, and was carried ashore by a dolphin.

As regards Trusty Ferdinand, the hero of the German story, we are told that he, seeing a fish struggling near the shore and gasping for water, takes it by the tail and restores it to its element. Whereupon the fish, in gratitude, puts its head out of the water, and presents Trusty Ferdinand with a flute. "Shouldst thou ever stand in need of my assistance," says the fish, "only play upon this flute, and I will come and help thee." Sometime afterwards Trusty Ferdinand embarks on a voyage to a distant country. While on board a ship he has the misfortune to let drop into the sea a precious ring, upon the possession of which depends the happiness of a beautiful princess as well as his own happiness. He takes up his flute; as soon as he begins to play, the fish appears and reaches back to him the precious ring.

THE WILD HUNTSMAN.

THE Wild Huntsman tears through the forest at night attended by a noisy host, pursuing his furious chase with unearthly singing, with sounding of horns, with the barking of dogs, the clattering of horses, and with fearful shouting and hallooing. This wide-spread conception has been ascertained to date from ancient pagan time, in which Wuotan, (or Woden), the principal deity of German mythology, exhibits the characteristics commonly attributed to the Wild Huntsman. But it is new as well as old; for it suggests itself not less naturally at the present day than it suggested itself in bygone times—as the reader will perhaps know from his own experience, if he has ever found himself alone on a stormy moonlight night in a forest of Bohemia or Germany. In any case, he may be sure that it is no joke to traverse in such a night a forest which still continues in almost its primeval state.

For awhile everything appears silent as the grave, and the lonely pedestrian, pursuing some old track which faintly indicates the way to a village, is only occasionally bewildered by the sudden darkness occurring when a cloud obscures the moon, or by the startling brightness, should he reach unexpectedly a clearing in the forest just at the moment when a cloud has passed across the moon, casting not far before him its shadow, which like a spectre rapidly flits over the brushwood, assuming various uncouth shapes. Soon his imagination is excited by distant sounds never heard in open day—yelping of foxes, howling of wolves, grunting of wild boars; and now by the piteous cry of agony emitted by a bird which has fallen a prey to some ravenous beast. Presently he is startled by an awful noise like the galloping of a cavalcade: a herd of stags is hastily fleeing through the wood. The cavalcade seems to come straight upon him; but soon the noise grows weaker, and quickly dies away. Now a whirlwind sweeping over the forest, and violently shaking the tops of the trees, gradually approaches the harassed pedestrian. At first only groaning and grumbling, it soon bursts forth into a terrific howl; and as it furiously passes over the head of the involuntary witness, it scares from their hiding-places sundry owls, the hooting and screeching of which alone would suffice to make his hair stand on end. And when the whirlwind has swept over, and is only heard faintly murmuring in the distance, other sounds and apparitions not less terrifying are sure soon to arise. In short, the lonely wanderer, be he ever so intelligent an observer of nature, will most likely feel his heart eased of a heavy weight when he has left the forest behind him. Soon, having reached the end of his journey, he may put on his slippers with that comfortable sensation of relief which people are sure to experience when they have escaped an imminent danger. It is all very well for him now to persuade himself that, after all, he has only witnessed some interesting natural phenomena; he may perhaps even smile at the superstitious notions of simple-minded peasants. But of what avail is this to him? The night is not yet over, and he cannot escape a fearful dream of a personal encounter with the Wild Huntsman and his furious host.

From what has been said it will not surprise the reader that the reports of witnesses who profess to have met with the Wild Huntsman are at variance in many points. Much evidently depends upon the nature of the locality in which the mysterious apparition shows itself. In some parts of Germany particular stress is laid upon the softness and sweetness of his music. This conception may have originated in the pine-forests where the delicate needle-shaped leaves of the trees are vibrated by the wind like the strings of an Æolian harp. But, the blowing of the huntsman's horn seems to be an indispensable attribute to the furious chase. The country-folks in Mecklenburg, and in some other provinces in the North of Germany where Low German is spoken, on hearing the mysterious noise in the wood, say, "*De Wode tüt!*" ("Woden is tooting!") thereby implying a series of unrhythmical sounds rather than a melodious succession of tones on the horn—in fact, sounds very much like the hooting of the owl. It is moreover a common belief that a kind of owl, called by the peasants *Tutosel,* always accompanies the Wild Huntsman with his furious host.

An account of an extraordinary occurrence given by an honest witness is, of course, generally preferable to a statement of the same occurrence merely obtained from hearsay; and the evidence of the witness deserves all the greater attention if he shows himself to be an intelligent and keen observer. The subjoined report of the German Baron Reibnitz may therefore interest the reader. It was communicated by the Baron to the Philosophical Society in Görlitz, Silesia. As Görlitz possesses a Philosophical Society, there must be clever fellows in the town. Be this as it may, the document is authentic, and has been faithfully translated from the German.

THE BOLD GERMAN BARON.

"THE popular tradition of the Wild Huntsman, current in many places, prevails also still at the present day in my village of Zilmsdorf. From my earliest years I had been acquainted with it, but only from hearsay; and as soon as I had come into possession of my paternal inheritance, I gave the most stringent orders, especially to the nightwatch, to inform me immediately, at any hour of the night, should this event come to pass.

"About thirty years ago, towards eleven o'clock on a clear night in the month of May, I heard a knocking at my window:—

"'Gracious Baron!' cried my nightwatch, 'The Wild Huntsman! In the upper wood of Teuplitz!'

"I directly gave orders to arouse Stäglich, my gamekeeper, who at that time—I being then a bachelor—was groom, gamekeeper, house-steward, in short all in all to me, and was moreover just of my own age, and certainly an excellent forester.

"'Go, fetch the horses! Make haste! Don't stop to saddle—only the horse-cloth; the Wild Huntsman is in the forest; we will welcome him!'

"This was the very thing for Stäglich. In less than ten

minutes we were mounted, well-armed, and were flying over meadows and ploughed fields towards the sounds of hunting-horns and the crying of hounds. Scarcely had we reached the heath when the noise ceased. We remained quiet. On a sudden we heard close by us a yelping much like that of a badger-dog when it has recovered the lost scent. Rapidly the yelping of dogs, large and small, with the sounds of horns, increased; and now commenced a truly furious chase, which moved towards the middle of the forest, where other hunting-horns besides were winding awfully. We spurred our horses and rushed forwards, but an impenetrable thicket compelled us to change our course, and to turn into a part of the forest where there was but little underwood, but where, notwithstanding the beautiful starlight night, it was so pitch dark that we really could not see the wood for the trees, as the saying is. The horses—which, as is well-known, are at night more nervous than men—shied several times.

"On a sudden the Wild Hunt appeared to come directly towards us, with a clamour so terrible that, as soon as we reached the summit of the hill where the highest forest trees stand, we called out to each other: 'Now at them!'

"Like a whirlwind it rushed past us, with awful music of voices and instruments, at a distance of scarcely forty paces. The horses snorted and shied, and that of my gamekeeper reared and fell backwards.

"'Heaven be merciful to us, and protect us!' we both cried. I hastened to his assistance, but he was already rising. Soon he was again at my side. Our horses nervously pressed close to each other. The Wild Hunt appeared to be over, when, after a little while, we heard it commencing anew a great distance off, in the open fields. Without waste of time we hastened in that direction, and soon reached the fields.

"The stars shone brightly and cheerfully. Now the Wild Hunt passed before us; but as we approached, it gradually went off in a curved line, with sounding of horns, crying of hounds, and clattering of horses. Soon it was far away on the distant heath.

"We rode home, where the nightwatch anxiously awaited us. He had already begun to doubt whether we should ever come back. It was past one o'clock."*

PROPHETIC CALLS OF BIRDS.

THE calls of birds are perhaps more frequently considered as good presages than as unlucky ones. Among the Slavonic nations, especially the Poles and Lithuanians, the hooting of the owl predicts misery and death. Also in Germany, if the little screech-owl makes its appearance in a village during a moonlight night, and settling on a farm-building emits its melancholy notes, some people are sure to hint that there will be ere long a death in the family of the householder. Moreover, a similar superstition prevails in Hindustan.†

The croaking of a raven is considered in Russia and Servia as foreboding the shedding of blood.‡ The ancient tradition of the singing of the dying swan is familiar to everyone. Although our common swan does not produce sounds which might account for this tradition, it is a well-known fact that the wild swan (*cygnus ferus*), also called the whistling swan, when on the wing emits a shrill tone, which, however harsh it may sound if heard near, produces a pleasant effect when, emanating from a large flock high in the air, it is heard in a variety of pitches of sound, increasing or diminishing in loudness according to the movements of the birds and to the current of the wind. With the idea of the song of the dying swan appears to be connected the Scandinavian tradition of the Valkyrjas, who were maidens in armour with wings of swans. During a

---

* 'Sagenbuch der Lausitz, von Karl Haupt. Leipzig, 1862.' P. 124. The descriptive music of the Wild Hunt in Weber's opera, 'Der Freischütz,' is probably in the recollection of most musicians. It agrees remarkably well with the popular traditions.

† 'A View of the History, Literature, and Religion of the Hindoos, by the Rev. W. Ward. Madras, 1863.' P. 160.

‡ 'Stimmen des Russischen Volks, von P. v. Götze. Stuttgart, 1828.' P. 17.

battle the Valkyrjas approached floating through the air, and hovering over the scene of carnage, they indicated who were to fall in the fight.*

The cuckoo is regarded by the Russians and by most other Slavonic nations as a bird of sadness. According to a Servian tradition the cuckoo (called *kukawiza*) was a girl who wept so continually for her deceased brother that she was transformed into a bird, which in two melancholy tones sends its unabating complaint through the air. A Servian girl who has lost her brother (lover?) never hears the cuckoo without shedding tears. Moreover, in Servia the cuckoo is considered as a prophetic bird, especially by the *heyduk*, or robber, who augurs from its earlier or later singing.†

Among the Germanic races the notes of the cuckoo, when in the spring it first makes itself heard, are generally considered as a good omen. It is still, as from Teutonic mythology it appears to have been in ancient time, a belief among the peasantry in Germany that if anybody counts the number of times this bird repeats its call, he may ascertain from it how many years he has still to live, or how many years will elapse before an event comes to pass which he has reason to expect. There is an old story told of a person who, having led a rather wicked life, in order to atone for it resolved to become a monk for the rest of his life. It happened that, just as he was entering the monastery, he heard the cuckoo crying its name the first time in the spring. He anxiously counted the number of calls; and finding them to amount to twenty-two repetitions, he at once changed his mind. "If I have to live twenty-two years longer," he argued with himself, "I may as well enjoy twenty years longer the pleasures of this world, and then I shall have two whole years left to denounce its vanities in a monastery." So he at once returned to the world.

The country-lasses in Sweden count the cuckoo's call to ascertain how many years they have still to remain un-

---

* 'Die Mythologie des Nordens, von K. F. Wiborg; aus dem Dänischen von A. v. Etzel. Berlin, 1847.' P. 147.

† 'Volkslieder des Serben, übersetzt von Talvj. Leipzig. 1853.' Vol. II., p. 380.

married; but they generally shut their ears and run away when they have heard it a few times. Should a girl hear it oftener than ten times, she will declare rather vexedly that she is not superstitious, and that she has not the least faith in the cuckoo's call.

WHISTLING.

"Why! he makes music with his mouth!" exclaimed a native of Burmah when he observed an American missionary whistling; and the missionary noted down the words in his journal, with the reflection: "It is remarkable that the Burmese are entirely ignorant of whistling."* But may not the simple-minded Asiatic only have been astonished in observing what he thought unbecoming in a gentleman who had come to Burmah to teach a new religion?

The Arabs generally disapprove of whistling, called by them *el sifr*. Some maintain that the whistler's mouth is not to be purified for forty days; while others are of opinion that Satan touching a man's person causes him to produce the offensive sound.†

The natives of the Tonga Islands, Polynesia, consider it wrong to whistle, as being disrespectful to their gods.‡

In European countries people are met with who object to whistling on a certain day of the week, or at certain times of the day. The villagers in some districts of North Germany have the saying, that if one whistles in the evening it makes the angels weep. The villagers in Iceland say that even if one swings about him a stick, whip, wand, or aught that makes a whistling sound, he scares from him the Holy Ghost; while other Icelanders, who consider themselves free from superstitions, cautiously give the advice: "Do it not; for who knoweth what is in the air?" §

---

* 'Travels in South-Eastern Asia, by Howard Malcolm. Boston, 1839.' Vol. I., p. 205.
† 'First Footsteps in East Africa, 1856, by Captain Burton, London.' P. 142.
‡ 'An Account of the Natives of the Tonga Islands, by Mariner and Martin. London, 1818.' Vol. II., p. 131.
§ 'Icelandic Legends, collected by Jón Arnason; translated by Powell and Magnússon. London, 1866.' P. 631.

There seem to have been, however, in all ages light-hearted persons who, defying the superstitious views of their compatriots, have whistled to their heart's content, or for the amusement of those who set at nought popular prejudices.

Joseph Strutt, in his 'Sports and Pastimes of the People of England' records the astonishing performance of a whistler who, assuming the name of Rossignol, exhibited at the end of the last century his talent on the stage of Covent Garden Theatre. Again, an amusing account is given in the 'Spectator' (Vol. VIII., No. 570) of a skilful whistler, who was the host of the tavern especially patronised by Addison and Steele; and the writer concludes his description of the host's surprising talent by recommending his readers to repair to the tavern and to order a bottle of wine for the sake of the whistling.

The Russians in the Ukraine tell a queer story about a whistling robber of old, who must have been a person of fabulously large dimensions, for he used to sit, we are told, on nine oak trees at once. His name is still known; but it would be an infliction upon the reader to put before him a name almost entirely made up of consonants, and only pronounceable by a Russian. This celebrated robber had, however, also a nickname signifying "Nightingale," which was given to him on account of his extraordinary whistling powers. Whenever a traveller happened to enter the forest in which the robber Nightingale had his domicile, it was pity for him if he had neglected to make his will; for the robber Nightingale whistled so impressively that the poor traveller must needs faint away, and then the wretched whistler stepped forward and killed him outright. But, at last, a great hero, who was besides a holy man, and whose name was Ilja Murometz, repaired to the forest to subdue the robber Nightingale. Having hit him with an arrow, and taken him prisoner, he bound him to the saddle of his horse and escorted him to Kiev to the court of the Grand-Prince Vladimir. Even there the fettered whistler proved most dangerous. For when the Grand-Prince, merely from curiosity, and perhaps to see whether his courtiers had told him the truth, commanded the robber to whistle before him

—the Grand-Princess and all the royal children being present—the man at once commenced whistling in a manner so overpowering that soon Vladimir with his whole family would inevitably have been dead, had not some brave courtiers, perceiving the danger, got up and shut the whistler's mouth.

Moreover, some enlightened Russians say that the story must not be taken literally. At the time of the introduction of Christianity into Russia there lived near Kiev, they say, a pagan high-priest who was so distinguished an orator that he actually succeeded in drawing many to his side to check the spread of Christianity. This man, whose powers of persuasion were so great that his adherents called him Nightingale, was at last vanquished by his Christian antagonist Murometz. The bones of Murometz, we are further informed, have never decayed, and are still annually exhibited in Kiev to be venerated by an assemblage of pious believers.*

---

* 'Stimmen des Russischen Volks, von P. von Götze. Stuttgart, 1828.' P. 58.

THE STUDIES OF OUR GREAT COMPOSERS.

An inquiry into the gradual cultivation of the genius of our great musical composers is as instructive as it is interesting to the lover of music. Before attempting this inquiry, it is advisable to ascertain exactly what is meant by the designation "our great composers."

To compose music does not only imply to invent musical ideas, but also to employ ideas which are already invented in such a way as to exhibit them in a new light. Certain modulations, passages, and rhythmical combinations occurring in our musical compositions may be regarded as common property; but how surprisingly original and fresh do they often appear to us through the new way in which they are employed by composers in connection with other ideas! Now, a composer who has the power to construct very beautiful works of art in a certain form, by inventing ideas and by showing in a new light ideas not invented by him, deserves to be regarded as a great composer.

However, in order to trace the gradual progress of his genius, it is not sufficient to examine his studies, or, so to say, to watch him in his workshop; we must commence our inquiry further back, and observe him first as a promising child.

Unfortunately, of the early initiatory lessons of our great composers but little is generally ascertainable. Celebrated musicians have more important occupation than to explain their earliest instructions; or they have to a great extent forgotten how they learnt in childhood the rudiments of their art. Still the initiatory lessons are especially noteworthy, since the foundation exercises an almost ineffaceable influence upon the subsequent direction of the musical student.

The talent for music in children is not always so easily discovered as might be supposed. Idleness, not unusual in fast-growing children, or indifference caused by injudicious training, may be mistaken for want of talent. There are records extant of distinguished musicians who in early childhood evinced neither talent nor fondness for music. Others, who, showing no inclination to learn the musical instrument on which they received instruction, have unexpectedly exhibited much talent and industry in practising on another kind of instrument of their own choice. Most of our distinguished musicians have manifested from early childhood a preference for a particular instrument which they perseveringly cultivated, and on which they afterwards excelled.

Parents are apt to see talent in their children where it does not exist, or, at least, not in the supposed degree. Some even find unmistakable evidence of musical talent in the shape of the head of their offspring. A peculiar formation of the skull, especially about the temples, is certainly observable in many clever musicians, and may be recognized in the few portraits which are known to be faithful likenesses of great composers. It would be interesting to know whether the infantine musical prodigies, of which there have been so many during the present century, generally possessed this phrenological indication. Be this as it may, they have become great composers in only exceptional instances. Indeed, early musical prodigies have but seldom achieved in after-life so much as was expected from them. There are, however, exceptions; for instance, Mozart. Dr. Crotch in his infancy displayed abilities as extraordinary as Mozart's. At the age of three years and a half he could play some harmonized tunes on the pianoforte, and when he was five years old he performed in public on the organ at a benefit concert in London. He afterwards achieved comparatively but little, and did not realise the expectations which as a child he had excited.

There are instances on record of musicians who in their early childhood were forced against their inclination to practise assiduously, and who must have been tortured by the incessant care for their progress bestowed on them by their parents. They became brilliant players, making music like a well-constructed machine. Our great composers have generally had a happier childhood. They were, in most instances, children whose physical development was especially attended to; who were permitted to ramble about in fields and forests, and by outdoor amusements and bodily exercises to lay the foundation for a healthy life. This, perhaps, sufficiently explains why not all of them have displayed a precocity of talent in early childhood. Indeed, their full development has been in many instances but slow, and several of them did not produce their best works until they had attained an age exceeding that generally allotted to musicians. Gluck composed his 'Iphigenia in Tauris' at the age of sixty-five; Haydn composed the 'Creation' in his sixty-ninth year, and the 'Seasons' in his seventy-second year. Handel was fifty-six years old when he wrote the 'Messiah,' and sixty-one when he wrote 'Judas Maccabæus.'

Some of our most gifted musicians have required much longer time than others for cultivating their talent, because they had not in childhood the same advantage of guidance which others had, and were consequently compelled to find out for themselves the best method of cultivation. Perhaps there now walks behind a plough a Handel, who has not shown that he is a man of genius because circumstances prevented his knowing and cultivating his powers. Happy is the artist who, in his childhood, was led by a judicious guide in the way which saves much time, trouble, and disappointment! Mozart had such a guide in his father; also Mendelssohn. Weber deserves, perhaps, all the greater praise from the fact of his father having been an impediment rather than a help to him.

A systematic education in childhood presents the greatest advantage; this is too self-evident to require further comment. It may also be taken for granted that the moral and mental education of the young composer is not less important than are his musical studies. Nay, his moral training is even of higher importance, since one *may* be a good musician, but *must* be a good man. Moreover, he is sure to become a better musician if he possesses an acute discernment of right and wrong, with love for the former and dislike to the latter.

As regards his mental education, it is more important for him to know *how* to think than *what* to think. A clear discernment is preferable to much information; at any rate, it is better to know but little and to understand that little clearly, than to know a great deal confusedly.

There can be no doubt that a classical education is of great advantage to the musician, not only on account of the refining influence which a familiarity with classical literature exercises upon the artistic mind, but also on account of the languages. An acquaintance with two or three modern languages is almost indispensable to the composer. Latin poetry occurs not unfrequently in Church music; and several old treatises on music have been written in Latin, and are therefore not accessible to musicians unacquainted with this language. It does not, of course, follow that to be a great composer one must know Latin; however, many musicians have thought it advisable in their later years to study this language, when they had not the opportunity of studying it in their youth.

Talented young musicians sometimes appear rather deficient in their mental cultivation. The enthusiasm with which they pursue their musical studies is apt to cause them to neglect other studies. But there is no real deficiency of intellectual gifts; on the contrary, they have generally a great versatility of talent. This often becomes apparent in their later years. Several eminent musicians have evinced much talent for painting. The humorous, witty, and clever remarks of some of our great composers are notorious.

Without having thoroughly mastered the technicalities of the art, it is impossible to achieve anything of artistic value. An assiduous and persevering cultivation of the talent is as necessary as the talent itself. It has generally cost a musical composer long and continued labour to produce a valuable work of art. He attained his aim by knowing what was requisite for its achievement, and by labouring perseveringly to attain it.

As has been already intimated, it is of great importance for the progress of the future composer that his initiatory lessons should be correct, so that there is nothing learnt which afterwards requires to be unlearnt. A bad touch on the pianoforte, or a wrong method of bowing in playing the violin, is scarcely ever entirely remedied in later years. Example is better than precept. A teacher who, by playing to his pupil, can show him how a passage ought to be executed, may save him much time and trouble. Our celebrated singers have generally learnt the most easily the best they are able to accomplish by having been sung to. However, music may be learnt by different methods, and each method may have something to recommend it. The teacher must study the pupil to find out what is the best for him.

Our great composers had generally instruction in singing very early. Indeed, a composer who has not cultivated his voice in childhood is not likely to write vocal music so effectively as would be the case if he had accustomed himself to sing his melodies while inventing them. Even the melodious phrases in his instrumental compositions are likely to be more impressive if he has been a singer from early age.

Furthermore, the young student has to learn to play in a high degree of perfection at least one musical instrument. The pianoforte is—in our time, perhaps—the best suited for his purpose, on account of the harmony and of the arrangement of orchestral works executable on the instrument. Most of our great composers were pianists, harpsichord players, or organists. There are, it is true, exceptions. Gluck's instrument was the violoncello; Spohr's, the violin. But even composers who are not pianists, generally, while composing for the orchestra, make use of the pianoforte.

The best musical performer is he who can play the most simple melody with the greatest expression; and the second best is he who can play the most difficult passages with the greatest correctness. Some pianists of astonishing manual dexterity are unable to play a simple tune with proper expression; others cannot execute well a technically easy sonata by Mozart, because they have not learnt—or, perhaps, have forgotten—the pure expression required for such unaffected music. The execution of many modern pianists is best suited for the performance of their own compositions.

If the young musician is bent upon becoming a distinguished *virtuoso*, it may easily be disadvantageous to him as a composer, not only on account of the time he will require for practising his fingers, but also because his fingers are apt to induce him to compose for them instead of for the heart. A great composer generally plays one instrument masterly; and he has, probably, found it expedient to learn another instrument or two besides that which he has principally cultivated. If, in addition to the pianoforte, he can play the viola or violoncello in a quartet, or Bach's pedal-fugues on the organ, he possesses the means of familiarising himself more thoroughly with many of our classical compositions than he could possibly do by merely hearing or reading them; and the familiarity thus acquired is beneficial to him. Moreover, some practical experience with wind-instruments is useful to the composer of orchestral works. Our great masters knew this, and acted upon it.

The exercise of the fingers takes up time, but not necessarily much. One hour of practice with great attention is better than three hours of careless practice. The former has not only the advantage that it advances the student more rapidly, but also that it leaves him the time required for other studies, reading, and recreation. Several of our great composers could be named who, notwithstanding their diligent studies from their youth, always found plenty of time for bodily exercise, and for amusements conducive to the preservation of health and energy—such as pedestrian tours, riding, fencing, swimming, dancing, etc.

The young musician has soon to commence the study of the theory of music, especially if he exhibits decided talent for composing. He must learn to write with facility any musical composition strictly according to the rules which have been laid down by our theorists as they found them observed in the works of the great masters. When he has acquired the skill to write correctly and fluently in the different forms of composition, it will be early enough for him to disregard the rules occasionally where he thinks it advisable for his purpose. Perhaps he may establish a new one. By far the greater number of our rules of composition are not dictated by any physical law traceable in acoustics, but only by human taste, which is continually undergoing modifications in the course of time. Thus, most of our great composers have caused some alterations in our theory of music. It is not only possible, but probable, that in a hundred years' time we shall have admirable musical compositions very different in form and construction from our present ones.

Several of our great composers in their youth excelled in extemporising. They were fond of it, and spent many an hour in pouring forth on their favourite instrument their momentary inspirations and fanciful conceptions. Extempore fantasias are sometimes so original and effective that it is a pity they cannot be preserved by being committed to notation at the moment of their creation. However, charming as such spontaneous effusions may be on account of their freshness, they do not possess the artistic value of an elaborately constructed and carefully finished work. At any rate, our great composers have in their youth derived greater benefit from carefully working out in notation a theme according to a certain form of composition, than from indulging in extempore fantasias. These have, however, often helped them in creating beautiful ideas for their works.

It may easily be understood that a retentive memory is of great value to the musician, be he composer or merely performer. Talented young musicians not unfrequently possess an astounding memory. Sonatas, symphonies, and even fugues, which they practise, they can soon play by heart. As they advance in years the power of memory generally becomes somewhat weaker. Blind musicians appear to preserve it undiminished for a longer period than others. The blind flutist Dulon knew 120 flute concertos by heart, which he had numbered, and any one of which he could play instantly on its number being mentioned to him. True, there is musically little gained by burdening the memory with compositions which chiefly consist of compilations of passages calculated to display the dexterity and skill of the performer. The works which the musician ought to be able to recall to his memory are the classical works, such as Gluck's 'Iphigenia in Tauris,' Mozart's 'Don Giovanni,' Beethoven's Symphonies, Handel's 'Messiah,' Bach's 'Passion according to St. Matthew.' There are not a few among our great composers who studied the masterworks of their predecessors so effectually that they knew by heart a considerable number of them from beginning to end, with the instrumentation of every bar.

As regards the different forms of composition, that of the sonata is the most important; for, if the composer is able to express his ideas with facility in this form, he possesses the key to all the other forms—except some of the older ones, as that of the fugue. Certain theorists recommend the student of composition to select a sonata by Mozart, or some other master, in which the established form is strictly adhered to, and to write a precisely similar sonata by imitating the model bar for bar, using the same time, tempo, modulations, changes in loudness, and so on—only substituting other notes. No doubt he may thus manufacture a sonata which is correct in form, whatever it may be in spirit. Our great composers did not arise from students trained to make music as the shoemaker makes shoes.

The form of the fugue has already become antiquated, and that of the sonata is more and more neglected by our present composers, and apparently will likewise become antiquated in the course of time. But until we have beautiful examples of some new form, it is not probable that those forms which have been gradually brought to a high degree of perfection will be entirely dispensed with, whatever modern composers may produce exhibiting an indifference to the rules observed by their predecessors.

Our great composers were particularly careful in the choice of the theme. This is only what might be expected. An orator who discourses on an uninteresting subject will not easily command the attention of his hearers. Still, if he is gifted with extraordinary powers of eloquence, he may discourse on almost any subject interestingly. Thus also in music. Beethoven and other great composers have occasionally chosen a theme which becomes significant only from its original and spirited treatment.

The artistic charm of a well-constructed composition consists in the development of the theme, so that it is exhibited in a variety of beautiful aspects—appearing, though always the same, yet always new. The skill of thus treating the theme, our great composers, by constant study and practice, have cultivated to an admirable degree of perfection. They were fully aware that it is as indispensable to the composer as is the power of creating an interesting musical idea. However, the development of the theme may be carried too far. It appears pedantic when it is contrived more with regard to the form than to the spirit of the music; and it disturbs the unity of the composition when the theme is so much changed as to appear an entirely new idea. Schubert, in his pianoforte sonatas, has not unfrequently altered the theme so much that its second exposition does not bear the required resemblance with its first; it becomes another theme, which is not wanted. For the clever development of a theme Schubert did not possess sufficient practical experience acquired by systematic study. Had he possessed a full command over the rules of the art—and especially, had he written less hastily—he might, with his wonderful gifts, have been as great a composer as Beethoven.

A few examples from Beethoven's book of sketches may find a place here, since they throw some light upon his studies. The alterations which he marked with "*meilleur*" are generally decided improvements upon the first notation of the idea to which they refer. This is, for instance, strikingly apparent in his sketches of his famous song 'Adelaide,' the beginning of which, noted down at first thus :—

he afterwards altered into :—

The following sketches from Beethoven's pocket-book refer to his Quartet in C♯ minor, Op. 131, with which they must be compared to render the several attempts at improvement more clearly intelligible:—

The first sketches for a tenth symphony, which Beethoven intended to compose, are noted by him thus:—

Beethoven wrote *As* over the little fragment of the Andante, evidently to indicate that he intended it to be in A flat major—*As* signifying in German *A flat*.

As an interesting specimen of Haydn's sketches, the following notation of his first design of the earthquake in the 'Seven Last Words' may serve. The entire sketch of which this is a fragment, has been published in the 'Allgemeine musikalische Zeitung,' Leipsig, 1848:—

Haydn, as well as Beethoven, generally used one staff for his first sketches; Mozart made them more clear by using two staves—one for the melody and another for the bass. Still, as the sketches are only indications to assist the memory, which is, as we have seen, in composers generally very strong, especially when their own inventions are concerned, a hasty notation is in most instances sufficient. In writing the score of an orchestral composition, Haydn, Mozart and Beethoven usually noted down the entire thread of a movement, or what may be called the melody and the bass of the piece; and having written this, they inserted the notation for the various instruments.

In submitting the manuscript of a composition to a final revision, or in preparing a new edition of a published work, our great composers have not unfrequently introduced improvements which testify to their unabating study as well as to their delicacy of taste and discernment. One or two examples in support of this opinion shall be pointed out here. Others will probably occur to the musical reader.

André, in Offenbach, has published the score of the overture to the 'Zauberflöte' (the Magic Flute), from Mozart's original manuscript, with its alterations and corrections. This interesting publication exhibits clearly the care bestowed by Mozart upon the work, and affords an excellent study for the musician.

A remarkable improvement by extension occurs in Mozart's famous Symphony in C major. Mendelssohn speaks of it with admiration in a letter to Moscheles as follows: " Just now André sends me for inspection the original score of Mozart's C major Symphony ('Jupiter'); I shall copy something from it for you which will amuse you. Eleven bars before the end of the Adagio it stood formerly thus :—

and so on, as it proceeds to the end. Mozart has written the entire repetition of the theme on an inserted leaf; he has struck out the passage, and has introduced it three bars before the end. Is that not a happy alteration ? The repetition of the seven bars belongs to my most favourite portions of the whole symphony."*

The Adagio of Beethoven's Sonata in B flat major, Op. 106, originally commenced with its present second bar thus :—

---

* 'Briefe von Felix Mendelssohn Bartholdy. Leipzig, 1863.' Vol. ii., p. 440.

Beethoven had sent, in the year 1819, a copy of the manuscript of this sonata to Ferdinand Ries, in London, who had undertaken to superintend its publication in England. Great must have been the astonishment of Ries when, soon after the arrival of the bulky manuscript of this gigantic sonata, he received a letter from Beethoven containing the notation of an additional single bar :—

to be placed at the beginning of the Adagio. The beautiful effect obtained by the alteration is especially noteworthy, inasmuch as it serves as an example of the incessant care which Beethoven bestowed upon the improvement of his compositions up to the last moment of their publication.

Probably no composer has revised his manuscripts more carefully, and re-written whole pieces with the view of improving them, than has J. S. Bach. His forty-eight Preludes and Fugues, entitled 'Das wohltemperirte Clavier,' afford instructive examples of improvements, which may be traced by a comparison of the several editions of the work, and especially by an examination of the several manuscripts of these preludes and fugues in Bach's handwriting which have been preserved.

The prelude in C major, in the first set, was originally longer than in subsequent revisions. The second half, which Bach has struck out, was a repetition of its first half.

The prelude in C♯ major, in the first set, he has curtailed by striking out thirty-five bars. This he did evidently for the purpose of increasing the unity of this charming composition by discarding what was foreign to its character, as indicated by the theme.

On the other hand, the beautiful prelude in D minor, in the same set, he has considerably enlarged.

These few remarks must suffice to draw the reader's attention to the careful reconsideration given by Bach to 'Das wohltemperirte Clavier.'

Beethoven generally kept his manuscripts a long time by him, and altered and polished them up gradually. This he did especially with the manuscripts of his earlier compositions. Gluck, in composing an opera, carried out in his mind the principal airs and choruses before he wrote down a note; so that, when he began to commit the music to paper, he considered his opera as almost finished. Mozart, too, had sometimes a whole new composition in his head before he commenced writing it down. The overture to 'Don Giovanni' he is recorded, by some of his biographers, to have composed a few hours before the first performance of the opera, so that the copied parts for the musicians were not yet dry when they were carried into the orchestra. Probably Mozart did not compose the overture when he committed it to paper, but had it ready in his head. He was often composing when otherwise occupied, and even while he was playing billiards.

A musical composer may have a good reason for preserving the manuscript of his new work though he considers it a failure. He may wish to refer to it after a time to ascertain whether his unfavourable opinion remains unchanged on a subsequent examination. Perhaps it contains ideas which he may be glad to employ in later years when his power of invention begins to flag. Still, a celebrated musician would do wisely to destroy any such manuscripts when he no longer requires them; otherwise they are sure to arise against him after his death as posthumous works. They will, at least, lower his fame, if it is too great to be seriously injured by them. In truth, there is often harm done to art as well as to artists by these posthumous publications—in most instances weak productions which have been permitted to live from carelessness of the composers, or perhaps from the natural affection which a father feels for even his most ill-favoured child.

Our great composers have generally been extremely cautious, especially during the earlier part of their lifetime, in selecting for publication only such of their manuscripts as they were fully justified in considering worthy of being published. As regards most musicians, it would be better for their reputation if they had published only half the number of their works, and destroyed the other half.

It is a noteworthy fact that our great composers have occasionally produced beautiful effects by disregarding the rules laid down in treatises on the theory of music. Beethoven has been not unfrequently a trespasser in this respect. Weber, in the Introductory Chorus of the elves, in 'Oberon,' produces really charming consecutive fifths. So does Handel, in the beautiful Pastoral Symphony in the 'Messiah':—

and Gluck repeatedly, in the beautiful air of Rinaldo, in 'Armida':—

Graun, in his cantata, 'Der Tod Jesu' (The Death of Jesus), introduces into the first chorale consecutive fifths upon the words "Zür Frevelthat entschlossen" (On evil deed resolved), thus :—

which, no doubt, was considered by some musicians as remarkably appropriate to the words, although, probably, they could not have heard it in the performance, had they not previously seen it in notation. Not such whims only, but even oversights and misprints occurring in the works of eminent masters have found admirers, who regarded them as strokes of genius; while, on the other hand, some of the most original and surpassingly beautiful ideas were thought to be misprints, and attempts have actually been made by theorists to correct them.

A curious instance of a misprint which by many admirers of Beethoven has been accepted as a beautiful inspiration occurs in the scherzo of his C minor Symphony. To dispel all doubt of its being a misprint, Mendelssohn caused the publishers of the Symphony to make known a letter addressed to them by Beethoven in the year 1810, in which he says: "The following mistake I still find in the C minor Symphony, namely, in the third piece, in ¾ time, where, after C major, the minor key recommences. It stands thus (I take at once the bass part):—

The two bars marked with * are redundant, and must be struck out; of course, also in all the other parts which have rests." A reference to the manuscript in the possession of the publishers revealed how the two superfluous bars had crept in. Beethoven had originally intended that the entire scherzo, with the trio, should be repeated, and then be concluded by the coda. He had marked in the manuscript the two superfluous bars with 1, and the two following ones with 2, and had written with a red pencil, "*Si replica con trio allora 2*," which the engraver had not exactly understood. As also the written parts for the instruments, which were used at the first performance of the C minor Symphony in Vienna, under Beethoven's direction, do not possess those two bars, there remains not the least doubt that they were never intended by the composer to be where they are now found to the delight of many enthusiastic admirers of Beethoven.

A misprint in Beethoven's 'Sinfonia Pastorale' (which Schumann points out in his 'Gesammelte Schriften,' Vol. IV.) is almost too evident to be left uncorrected, even by those who find it beautiful. In the second part of the first movement, where the theme recommences, with the accompaniment of triplets, the score has the following notations:—

110   THE STUDIES OF OUR GREAT COMPOSERS.

That here, by mistake, three rests for the first violins have been inserted by the engraver, instead of three simile-signs, ▬, is evident from the sudden interruption of the flow of the triplet accompaniment, as well as from the fact that immediately afterwards, in the inversion of the same passage, the violas have the same accompaniment without any interruption. Otto Jahn, in his 'Gesammelte Aufsätze über Musik,' notices a misprint in the score of Beethoven's last Quartet, Op. 135, which is very extraordinary. He says: "In the last movement the copyist has omitted two bars in the first violin part, so that during twelve bars it is two bars in advance of the other instruments. After the twelve bars, the corrector perceiving that two bars were wanting to restore the equilibrium, has inserted two there according to his own fancy." Jahn gives side by side the genuine reading and the interpolated one. The wonder is that the latter is playable at all,—or rather, that the musicians, in playing it, should not have discovered at once that there must be something radically wrong. However, as Jahn justly remarks, the respect for the eccentricities of Beethoven's last quartets was so great, that no one ventured to think there could be a mistake here which required rectifying.

A carefully-compiled manual, containing reliable corrections of the most important misprints occurring in our classical compositions, would be a boon to the musical student. There are many in Bach's fugues, and even in Beethoven's sonatas, which are not easily detected, but which are on this account all the more noteworthy.

The following beautiful conception, which occurs in the first movement of Beethoven's Sinfonia Eroica, was regarded by many, on the first publication of the symphony, as a misprint :—

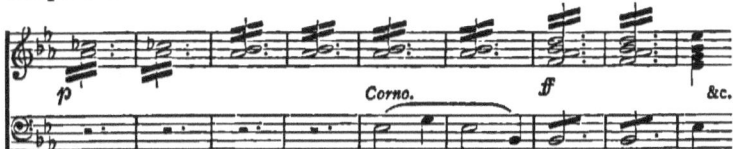

Ferdinand Ries, the pupil of Beethoven, was unable to appreciate the charm of this soft and timid indication of the theme on a dissonance immediately before it gloriously breaks out on the harmonious triad. In his biographical notices of Beethoven he thus speaks of it: "In the first Allegro of the Symphony there occurs a bad whim of Beethoven for the horn. Some bars before the theme enters again, in the second part of the Allegro, Beethoven indicates it by the horn, while the violins continue to sound the second-chord. This must always convey to those who are unacquainted with the score, the impression that the horn-player has counted incorrectly, and that he falls in at a wrong bar. At the first rehearsal of the symphony, which was very unsatisfactory, but in which the horn-player kept proper time, I was standing near Beethoven, and, in the belief that it was wrong, I cried: 'That confounded hornist! Can he not count! It sounds so infamously wrong!' Beethoven was near to giving me a box on the ear. It took him a long time to forgive me."

By making beautiful "mistakes," Beethoven has extended the rules of composition. Ries relates, "During a walk I took with him, I spoke to him of certain consecutive fifths which occur in his C minor Quartet, Op. 18, and which are so eminently beautiful. Beethoven was not aware of them, and maintained that I must be in error as to their being fifths. As he was in the habit of always carrying music paper with him, I asked for it, and wrote down the passage in all its four parts. When he saw that I was right, he said, 'Well, and who has forbidden them?' Not knowing how to take this question, I hesitated. He repeated it, until I replied in astonishment, 'But, they are against the first fundamental rules!' 'Who has forbidden them?' repeated Beethoven. 'Marpurg, Kirnberger, Fuchs, etc., etc.—all theorists,' I replied. 'And I permit them!' said Beethoven."

The harsh beginning of Mozart's C major Quartet (No. 6 of the set dedicated to Joseph Haydn) has been the subject of fierce attacks and controversies. Many musicians have supposed that misprints must have crept into the score; while others have endeavoured to prove in detail that all the four instruments are treated strictly according to the rules of counterpoint. Otto Jahn (in his 'Biography of Mozart,' Vol. IV. p. 74) finds it beautiful as "the afflicted and depressed spirit which struggles for deliverance." This may be so; and it is needless to conjecture what the admirers of the passage would have said, if it had emanated from an unknown composer. As it stands, it is, at any rate, interesting as an idea of Mozart, whose compositions are generally distinguished by great clearness of form and purity of harmony.

The adherence to a strictly prescribed form may easily lead the composer to the re-employment of some peculiar idea which he has already employed in a previous work. In fugues especially this may be often observed. Beethoven, in his sonatas, and likewise in his other compositions written in the sonata form, as trios, quartets, etc., introduces not unfrequently in the modulation from the tonic to the dominant certain favourite combinations of chords and modes of expression; and he has one or two phrases which may be recognised with more or less modification, in many of his compositions. Mozart, too, has his favourite successions of chords; for instance, the interrupted cadence which the German musicians call *Trugschluss*. Spohr repeats himself perhaps more frequently than any other composer. Mendelssohn has a certain mannerism in the rhythmical construction of many of his works, which gives them a strong family likeness. Weber has employed a certain favourite passage of his, constructed of groups of semi-quavers, so frequently, that the sight of a notation like this:—

is to the musician almost the same as the written name Carl Maria von Weber.

Some of the best examples for illustrating the studies of our great composers are to be found in those compositions which originally formed part of earlier and comparatively inferior works, and which were afterwards incorporated by the composers into their most renowned works. In thus adopting a piece which would otherwise probably have fallen into oblivion, the composer has generally submitted it to a careful revision; and it is instructive to compare the revision with the first conception. Gluck has used in his operas several pieces which he had originally written for earlier works, now but little known. For instance, the famous ballet of the Furies in his 'Orfeo,' is identical with the Finale in his 'Don Juan,' where the rake is hurled into the burning abyss; the overture to 'Armida' belonged originally to his Italian opera, 'Telemacco;' the wild dance of the infernal subjects of Hate, in 'Armida,' is the Allegro of the duel-scene in his 'Don Juan.'

As an instance of adoption from a former work wonderfully improved by reconstruction, may be noticed Handel's Sarabande, in his opera 'Almira,' performed the first time at Hamburg in the year 1705:—

From this Sarabande, Handel, six years later, constructed the beautiful air "Lascia ch'io pianga," in his opera 'Rinaldo,' performed in London in the year 1711:—

Beethoven's third overture to his opera 'Leonora' (later called 'Fidelio') is a reconstruction of the second. A comparison of these two overtures affords an interesting insight into Beethoven's studies. It must be remembered that Beethoven, not satisfied with the first overture, wrote a second, and subsequently a third, and a fourth. The first three, which are in C major, he wrote when the opera was known by the name of 'Leonora;' and the fourth, which is in E major, when the opera was brought anew on the stage in its revised form under the name of 'Fidelio.' The air of Florestan is indicated in Nos. 1, 2, and 3, composed in 1805 and 1806. No. 2 has the distant trumpet-signal, produced on the stage; and in No. 3 this idea is further carried out; but in No. 4, written in 1814, it is dropped.

A composer who borrows from his former works deserves reproach as little as a person who removes his purse from one pocket into another which he thinks a better place. To borrow from the works of others, as some composers have done, is altogether a different thing. However, it would be unreasonable to regard such a plagiarism as a theft unless the plagiarist conceals the liberty he is taking by disguising the appropriation so as to make it appear a creation of his own. Some inferior musicians display much talent in this procedure. Our great composers, on the other hand, have often so wonderfully ennobled compositions of other musicians which they have thought advisable to admit into their oratorios, operas, or other elaborate works, that they have thereby honoured the original composers of those pieces as well as benefited art. It is a well-known fact that Handel has, in several of his oratorios, made use of the compositions of others. As these adoptions have been pointed out by one or two of Handel's biographers, it may suffice here to allude to them. Beethoven has adopted remarkably little. His employment of popular tunes where they are especially required, as for example in his Battle Symphony, Op. 91, can hardly be regarded as an instance to the contrary. At any rate, popular tunes have frequently been adopted by our great composers for the purpose of giving to a work a certain national character. Weber has done this very effectively in his 'Preciosa.' Gluck, in his 'Don Juan,' introduces the Spanish fandango. Mozart does the same in his 'Le Nozze di Figaro,' twenty-five years later. Here probably

Mozart took a hint from Gluck. However this may be, there can be no doubt that Gluck's 'Don Juan' contains the germs of several beautiful phrases which occur in Mozart's 'Don Giovanni.' Even on this account it deserves to be better known to musicians than it is, independently of its intrinsic musical value. A detailed account of it here would, however, be a transgression. Suffice it to state that Gluck's 'Don Juan' is a ballet which was composed at Vienna in the year 1761, twenty-six years before Mozart produced his 'Don Giovanni.' The programme of the former work, which has been printed from a manuscript preserved in the Bibliothèque de l'Ecole Royale de Musique of Paris, shows that it is nearly identical with the scenarium of the latter work. The instrumental pieces, of which there are thirty-one, are mostly short, and increase in beauty and powerful expression towards the end of the work. The justly-deserved popularity in Vienna of Gluck's 'Don Juan' probably induced Mozart to have his 'Don Giovanni' first performed under the title of 'Il Dissoluto Punito,' and the great superiority of this opera may perhaps be the cause of Gluck's charming production having fallen into obscurity.

Mozart's facility of invention was so remarkably great that he can have had but little inducement to borrow from others. Plagiarisms occur but rarely in his works, but are on this account all the more interesting when they do occur. Take for instance the following passage from 'Ariadne of Naxos,' a duodrama by Georg Benda. It is composed to be played by the orchestra while Ariadne exclaims: "Now the sun arises! How glorious!"

Mozart was in his youth a great admirer of this duodrama. He mentions in one of his letters that he carried its score constantly with him. The great air of the Queen of Night in 'Die Zauberflöte,' Act I, commences thus:—

It is, however, quite possible that Mozart had made Benda's work so thoroughly his own that he borrowed from it in the present instance without being aware of the fact.

Again, Johann Heinrich Rolle published in the year 1779 an oratorio entitled 'Lazarus, oder die Feier der Auferstehung' (Lazarus, or the Celebration of the Resurrection). The second part of this oratorio begins with an introductory symphony, as follows:—

Perhaps Mozart was not acquainted with Rolle's oratorio when he wrote his overture to the 'Zauberflöte,' in the year 1791. The curious resemblance in the two compositions may be entirely owing to the form of the fugue in which they are written.

Moreover, the theme of Mozart's overture to the 'Zauberflöte' resembles also the theme of a Sonata by Clementi which was composed ten years earlier than the overture. In Clementi's Sonata it is as follows:—

In the complete edition of Clementi's pianoforte compositions this Sonata is published with the appended notice that Clementi played it to the Emperor Joseph II. when Mozart was present, in the year 1781. Mozart appears to have been fond of the theme, for he introduces a reminiscence of it into the first movement of his Symphony in D major, dating from the year 1786.

The first chorus in Mozart's 'Requiem' was evidently suggested by the first chorus in Handel's 'Funeral Anthem for Queen Caroline.' The *motivo* of both is however an old German dirge dating from the sixteenth century, which begins thus :—

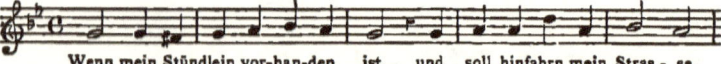

and which may have been familiar to Mozart as well as to Handel.

The *motivo* of the Kyrie Eleison in Mozart's 'Requiem:'—

occurs also in Handel's oratorio 'Joseph:'—

and in Handel's 'Messiah:'—

Likewise in a Quartet for stringed instruments by Haydn, Op. 20, thus:—

In the solemn phrase of the Commendatore, in 'Don Giovanni,' we have an interesting example of the happy result with which Mozart has carried out ideas emanating from Gluck. In the opera 'Alceste,' by Gluck, the Oracle sings in one tone, while the orchestral accompaniment, including three trombones, changes the harmony in each successive bar, as follows:—

That Mozart was much impressed with the effect of Gluck's idea may be gathered from the circumstance of his having adopted it in 'Don Giovanni,' and likewise, to some extent, in 'Idomeneo.' The Commendatore in 'Don Giovanni' sings, accompanied by trombones:—

There can hardly be a greater difference in the styles of two composers than exists in the style of Gluck and that of J. S. Bach. The masterly command of Bach over the combination of different parts according to the rules of counterpoint is just the faculty in which Gluck is deficient. It is on this account especially interesting to observe how Gluck has employed an idea which he apparently borrowed from Bach. The student may ascertain it by carefully comparing the air, 'Je l'implore, et je tremble,' in 'Iphigenia in Tauris,' with J. S. Bach's beautiful gigue in B flat major, commencing :—

Clementi, a pianoforte composer, who has certainly but little in common with Gluck, has for his B minor Sonata dedicated to Cherubini—perhaps his best work—a theme which may be recognised as that of the dance of the Scythians in 'Iphigenia in Tauris.'

Again, Beethoven's style, especially in his later works, is as different from Haydn's as possible; nevertheless we occasionally meet with a phrase in Beethoven's later works which appears to have been suggested by Haydn. For instance, Haydn, in his Symphony in B flat major (No. 2 of Salomon's set) has a playful repetition of a figure of semi-quavers leading to the re-introduction of the theme, thus:—

In Beethoven's famous E minor Quartet, Op. 59, a similar figure leads to the theme, thus:—

A more exact comparison of the two passages than the present short notations permit will probably convince the student of the great superiority of Beethoven's conception. He was one of those rare masters who convert into gold whatever they touch.

But it is not the object here to give a list of the similarities and adaptations which are traceable in the works of different musical composers. Such a list would fill a volume, even if composers of secondary rank, who are often great borrowers, were ignored. For the present essay a few examples must suffice, especially as others will probably occur to the reflecting reader.

Some insight into the studies of our great composers may also be obtained by comparing together such of their operas or other elaborate vocal compositions with instrumental accompaniment as are founded on the same subject. Note, for instance, the love-story of Armida, taken by the compilers of the various librettos from the episode of Rinaldo

I

and Armida in Tasso's 'Gerusalemme Liberata.' The story had evidently a great attraction for the musical composers of the eighteenth century. There have been above thirty operas written on it, several of which it might now be difficult to procure, nor would an examination of them perhaps repay the trouble. However, the operas on the subject composed by Lulli, Gluck, Graun, Handel, Traetta, Jomelli, Naumann, Haydn, Sarti, Cimarosa, Rossini, Sacchini, etc., would suffice for the purpose. Thus also, a comparison of several compositions depicting a storm —most of our masters have written such a piece—elicits valuable hints for the musical student. Compare, for instance, with each other the storms in Gluck's 'Iphigenia in Tauris,' Haydn's 'Seasons,' Beethoven's 'Sinfonia Pastorale,' Cherubini's 'Medea.'

Even arrangements may illustrate the studies. Take, for instance, the arrangements of Vivaldi's violin concertos by J. S. Bach. It is, however, but seldom that eminent composers have occupied themselves with arranging the works of others. Instructive examples of this kind are therefore rare.

It is recorded of some composers that they were in the habit of founding their instrumental works on certain poetical ideas. Haydn is said to have done this almost invariably. Schindler, in his biographical notices of Beethoven, states that the two pianoforte Sonatas, Op. 14, of Beethoven, were explained to him by the composer as representing a dialogue between two lovers. When Schindler asked the meaning of the motivo of the C minor Symphony,

Beethoven exclaimed, "Thus Fate knocks at the gate!" And being requested by Schindler to supply him with the key to the Sonatas in D minor, Op. 31, and in F minor, Op. 57, Beethoven's answer was: "Read Shakespeare's 'Tempest!'" Beethoven probably resorted to such replies merely to satisfy troublesome inquirers somewhat resembling the inquisitive gentleman in Washington Irving's 'Tales of a

Traveller,' who "never could enjoy the kernel of the nut, but pestered himself to get more out of the shell." Several of the titles of Beethoven's instrumental compositions ('Pastoral Sonata,' 'Moonlight Sonata,' 'Sonata appassionata,' etc.) did not originate with the composer, but were given to the pieces by the publishers to render them more attractive to the public. The title of his sonata Op. 81, 'Les Adieux, l'Absence et le Retour,' emanates however from Beethoven himself. This is noteworthy inasmuch as it has brought the advocates of descriptive music into an awkward dilemma. They found in this sonata an unmistakable representation of the parting and ultimate reunion of two ardent lovers,—when, unhappily for them, Beethoven's autograph manuscript of the sonata was discovered, in the library of Archduke Rudolph, bearing the inscription (in German), "The Farewell, Absence, and Return of His Imperial Highness the Venerated Archduke Rudolph."

A similar subject is treated by J. S. Bach, in a capriccio for the harpsichord, entitled, 'On the Departure of a very dear Brother,' in which the different movements are headed as follows:—"No. 1. Entreaty of friends to put off the journey.—No. 2. Representation of the various accidents which might befall him.—No. 3. General lament of friends. —No. 4. Entreaty being of no avail, the friends here bid farewell.—No. 5. Air of the postillion.—No. 6. Fuga in imitation of the post-horn."

This is but a modest essay in tone-painting compared with a certain production by Johann Kuhnau, a predecessor of Bach, who depicted entire biblical stories in a set of six sonatas for the clavichord, which were published in Leipzic in the year 1700. Each sonata is prefaced by a programme, which informs the player what is meant by the several movements—a very necessary proceeding. The stories depicted are from the Old Testament. One of the sonatas is entitled, 'Jacob's Marriage;' another, 'Saul cured by David's Music;' another, 'The Death of Jacob;' and so on. To show how far Kuhnau ventures into detailed description, the explanation printed with the sonata called 'Gideon' may find a place here. It runs as follows:—"1. Gideon mistrusts the promises made to him by God that he should be victorious.—2. His fear at the sight of the great host of the enemy.—3. His increasing courage at the relation of the dream of the enemy, and of its interpretation.—4. The martial sound of the trombones and trumpets, and likewise the breaking of the pitchers and the cry of the people.—5. The flight of the enemy and their pursuit by the Israelites.—6. The rejoicing of the Israelites for their remarkable victory."

Still earlier, in the seventeenth century, Dieterich Buxtehude depicted in seven suites for the clavichord, 'The Nature and Qualities of the Planets;' and Johann Jacob Frohberger, about the same time, composed for the harpsichord a ' Plainte, faite à Londres, pour passer la mélancolie,' in which he describes his eventful journey from Germany to England—how in France he was attacked by robbers, and how afterwards in the Channel, between Calais and Dover, he was plundered by Tunisian pirates. Frohberger composed also an *allemande* intended to commemorate an event which he experienced on the Rhine. The notation is so contrived as to represent a bridge over the Rhine. Mattheson is said to have cleverly introduced into one of his scores, by means of the notation, the figure of a rainbow. Such music one must not hear; enough if one sees it in print. It deserves to be classed with the silent music mentioned in Shakespeare's 'Othello,' Act III., Scene 1:—

"*Clown.*—But, masters, here's money for you: and the General so likes your music, that he desires you, for love's sake, to make no more noise with it.

"*First Musician.*—Well, sir, we will not.

"*Clown.*—If you have any music that may not be heard, to't again: but, as they say, to hear music the General does not greatly care.

"*First Musician.*—We have none such, sir.

"*Clown.*—Then put your pipes in your bag, for I'll away: go, vanish into air; away!"

It may afford satisfaction to the lover of descriptive music to imagine he hears in certain choruses by Handel the leaping of frogs, the humming of flies, or the rattling of hailstones; but the judicious admirer of these compositions values them especially on account of their purely musical beauties. These may in a great measure be traced to euphony combined with originality. Music must be above all things melodiously beautiful. Our great composers bore this in mind, or acted upon it as a matter of course; hence the fascinating charms of their music. The euphony does not depend upon the consonant harmony prevailing in the composition; if this were the case, music would be the more euphonious the fewer dissonant chords it contains, and the major key would be more suitable for euphony than the minor key, since the major scale is founded upon the most simple relation of musical intervals yielding concords. However, our finest compositions contain numerous dissonant chords; and many—perhaps most—are in the minor key. Some of our great composers have certainly written more important works in minor than in major keys. Mozart, in those of his compositions which are in major keys, often manifests extraordinary inspiration as soon as he modulates into a minor key.

Remarkably devoid of euphony are the compositions of some musicians who, having taken Beethoven's last works as the chief models for their aspirations, have thereby been prevented from properly cultivating whatever gift they may naturally possess for expressing their ideas melodiously and clearly. Moreover, they talk and act as if affected originality, or far-fetched fancies, constituted the principal charm of a composition. Not less tedious are the works of some modern composers who possess no originality, but who write very correctly in the style of some classical composer. There has been published a vast amount of such stale and unprofitable productions. Music, to be interesting, must possess some quality in a high degree. If it is very good, it is just what it ought to be; if it is very bad, one can honestly condemn it, and leave it to its fate. But music which is neither very good nor very bad—which deserves neither praise nor blame, and which one cannot easily ignore because it is well meant—this is the most wearisome. And often how long such productions are! The composers show with many notes that they have felt but little, while our great composers show with but few notes that they have felt much.

An inferior composer has, however, not unfrequently a better chance of becoming soon popular than a superior one. The latter is likely to be properly appreciated only by a few unbiassed judges—at least during his earlier career—while the former may possess qualities which at once please the uncultivated taste, and the voice of the unrefined majority may silence the voice of the few whose opinion is correct. If you become acquainted with a celebrated musician, you will perhaps find that he is not so talented as you expected; and if you become acquainted with a musician of no reputation, you will perhaps find that he is much more talented than you expected. Diffidence is apt to be mistaken for want of ability. Even some of our deepest thinkers, on acknowledging that they did not understand a certain subject, have been set down by ignorant people as dunces.

Composers who have made good studies sometimes write ingenious contrivances or "learned music," instead of inventing a beautiful melody. They are apt to introduce fugues into their works when they are short of ideas or at a loss how to proceed. Even our great composers have done this occasionally, when their power of invention began to flag. But they were careful, when resorting to mere headwork, to use it only in places most appropriate; and they generally succeeded in imparting to it some musical charm.

Always striving to attain a higher degree of perfection, they were in fact students all their lifetime. The more they learnt, the clearer they saw that they had much to learn, and that time was precious to them. Beethoven on his death-bed was studying the scores of Handel's oratorios, and Mozart to the end of his life investigated the intricate works of Johann Sebastian Bach.

Many examples from different composers might have been cited in support of the opinions advanced in this essay. But, not to lengthen it unnecessarily, only a few examples, referring to such of our composers as are universally acknowledged to be truly great, have been selected. No doubt many more will occur to the reflecting reader, if he is familiar with our classical compositions.

SUPERSTITIONS CONCERNING BELLS.

Much is said about church-bells which formerly sometimes used to toll entirely by themselves on occasions of extraordinary importance. In some countries places are pointed out where church-bells which have fallen into a lake or river, or have sunk deep into the ground, will toll on certain days of the year, or on certain solemn occasions. The believers in these wonders go to the place where a bell is said to be hidden, and listen attentively. Generally they soon hear the distant sounds which they anxiously wish to hear.

A wonderful bell is mentioned by Abraham à Sancta Clara, who so forcibly preached during the latter half of the seventeenth century; and some account of the same bell is given by Montano in his 'Historische Nachricht von denen Glocken,' published in the year 1726. Montano says that "it may be seen at Vililla, a small town in the kingdom of Arragon." When this bell was being cast, one of the thirty pieces of silver for which the arch-traitor Judas Iscariot delivered up Jesus Christ to the chief priests, was melted down with the metal, which had the effect of causing the bell to sound occasionally by itself without being touched, especially before the occurrence of some great national calamity, such as a disastrous issue of a warlike expedition, or the death of a king. In the year 1601, Montano records, it continued to ring by itself for three days unintermittingly,—viz., from Thursday the 13th of June until Saturday the 15th; but whether it had some particular reason for this extraordinary procedure, or whether it was merely actuated by some capricious impulse, we are not informed by the learned writer.

Spain appears to have been pre-eminently favoured with such miraculous bells. This is perhaps not to be wondered at considering that miracles occur most frequently in countries where the people are best prepared to accept them.

A lamentable misunderstanding occasioned by a little house-bell is recorded by Grimm as having occurred in a German town; but we are not informed of the name of the town, nor of that of the citizen in whose house it occurred. The inmates of the house, with the exception of the mistress, heard distinctly the sound of the bell, and were quite certain that no one had touched it. Moreover, a few days afterwards, they heard it a second time. The master of the house, a strong and healthy man, made up his mind at once that this omen portended the decease of his wife, who was keeping her bed, very much reduced indeed. He forbade the servants to tell their mistress what had occurred, lest it might frighten her and hasten her dissolution. The state of suspense, after the bell had given warning the second time, lasted for about six weeks, when suddenly—the husband died, and the wife became better! Even after the widow had married again, the bell rang by itself on several occasions; and whenever this happened, there was sure to be a death in the house—sooner or later.*

PROTECTIVE BELL-RINGING.

The notion that the tinkling and clanging of bells is a safeguard against the influence of evil spirits, so common among Christian nations, evidently prevailed also with the ancient Egyptians. Some little hand-bells with representations of Typhon have been found in Egyptian tombs, and are still preserved. The Hebrew high-priests had bells attached to their garments, and the reason assigned to this usage, given in Exodus xxviii., verse 35, is: "His sound shall be heard when he goeth into the holy place before the Lord, and when he cometh out, that he die not." Whatever

---

* 'Deutsche Sagen, herausgegeben von den Brüdern Grimm. Berlin, 1816.' Vol. I., p. 355.

may be the right interpretation of this sentence—there are more than one—it cannot but remind us of the use made by the ancient Egyptians of the Sistrum, the tinkling sounds of which were considered indispensable in religious ceremonies. Nay, what is more remarkable, the sistrum is still in use, being employed by the priests of a Christian sect in Abyssinia; while the Copts, in Upper Egypt, who are likewise Christians, shake in their religious performances a tinkling instrument of metal, called *maràoueh*, avowedly for the purpose of keeping off the Evil One. Moreover, the Shamans, in Siberia, when preparing themselves for performing incantations, and for prophesying, dress themselves in garments to which are attached tinkling and rattling appendages. Likewise the "medicine men," or prophets of the American Indians, when they engage in sorcery and invocation of spirits, employ, if not tinkling metal, at least dried and rattling seed-pods, loose bills of certain water birds, gourds containing pebbles, and similar contrivances.

The old belief, even at the present day not uncommon, that bell-ringing on the approach of a thunderstorm, and during its continuance, is a protection against lightning, may not unfrequently have been conducive to a deplorable accident, since the current of air produced by the swinging of a bell is more likely to attract the electric fluid than, as is supposed, to drive it away. In Prussia the old and cherished custom of ringing bells during a thunderstorm was wisely forbidden by Frederick the Great, in the year 1783, and his ordinance directed the prohibition to be read in all the churches of the kingdom.

SIGNIFICANT SOUNDS OF BELLS.

The erroneous opinion that an admixture of silver with the bell-metal, consisting of copper and tin, greatly improves the sound of the bell, is very common.

The old church at Krempe, in Holstein, possessed formerly a bell of extraordinary sonorousness, which, people say, contained a great deal of silver. When this bell was being cast, the people brought silver coins and trinkets to be thrown into the fusing metal, in order to ensure a very fine tone. The avaricious founder had a mind to retain these valuable offerings for himself, so he put them aside. But, during his temporary absence, the apprentice took all the silver and threw it into the melting mass. When, on the master's return, his apprentice told him that he had applied the silver to the purpose for which it was presented by the donors, the master waxed angry, and slew the lad. Now, when the bell was cast, and hung in the tower of the church, its sound proved indeed most sonorous, but also very mournful; and whenever it was rung it distinctly sounded like "Schad' um den Jungen! Schad' um den Jungen!" ("Pity for the lad! Pity for the lad!")

The church-bell at Keitum, on the Isle of Silt, in the North Sea, off the coast of Denmark, distinctly says "Ing Dung!" which are the names of two pious spinsters at whose expense the old bell-tower of the church was erected long ago. There exists an old prophecy in the place that, after the bell shall have fallen down and killed the finest youth of the island, the tower will likewise fall, and will kill the most beautiful girl of Silt. A fine youth was actually killed by the fall of the bell in the year 1739; and since that time the young girls of Silt are generally very timid in approaching the tower, for each one thinks that she may be the destined victim.

The good people of Gellingen, in the district of Angeln, on the borders of Denmark, once ordered two bells to be cast for them in the town of Lübeck. These bells were brought by water to Schleimünde; but as ill-luck would have it, one of them fell into the sea and was lost. Now, whenever the remaining bell is being rung, it distinctly proclaims, of which everyone may convince himself, "Min Mag ligger i ä Minn!" ("My companion lies in the Schleimünde!")*

The church at Dambeck, in Mecklenburg-Schwerin, is so very old that the oldest inhabitants of the place affirm that its outer walls, which only are now remaining, were built

---

* 'Sagen, Märchen und Lieder der Herzogthümer Schleswig, Holstein und Lauenburg, herausgegeben von Karl Müllenhoff. Kiel, 1845.' Pp. 116, 118.

before the deluge. The tower with the bells is sunk in the Lake Müritz; and in olden time people have often seen the bells rising to the surface of the water on St. John's Day. One afternoon some children, who had carried the dinner to their parents labouring in an adjacent field, stopped by the lake to wash the napkins. These little urchins saw the bells which had risen above the water. One of the children, a little girl, spread her napkin over one of the bells for the purpose of drying it; the consequence was that the bell could not descend again. But though all the rich people of the town of Röbel came to secure the bell for themselves, they were unable to remove it, notwithstanding that they brought sixteen strong horses to draw it from the place. They were still unsuccessfully urging the horses, when a poor man happened to pass that way from the fields with a pair of oxen. The man, seeing what the rich people were about, at once told them to put their horses aside; he then yoked his pair of oxen to the bell, and said : "Nu met God foer Arme un Rieke, all to gelieke!" ("Now with the help of God, alike for poor and rich.") Having pronounced these words, he drove the bell without the least difficulty to Röbel, where it was soon hung in the tower of the new church. Whenever a really poor man dies in Röbel, this bell is tolled for him free of charge, and it distinctly says "Dambeck! Dambeck!"*

A hundred other instances could be noticed of church-bells being said to pronounce some sentence referring to a remarkable incident which occurred in very remote time. The people, in reciting these sentences, generally imitate the sound of the bell, which of course, greatly heightens the effect of the story. Switzerland is especially rich in such old and cherished traditions.

Every true-born Briton is familiar with the prophetic words chimed by the bells of Bow Church to Whittington on his return to London, which signified to him that he was destined to fill one of the highest posts of honour to which an Englishman can aspire. Some people scout the tradition,

---

* 'Norddeutsche Sagen, Märchen und Gebräuche, herausgegeben von Kuhn und Schwartz. Leipzig, 1848.' P. 4.

bluntly saying, "I don't believe a word of it!" Others reply, "Only just prove that it is a myth, and I shall not believe it any longer, of that I am quite certain."

BAPTIZED BELLS.

Baptized bells are still by many people believed to possess marvellous powers. In Roman Catholic countries the large church bells are most frequently named after particular saints. The baptism, or the dedication to a saint, as the case may be, is performed with solemn ceremonies. The words of consecration pronounced by the priest are " May this bell be sanctified and consecrated in the name of the Father, and the Son, and the Holy Ghost, in honour of Saint ———." A real baptism does not always take place, but the solemn consecration resembles so closely a baptismal ceremony that it is not surprising the people should generally regard it as such; neither is it surprising that with these exhibitions there should still prevail many superstitious notions relating to miraculous bells.

The uneducated man in Lithuania believes that a newly-cast church bell emits no sound until it has been consecrated and baptized; and the sound of a baptized bell, he fancies, frightens away all sorcery, and even the devil. Moreover, the Lithuanians have a poetical and beautiful conception, according to which the souls of the deceased are floated on the sounds of baptized bells into Heaven.*

If we look back a century or two, we meet with popular traditions implying that baptized bells were regarded by many persons much as living beings. Take, for instance, the following story, recorded by Montano:— "When the French, anno 1677, in their cruel madness held possession of the town of Deux-Ponts (or Zweibrücken), they took the bell from the church-tower and endeavoured to destroy it by knocking it to pieces. This they were, however, unable to accomplish. They, therefore, made a large fire, upon

---

* 'Die Sprichwörter der Polen, von C. Wurzbach. Wien, 1852.' P. 135.

which they placed the bell with the intention of melting it. All the military officers stood by to watch the process. How great was their surprise when they saw that the tortured bell begin to sweat blood! The highest officer took his handkerchief, stained it with the blood, and sent it to the King of France; for he thought it possible that, without this irrefragable evidence, neither the king nor anyone else would believe the miracle."

The Swiss preserve some curious traditions respecting baptized bells. They have even had a medal struck commemorating some miracle which occurred when the Pope sent such a blessed bell to the canton of Valais. Moreover, all the bells of the Roman Catholic churches in Switzerland wander annually to Rome for the purpose of confession. They leave on Thursday in Passion Week, and return on the following Saturday; at any rate, there is no bell-ringing during the time indicated. Rochholz says that it is a usual custom in Switzerland to have sponsors at the baptismal ceremony of a church-bell; to dress the bell for the occasion in a garment called "Westerhemd;" to pronounce the Creed in its name; and to sprinkle it with holy water. All these rites were, for instance, observed in the village of Ittenthalen situated in the valley of Frickthal, canton Aargau, where the new bell received not only the name of the godmother, but also was presented by her with a baptismal gift of 200 francs.*

Unbaptized bells have, according to accounts from various countries, often proved troublesome, and instances are mentioned of their having flown out of towers, several miles distance through the air, and having fallen into a pond believed to be bottomless. In Moringen, a small town south of Hanover, is a bottomless pond called "Opferteich" ('Pond of Sacrifice') near which, according to an old tradition, the pagan ancestors of the people of Moringen used to offer sacrifice. A bell which through some neglect had not received the rite of baptism, flew into the pond, where it is

---

* 'Allemannisches Kinderlied und Kinderspiel aus der Schweiz; gesammelt von E. L. Rochholz. Leipzig, 1857.' P. 58.

said to be chained fast and guarded by a ferocious dog. Another unbaptized bell was carried by an awful storm from the church of Grone, a village not far from Moringen, a long distance through the air, and sunk into a pond, where it rests on a table covered with black. At least, a diver, whom the peasants engaged to recover it, reported that he had seen it so placed. But when they sent the diver down a second time, provided with a rope to secure the bell, they found, on drawing up the rope, the diver and not the bell fastened to it, and he was dead.*

In a morass near the town of Lochen, in Holland, are two ponds of stagnant water, in which the Evil One has hidden two fine bells which, many years ago, he suddenly carried off from the church-tower of Lochen, as they had not been baptized. These bells are still heard by the people, tolling every year on Christmas Eve precisely at twelve o'clock. The Dutch call these two ponds " Duivelskolken." †

INSCRIPTIONS ON CHURCH BELLS.

The inscriptions on church bells are sometimes so quaint, and in some countries so characteristic, that a collection of them would probably be amusing. Take, for instance, the following English specimens, in which the names of the donors are immortalised :—

On a bell at Alderton are the words :—

"I'm given here to make a peal,
And sound the praise of Mary Neale."

And on a bell at Binstead :—

"Doctor Nicholas gave five pounds,
To help cast this peal tuneable and sound."

An alarm-bell in the church of Sherborne, cast in the year 1652, bears the inscription :—

"Lord, quench this furious flame!
Arise, run, help, put out the same!"

---

* ' Niedersächsiche Sagen und Märchen, gesammelt von Schaumbach und Müller. Göttingen, 1855.' P. 57.

† ' Niederländische Sagen, herausgegeben von J. W. Wolf. Leipzig, 1843.' P. 562.

On the bell which emits the highest sound in the peal of St. Mary's, at Devizes, are the words:—

"I am the first, altho' but small,
I will be heard above you all."

St. Helen's Church, at Worcester, possesses a set of eight bells, cast in the time of Queen Anne, with inscriptions recording the victories gained in her reign.

A recent traveller in Iceland saw in a village of that country a church-bell which had the inscription in the German language:—

"Aus dem Feuer bin ich gegossen,
Hans Meyer in Kopenhagen hat mich geflossen, Anno 1663." *

recording that it had been cast, more than two hundred years ago, by a German founder residing in Denmark. The great bell in the cathedral at Glasgow contains a statement of its having been cast in the year 1583, in Holland, and recast in the year 1790 in London; and a bell in the cathedral of St. Magnus, at Kirkwall, Orkney, records that it was sent to Amsterdam to be recast in the year 1682. Still more frequent than historical statements are scriptural sentences and religious admonitions.

The Burmese, in order to protect a newly-cast bell from being defiled by their European aggressors, have hit upon the expedient of supplying it with a threatening sentence. The bell is in a Buddhist temple at Moulmein. Besides an inscription in Burmese characters it has a sentence in bad English running thus:—

"This bell is made by Koonalinnguhjah the priest, and the weight 600 viss. No one body design to destroy this bell. Moulmein, March 30, 1855. He who destroyed this bell, they must be in the great heell and unable to coming out."

THE CHURCH BELLS BANISHING THE MOUNTAIN-DWARFS.

Curious traditions are still found among the country people in Sweden, Denmark, Germany and some other

---

* 'Iceland, its Scenes and Sagas, by Sabine Baring-Gould. London, 1863.' P. 194.

European countries, of mountain-dwarfs, and suchlike mysterious inhabitants of the country, having been forced to emigrate on account of the bell-ringing. To note one instance:—

In Holstein, people say, a large number of mountain-dwarfs, greatly troubled by the sounds of the many new church-bells introduced, made up their mind to leave the country. Accordingly, having arranged their affairs, they set out in a body and travelled northwards until they came to the River Eider, at a place where there is a ferry. It was late in the night when a knock at the door aroused the ferryman from his sleep. He thought he must have been dreaming; for, it had never happened that anybody had called him up in the middle of the night to be ferried over the river. He therefore took no notice of it, and soon fell asleep again. But after awhile he was awakened by the sound of another knock at the door; and this time he felt sure he had not been dreaming. So he dressed himself quickly, and opened the house-door to see who was there. But, strange enough, he saw no one at the door; and when he called out in the dark, inquiring who wanted him, he got no reply. Then he thought the best thing he could do would be to go to bed again. However, he had scarcely taken his coat off, when there came a bang at the door which quite startled him, so loud it was. Taking up a bludgeon from a corner of the room, and putting on his hat, he at once went out of the house to scrutinise the place.

He had gone only a few steps in the direction towards the river, when to his great surprise he saw before him in a field a multitude of gray-looking dwarfs, who moved restlessly to and fro like ants when you open an ant-hill. Presently one of them, a very old fellow with a long white beard, approached the ferryman and requested him to convey the whole company over the Eider.

"You will be duly paid for your services," said the pigmy with the long beard. "Only place your hat upon the bank of the river for our people to throw the money into as they enter the boat."

The ferryman did as he was desired; but he would

rather not have had anything to do with these people. The boat was soon crowded with them. They scrambled about everywhere like insects, and he had to make the passage several times before he had carried them all over to the opposite bank of the river. He observed that each of them threw what appeared to be a grain of sand into the hat; but this he did not mind—thinking only how glad he should be when he had got rid of them all. In fact, he did not trust them, especially as the fellow with the long beard informed him that they were compelled to migrate to some other part of the world on account of the church bells and the hymn-singing, which they could not put up with any longer.

When the ferryman had carried over the last load of the little emigrants, he saw that the whole field near the place where he had landed them was glittering with lights, which flitted about in every direction. The little wanderers had all of them lighted their lanterns. But when he had returned to the bank near his house, and came to take up his hat, how he opened his eyes! Certainly he had never been so surprised in all his life. The hat was full of gold!

He joyfully carried the treasure into his house, and was immensely rich ever after. In short, this simple man became in no time one of the most respectable gentlemen in the country, and died actually worth thousands of pounds.

THE EXPULSION OF PAGANISM IN SWEDEN.

If the reader should ever happen to visit Lagga, a parish in the south-west of Sweden, the people will point out to him an enormously large stone which a giant once threw at a church, and in which the marks of his strong fingers are still discernible. It was, Afzelius says, a common practice with giants in Sweden to hurl stones at the churches, but they never hit them. Moreover, the sound of the church bell was very hateful to them. Near Lagga is a mountain celebrated as the former domicile of a giant, who lived there until the time of the Reformation, when the church of the place was provided with bells. One morning the dejected giant addressed a peasant from Lagga, whose name was Jacob, and who happened to be at the foot of the mountain. "Jacob!" said the giant in a subdued tone of voice, "come in, Jacob, and eat of my stew!"

But Jacob, alarmed at the kind invitation, replied rather hesitatingly: "Sir, if you have more stew than you can consume, you had better keep the rest for to-morrow."

Upon this sensible advice, the dejected giant complained: "I cannot stay here even till to-morrow! I am compelled to leave this place because of the constant bell-ringing, which is quite insupportable!"

Whereupon Jacob, getting a little courage, asked him: "And when do you intend to come back again?"

The dejected giant, hearing himself thus questioned, ejaculated whiningly: "Come back again? Oh! certainly not until the mount has become the bottom of the sea, and the sea itself arable and fertile land; if this should ever happen, then I may perhaps come back again."

CURIOSITIES IN MUSICAL LITERATURE.

Anything which is new and unprecedented in music is seldom at once properly appreciated by the majority of musicians however beautiful it may be. Hence the diversity of opinion concerning certain important musical compositions which we meet with in our literature.

The 'Letters on Musical Taste' written by J. B. Schaul ('Briefe über den Geschmack in der Musik. Carlsruhe, 1809,') contain many sensible observations which are blemished by unreasonable attacks on Mozart, because the then new composer did not in his operas restrict himself to the same treatment of the orchestra to which previous masters had accustomed the ear. Schaul was a great admirer of Boccherini. "What a difference between a Mozart and a Boccherini!" he exclaims. "The former leads us among rugged rocks in a thorny forest but sparingly strewn with flowers; whereas the latter conducts us into a smiling landscape with flowery meadows, clear and murmuring brooks, and shady groves, where our spirit abandons itself with delight to a sweet melancholy, which affords it an agreeable recreation even after it has left these pleasant regions."

There are several other remarks of this kind in the book, which aroused the ire of Carl Maria von Weber, and induced him to take up his pen in defence of Mozart,* which he probably would have thought unnecessary, if the book were not otherwise rather clever.

---

* 'Hinterlassene Schriften von C. M. von Weber. Zweite Ausgabe, Leipzic, 1850.' Vol. II., p. 14.

When, in the year 1790, Mozart's 'Don Giovanni' was performed in Berlin for the first time, the new opera found favour with the public, but by no means with the critics. The following extract is translated from the 'Chronik von Berlin,' Vol. IX., p. 133 :—"It is not by overcharging the orchestra, but by expressing the emotions and passions of the heart, that the composer achieves anything great, and transmits his name to posterity. Grétry, Monsigny, and Philidor are, and ever will be, examples of this truth. Mozart, in his 'Don Giovanni,' aimed at producing something extraordinary, thus much is certain, and something extraordinary surely he has produced; nothing however, which could not be imitated, or which is great. Not the heart, but whim, eccentricity, and pride are the sources from which 'Don Giovanni' has emanated. . . . . . This opera, nevertheless, proved remunerative to the manager; and gallery, boxes and pit will also in future not be empty; for a ghost in armour and furies spitting fire are a powerful magnet."*

The chord with the augmented octave, which occurs several times in Mozart's overture to 'Don Giovanni':—

has caused more than one honest theorist to shake his head. No doubt, if seen in notation disconnected from the preceding and following bars, it looks deterrent enough; but ought it thus, to be judged? Still, Schilling in his Musical Dictionary,† has thought it necessary to excuse Mozart for having used this chord. In the article headed "Accord" he remarks: "Türk says we possess no chord with an augmented octave. Until Mozart, this interval was only used as a Suspension. Mozart, however, makes it stable enough by filling with

---

* 'Geschichte der Oper in Berlin, von L. Schneider. Berlin, 1850,' P. 240.

† ' Universal-Lexicon der Tonkunst. Stuttgardt, 1835.'

it a whole bar of ¾ time. The master always knows why he acts in a certain particular way and not otherwise; and as in 'Don Giovanni' the extraordinary is predominant, this long-sustained augmented interval—this premeditated poignard-stab—may stand there as a warning to our libertines. We, for our part, know nothing more frightful than this sustained chord, and the sudden energy with which it is intended to be executed."

If Mozart could provoke adverse criticism, it is not surprising that Beethoven did, considering his great originality. Dr. Crotch therefore, should not be thought a worse critic than many others when he says (in his 'Lectures,' London, 1831, p. 146) of Beethoven: "That he has ever disregarded the rules of composition is to be regretted, as there does not seem to have been the least good obtained by it in any one instance."

Rochlitz, in criticising Beethoven's last violin quartets, which he evidently did not like, cautiously observes: "When Beethoven had published his first three Trios for pianoforte, violin and violoncello—and soon afterwards, his first Symphony in C major—a certain reviewer thought it right and good to speak of the Trios almost jokingly, treating them rather as confused explosions of the bold wantonness of a young man of talent; and the symphony he earnestly and warningly declared to be an odd imitation of the style of Haydn, amounting almost to caricature. Yet this critic was really an able musician of much experience, and standing firm as a rock in his time and its theory. He had also produced many works which are justly appreciated, and he liked Beethoven in a degree. Had the man given his name, or did we not owe reticence to the dead, every reader would concede this, and even more, if we named him. Again, when Beethoven had finished his second Symphony in D major, and Prince Lichnowsky brought the manuscript to Leipzig, Spazier, after the performance of the symphony, gave his opinion about it in his new journal, entitled 'Zeitung für die elegante Welt.' He called it a coarse monster—a pierced dragon writhing indomitably, which will not die, and which in bleeding to death (Finale) flourishes its uplifted tail furiously in all directions in vain. Now, Spazier was a clever fellow, a many-sided and versatile man, and by no means inexperienced. As musician, he was acquainted with every composition which in his time was considered as superior. Having been a pupil and faithful assistant of Reichardt, he enjoyed as a critic a by no means small reputation, and was even feared. Since then, twenty-five years have elapsed; and what is now thought of these works by the whole world?"[*]

A collection of the musical reviews emanating from critics of reputation, which condemn our master-works, might be amusing, but would probably be more ridiculous than instructive. England especially could contribute a large share of such curiosities in musical literature. No doubt some of the judges were clever enough; they cannot exactly be said to have been unable to understand what they criticised; but they had compiled a certain code of rules for their own guidance in judging, gathered from the works of some favourite composer, which rules they considered as the only right ones. Consequently they denounced whatever they found in disagreement with their adopted code.

J. N. Forkel, the learned and justly-esteemed author of a 'History of Music,' and of several other useful works, possessed for J. S. Bach so intense an admiration, that he had at last no ear for any composer who differed from his idol. Hence his unwarrantable attacks on Gluck in his 'Musikalisch-Kritische Bibliothek,' Gotha, 1778.

We possess in the German language a cleverly written book entitled 'Ueber Reinheit der Tonkunst' (On the Purity of Music), the first edition of which appeared in the year 1825. The author of this book, A. C. J. Thibaut, a distinguished Professor of Law in Heidelberg, had studied the old Italian and Dutch Church composers of the time of Palestrina, whose works he delighted in having performed at regular meetings of a number of well-trained

---

[*] Rochlitz wrote this in the year 1828. See 'Allgemeine musikalische Zeitung,' Jahrgang XXX, p. 489.

choristers in his house. Thibaut's enthusiasm for the old writers of vocal music without instrumental accompaniment was so unbounded that the great instrumental compositions by Beethoven and others had but little attraction for him. He ridicules with much sarcasm Weber's overture to 'Oberon.' Celebrated pianists evidently found but little favour with him. Still, Thibaut has had a beneficial influence on musicians, and his strange and spirited book deserves a prominent place among our curiosities in musical literature.

Distinguished composers sometimes prove but unreliable judges of the merits of other composers, especially if the latter are their contemporaries, and perhaps their rivals. We know from the biographies of the composers how greatly Weber disliked Rossini; how lightly Spohr appreciated Weber's 'Der Freischütz' when all the world was in ecstasy about the opera; how Spohr found fault with Beethoven's symphonies. And we know what Beethoven, in an unguarded moment, said of these composers. We remember Mozart's unfavourable opinions concerning Clementi, Abbé Vogler and some other musical celebrities of his time; likewise J. S. Bach's joking remarks to his son Friedemann about their going to Dresden to listen to the "pretty little songs" of Hasse; and Handel's hard words about Gluck: "He knows no more of counterpoint than my cook!"—not to record other such gossip which is rather scandalous. Being reminded of these musical discords, it is all the more agreeable to remember the sincerity with which many of our great musicians have acknowledged the merits of their compeers. Haydn's esteem for Mozart was only equalled by Mozart's esteem for Haydn. Beethoven's high appreciation of Cherubini is notorious. Likewise, Schubert's admiration of Beethoven. But it is unnecessary here to point out instances of the kind.

Musical amateurs often evince a preference for a certain composer merely because they have accidentally become more familiar with his works than with those of other composers. No wonder that in their literary productions referring to music they should have largely contributed to the curiosities.

In noticing here M. Victor Schœlcher's 'Life of Handel,' it is with sincere esteem for his enthusiasm and perseverance, which enabled him to collect interesting information respecting the great composer. However, in order to write the 'Life of Handel' it is not sufficient to be an enthusiastic admirer of his works. One must be well acquainted with the musicians contemporary with the great composer, and with the stage of progress of the art at the time when the little boy Handel took his initiatory lessons. One must also have practical experience in musical composition. The following opinion expressed in the work alluded to may serve as an example of a literary curiosity from a musical amateur:—"When a great artist like Handel is accused of theft, the proofs should be exhibited openly . . These pretended thefts are nothing but accidental resemblances, fugitive, and quite involuntary . . . . If Dr. Crotch is to be believed, Handel was never anything but a plagiarist, who passed his life in seeking ideas out of every corner!" and so on. Now, it is a well-known fact that Handel did in several instances make use of the compositions of others. But, no discerning biographer would for this reason regard him as a thief. The really musical inquirer would find it interesting to examine carefully how the great composer has treated and ennobled ideas emanating from others.

An autobiography of a celebrated musician may be instructive, if the author possesses the moral courage to record candidly what he has thought and felt. He must tell the truth, and nothing but the truth. How seldom is this the case! Be it from a praiseworthy consideration for others, or perhaps from personal vanity, statements of committed mistakes, unsuccessful struggles, and such like facts, are often omitted or gilded over. The letters of celebrated musicians, published after their death by their friends, are generally so much polished, and sentences thought to be injurious to the reputation of the great artist so carefully expunged, that we obtain only occasionally a glimpse at the real life of the man. Perhaps the most amiable, but also the weakest publications of this kind are generally the biographical notices which have been edited by the widow of a celebrated musician. To note one instance: 'Spohr's Autobiography' is interesting, although it is somewhat tinged with self-complacency. After Spohr's death his widow published the Autobiography, supplementing it with laudatory remarks such as the following :—

"During the last few years of his life he often expressed his conviction that there must certainly be music in Heaven, although it might be very different from our own music. When his wife replied with all her heart: 'Yes, perhaps different; but more beautiful than yours it cannot be!'— Then, a smile of happy contentment and blissful hope spread over his face."*

The musician acquainted with the frequent repetitions in Spohr's works of certain modulations and mannerisms in favour with the composer, may well be excused if he shudders at the thought that he should have to listen to them eternally.

Let us now direct our attention for a moment to books relating to musical controversy. The reader is probably aware of the dispute occasioned by Gluck and Piccini, in France, towards the end of the last century, and of the large number of pamphlets which it caused to be published, including some which were written by the most distinguished thinkers of the time. The dispute concerning the genuineness of Mozart's Requiem likewise supplies some curious specimens of musical literature. The paper-war commenced with an article by Gottfried Weber, published in the musical journal 'Cæcilia,' in the year 1825. The gauntlet thrown down was taken up, in the same year, by the Abbé Stadler. After this beginning of the controversy, other champions, *pro* and *contra*, made their appearance; and the quarrel, conducted not entirely without personal insult, soon grew to be as formidable as the fray between the Montagues and the Capulets,—when, fortunately for the sake of concord, Mozart's MS. score of the Requiem was

---

* 'Louis Spohr's Selbstbiographie. Cassel, 1861.' Vol. II., p. 404.

discovered, and revealed which portions of the work had been committed to paper by himself, and which were written after his death by his instructed disciple, Süssmayr.

Another controversy of a peculiar kind, in which many musicians took part, and upon which several dissertations were published, originated in a violent attack by Giovanni Spataro upon Franchino Gafori, in the beginning of the sixteenth century. An account of this dispute, which related to some theoretical questions, is given in Hawkins's 'History of Music,' London, 1776, Vol. II., p. 335. As regards the style of language of the combatants, it reminds us more of fists and clubs than of needle-guns; but this is only what might be expected.

Again, as regards the learned inquiries respecting the origin and use of music, some curious treatises may be noticed.

The opinion that man learnt the art of music from the songs of birds is very old, and was already held by the Roman poet Lucretius, nearly a century before our Christian era. Guido Casoni, in his 'Della Magia d'Amore,' Venice, 1596, finds the origin of music in Love. J. C. Ammon, a German clergyman, wrote in the year 1746, an essay entitled 'Gründlicher Beweis dass im ewigen Leben wirklich eine vortreffliche Musik sei' ('A Clear Proof that there is in Eternal Life really excellent Music'). Also Mattheson, of whose literary productions more than one might be classed with the curiosities, wrote circumstantially about the music in Heaven. A book of his on the subject, published in the year 1747, bears the title—'Behauptung der himmlischen Musik aus den Gründen der Vernunft, Kirchen-Lehre, und Heiligen Schrift' ('An Assertion that there is Music in Heaven, proved from conclusions of reason, from the teaching of the Church, and from Holy Scripture'). Latrobe, in his treatise entitled 'The Music of the Church,' London, 1831, settles this question by citing passages from the Revelation; for instance, the nature of the instrumental accompaniments to the vocal music in Heaven, is in his opinion clearly revealed by the passage "Harpers harping upon their harps." (Rev. XIV., 2).

The erroneous conjecture, that the art of music suggested itself originally to man, from his hearing the various sounds in nature, instead of being innate in him, has been entertained by several writers. Suffice it to notice two books on this hypothesis, written in the present century: 'The Music of Nature; or an attempt to prove that what is passionate and pleasing in the art of singing, speaking, and performing upon musical instruments, is derived from the sounds of the Animated World,' by William Gardiner; London, 1832. 'La Harpe d'Eole et la musique cosmique; études sur les rapports des phénomènes sonores de la nature avec la science et l'art;' par J. G. Kastner; Paris, 1856.—Kastner is the author of several musical treatises which might be enumerated with the literary curiosities.

Feyoo y Montenegro, a Spanish ecclesiastic, about the middle of the eighteenth century, wrote a dissertation, the title of which, translated into English, is: 'The Delights of Music accompanied by Virtue are upon Earth the foretaste of Heaven.' By way of contrast to this may be noticed Francesco Bocchi's 'Discorso sopra la Musica,' Florence, 1580, in which the learned author maintains that music is injurious to morals and good manners. Vicesimus Knox, in his 'Essays moral and literary,' London, 1778, recommends the acquirement of musical accomplishments as a means of protecting oneself in old age from contempt and neglect.

The oddities of the following English works are sufficiently indicated by their titles:— 'The Schoole of Abuse conteining a pleasaunt Inuective against Poetes, Pipers, Plaiers, Jesters, and such like Caterpillers of a Commonwelth,' by Stephen Gosson; London, 1579. 'Histrio-mastic; The Player's Scovrge, or Actors' Tragedie,' by William Prynne; London, 1633. For the publication of this work, which contains a satire against vocal music, the author was condemned by King Charles I. to have his ears cut off, and to stand in the pillory.

Curious specimens of English treatises on sacred music are:—'A Treatise concerning the lawfulness of Instrumental Musick in Holy Offices,' by Henry Dodwell. Second edition; London, 1700. 'The Temple Musick; or an Essay concerning the Method of Singing the Psalms of David, in the Temple, before the Babylonish Captivity,' by Arthur Bedford; London, 1706. 'The Great Abuse of Musick,' by Arthur Bedford, London, 1711.

A German philosopher, in the beginning of the present century, wrote 'On our Inclination to sing when we are in a cheerful Mood.' Others have shown that cheerful music makes some persons feel sad. Shakespeare knew this, to conclude from Jessica's words (The Merchant of Venice, Act V., Scene I.): 'I am never merry when I hear sweet music.'

As regards curious illustrations of musical instruments, the following works are especially deserving of notice :—

'Musica getutscht und ausgezogen,' Basel, 1511, by Sebastian Virdung.—'Musica instrumentalis,' Wittenburg, 1529, by Martin Agricola.—'Musurgia seu Praxis Musicæ,' Strassburg, 1536, by Ottomarus Luscinius.—The last-named work is written in Latin; the other two are in German. All these contain illustrations of the instruments described by the authors. Sebastian Virdung's book is written in dialogue. Virdung and Luscinius (whose German name was Nachtigall) were priests. Martin Agricola was a professional musician, and conductor of a choir and orchestra at Magdeburg. His book is written in wretched doggerel rhymes, but the wood-engravings are very exact, and his explanations are lucid. The circumstances of Martin Agricola having been practically experienced in the art, and having lived, so to say, in the midst of the instruments on which he treats, render his observations especially reliable.

The same may be said of Michael Prætorius, a distinguished Kapellmeister at Brunswick, who is the author of 'De Organographia,' Wolfenbüttel, 1619. This valuable treatise forms the second volume of a work entitled, 'Syntagma Musicum,' etc. The first volume treats on the history of music, chiefly sacred; it is written in Latin, and was published in 1615. The third volume, which like the second is written in German, contains an account of the different vocal compositions in use at the time when the work was written. The wood-engravings of 120 instruments belonging to Volume II. were published with the separate title: 'Theatrum Instrumentorum seu Sciagraphia,' Wolfenbüttel, 1620. The proper German name of Prætorius is Schulz. It was not unusual with the old German authors to Latinize their names on the title-page of their books.

The works just noticed are now so scarce that the musician rarely finds an opportunity to consult them. Hardly more accessible is the 'Harmonie universelle,' Paris, 1636, by F. Marin Mersenne,—a work which is valued especially on account of its comprehensiveness. The second volume contains descriptions with illustrations of the musical instruments in use about the year 1600. Mersenne was a monk,—as was also Athanasius Kircher, whose 'Musurgia universalis' appeared in Rome in the year 1650. Kircher's work is less scarce than that of Mersenne, but also less important. The illustrations in 'Musurgia universalis' are however, interesting, and it is principally on account of them that the work is still appreciated by musical historians. The 'Musurgia universalis' is written in Latin. Athanasius Kircher occupied himself also in making acoustic experiments, and he wrote a treatise on the subject, illustrated by engravings. He also constructed various acoustic instruments, which after his death, were deposited with other curiosities left by him, in a Museum at Rome. Dr. Burney, who saw them in Rome in the year 1770, remarks in his Journal: "They are now almost all out of order; but their construction is really curious, and manifests an ingenuity as well as zeal of this learned father in his musical inquiries and experiments."

Filippo Bonanni, who like Athanasius Kircher was a Jesuit Father, published at Rome in the year 1722, a work entitled 'Gabinetto armonico pieno d'istromenti sonori,' which contains 138 copper-plate engravings of musical instruments, most of them with representations of the performers. It is written in Italian. A second edition, in Italian and French, appeared in 1776. Bonanni's work is an amusing picture-book rather than a scientific treatise. The illustrations are inexact, and the explanations are meagre and unsatisfactory. The author had evidently never seen most of the instruments which he describes, and many of the illustrations appear to have been drawn from his description and not from actual specimens.

It is however, from Bonanni and kindred writers that Laborde has compiled his 'Essai sur la Musique,' Paris, 1780. It would be more easy than pleasant to cite misstatements copied from old authors by Laborde which have been recapitulated almost verbally by subsequent writers down to Fétis. In consulting the 'Essai sur la Musique' with its illustrations, many of which are fanciful, it must be borne in mind that Laborde was a musical dilettante more distinguished for his enthusiasm for the art, than for any particular qualification as an author on the subject in question.

Sir John Hawkins, likewise a musical dilettante and ardent lover of the art, by persevering diligence succeeded in accumulating a large mass of material for the compilation of a history of music, published in 1776, which contains many interesting accounts of scarce works on music, with extracts from them; but he was evidently not much of a musician, and the information he offers is arranged without sufficient discernment or order.

Hawkins was probably unacquainted with the original German works from which he gives extracts in translation. At any rate, he has made some funny mistakes. For instance, in noticing a publication of a series of letters on music by Steffani, he says (Vol. IV., p. 303): "Mattheson, in his 'Orchestra', mentions two persons, namely John Ballhorn and (   ) Weigweiser, as the authors of observations on these letters by Steffani; but, according to Mattheson, neither of them was either able to read the original, or in the translation to distinguish between the sense of the author as delivered in the text, or the opinions of the translator contained in the notes."

Now, the fact is that neither John Ballhorn nor Wegweiser—or Weigweiser as Hawkins spells the word,—were distinguished men deserving a place in a 'General History of Music.' "Johann Ballhorn" merely signifies "a Blunderer," just as "Jack of all Trades" signifies a person who can turn his hand to anything. Old Mattheson was a quaint and sarcastic writer. He calls the translator of Steffani's treatise from Italian into German a "Johann Ballhorn" on account of the blunders in the translation; and another writer, who commented upon the subject, and who put himself forth as a true Mentor, he nicknames Wegweiser, which simply means " Guide." The student ought, however, to acknowledge the literary scrupulosity of Hawkins evinced by his leaving a small blank space open before "Weigweiser" to enable any reader who may happen to be informed of the christian name of this gentleman, to insert it there. Still, Hawkins may well be excused, considering that even Nagler, in his well-known Lexicon of Artists, written in German, exhibits a somewhat similar "John Ballhorn." He mentions a Mr. "Somebody" among the English engravers, and states that this artist has engraven the Death of General Wolfe painted by West.

A writer on musical history must above all be a musician of practical experience—an accomplished executant on at least one instrument, so that he is enabled to familiarize himself with the compositions of different masters more thoroughly than could otherwise be possible ; and a composer in order to form a correct judgment of the compositions of others. The opinion about Handel or Bach of a writer who is but imperfectly practised in counterpoint, and who is incompetent to produce correctly a fugue or other intricate composition constructed according to fixed rules, is not likely to prove of use to the student of musical history. Burney possessed many of the qualities requisite for a musical historian. He was a professional musician systematically trained in the art, and an intelligent inquirer without pedantry or prejudice. Moreover, he had the moral courage to rescind an opinion when he discovered that it was erroneous. For instance, respecting n opinion which he formerly held on German music, he candidly avows ('History of Music' Vol. IV., p. 606), "It was inconsiderately inserted in the first edition of my 'German Tour' before I was able to examine the truth. . . . . . . So far, therefore from letting a second-hand prejudice warp my judgment, or influence my opinions in writing my General History, I have long been keeping double guard over my pen and my principles."

The most valuable literary productions are generally to be found among the investigations which are confined to a certain branch of the art. The works which pretend to embrace its whole science are often but mere compilations by writers who, like Bottom the weaver, want to act not only Pyramus, but at the same time also Thisbe and the lion.*

With the objectionable curiosities in musical literature might also be classed certain compilations which contain acute observations interspersed with silly remarks. In the preface the author states that he considers it an agreeable duty to acknowledge his obligations to other writers; but, as he does not indicate in the course of the book the sources from which he has drawn, most readers remain ignorant of the fact that the acute observations ought properly to have been given in inverted commas.

Equally objectionable are certain productions bearing on the æsthetics of music, in which the author shows with highflown words that he is himself not quite clear about what he propounds. It certainly seems odd that just such worthless productions are often prefaced with the remark that the subject of the book has never been properly treated before, whereas there are generally much better works on the same subject well known to musicians.

Here also may certain puffing publications be alluded to, which resemble the literary productions of quack doctors. Some are curious, however objectionable they may be. We have guides professing to teach how to become a brilliant player without the trouble of practising an instrument; how to compose fine music with the aid of dice instead of musical knowledge; how to sing in chorus without having a voice; and suchlike tempting propositions.

Nor must the fanciful schemes for reform relating to the theory of music, to musical notation, to the construction of instruments, etc., be left unnoticed. Some of these are very extravagant, while others have proved to be of greater practical

---

* A Midsummer-Night's Dream, Act I., Scene 2.

utility than was expected. Space can only be afforded here for three curious examples of proposed innovations, two of which shall be selected from English publications of this description.

'An Essay to the Advancement of Musick, by casting away the Perplexity of different Cliffs, and uniting all Sort of Musick,—Lute, Viol, Violin, Organ, Harpsechord, Voice, etc.—in one Universal Character;' by Thomas Salmon, London, 1672.

'A New System of Music, both theoretical and practical, and yet not mathematical; written in a manner entirely new; that's to say, in a Style plane and intelligible; and calculated to render the Art more Charming, the Teaching not only less tedious, but more profitable, and the Learning easier by three Quarters. All which is done by tearing off the Veil that has for so many ages hung before that noble Science;' by John Francis De La Fond, London, 1725.—The author proposes to abolish the clefs entirely, as he finds them only troublesome.

Wilhelm Kühnau published in Berlin, in the year 1810, a book entitled " Die Blinden Tonkünstler," which contains the biographies of seventy blind musicians. The author discards all the foreign words used in German music, and substitutes for them German words of his own coining. For Kapellmeister he proposes 'Tonmeister;' for Clarinette, 'Gellflöte;' for Harmonika, 'Hauchspiel;' and so on. He, however, does not stand alone as such a whimsical innovator. Beethoven, ten years later, coined the word 'Hammer-Klavièr' for Pianoforte, and used it on the title-page of his large sonata in B flat major, Op. 106.

As specimens of Lampoons may be mentioned :—Joel Collier's 'Musical Travels through England,' London, 1774, written in ridicule of Dr. Charles Burney; and L. Rellstab's 'Henriette, oder die schöne Sängerin,' Leipzig, 1826, which caricatures certain admirers of the celebrated songstress and estimable lady, Henriette Sontag, in Berlin. These musical enthusiasts included several noblemen of the highest position, and a foreign ambassador at the Prussian Court, who were described under fictitious names so as to be easily recognised. The scandalous gossip thereby occasioned induced the government to confiscate the obnoxious though witty book, and to condemn Rellstab to be imprisoned three months in the fortress of Spandau. The punishment of the author, of course, greatly increased the popularity of the book. Being forbidden by high authority, it was read everywhere,—even aloud to circles of guests in the coffee-rooms and wine-houses of Berlin,—until curiosity was satisfied.

As regards musical novels, those which may be called curious are mostly so on account of their eccentricities and improbabilities. Some interesting exceptions could, however, be pointed out. The heroes of the novels are not unfrequently drawn from life, inasmuch as they represent certain celebrated musicians.

E. T. A. Hoffmann, the spirited and highly imaginative novelist, has taken, it is generally believed, the eccentric musician Louis Böhner as a model for his famous 'Kapellmeister Kreisler.' After having travelled for several years through Germany, and performed his own compositions in concerts at different courts, Louis Böhner, more estimable as an artist than otherwise, retired to his native village in Thuringia, where he died in great poverty. His concerto in D major for the pianoforte, Op. 8, which was published about ten years before Weber composed 'Der Freischütz,' contains the following passage—

in which may be recognised the melody of Agatha's grand Scena. Besides this, there occur in Böhner's concerto some other slight resemblances with phrases in 'Der Freischütz.' It is said that on a certain occasion Böhner played the concerto in the presence of Weber. The resemblances are not very striking, and may be accidental. Their discovery, however, did not fail to cause some contributions to our literary curiosities.

The journals of musicians travelling in distant parts of the world often contain, as might be expected, interesting observations about music, which are not likely to be found in the journals of other travellers. If not particularly instructive, they are at least often amusing to musicians who prefer to read something about their art more novel and refreshing than they are likely to find in their treatises on thoroughbass. A. Anton, a German by birth, who was band-master in the Bengal army, published, after his return to the Fatherland, some unpretending extracts from his journal, under the title 'Von Darmstadt nach Ostindien; Erlebnisse und Abenteuer eines Musikers auf der Reise durch Arabien nach Lahore. Die denkwürdigen Ereignisse der letzten Jahre nach seinem Tagebuch wahrheitsgetreu geschildert.' ('From Darmstadt to the East Indies; Life and Adventures of a Musician during his journey through Arabia to Lahore. The memorable occurrences of the last years truthfully depicted from his journal;' Darmstadt, 1860.)

M. Hauser, an accomplished violinist, has given an account of his travels round the world, in a series of letters published with the title: 'Aus dem Wanderbuche eines österreichischen Virtuosen; Briefe aus Californien, Südamerika, und Australien.' ('From the Journal of Travels of an Austrian Virtuoso; Letters from California, South America, and Australia;' Leipzig, 1859.) Hauser's grand show-piece was evidently a sort of descriptive composition of his own, called 'The little Bird in the Tree,' in which he cleverly imitated the chirping of the tiny feathered songster. Whether he imitated it by bowing above or below the bridge, he does not state. In Tahiti he played it with success to queen Pomare; and at the gold-fields he charmed the diggers with it to such a degree, that they rewarded him with pinches of gold-dust and nuggets fresh from the soil. Having himself become thoroughly tired of 'The little Bird in the Tree,' although it was his own composition, and wishing to treat the people with some really good music, he ventured, at a concert in a town of the Isthmus of Panama, to play Beethoven's famous violin concerto. His audience were at first puzzled, not knowing what to make of the music; soon, however, silence changed into general conversation about the news of the town and suchlike topics.

In order to gain a hearing and money, there was no choice for the *virtuoso* but to resort to 'The little Bird in the Tree.' With this conviction he laid aside the classical music, determining at the same time to enjoy it all the more heartily at home after having made his fortune. His jottings contain interesting statements concerning the cultivation of music in the various countries which he visited.

A journal of a vagabond musician may, perhaps, be thought to possess but little attraction. If, however, the vagabond musician is an intelligent man who has had the advantage of a University education, his observations may be much more interesting than those of a fashionable *virtuoso* who moves in the highest circles of society, but whose knowledge is almost entirely confined to his profession. Ernst Kratz was such a man. He published his journal in two volumes entitled 'Kunstreise durch Nord-Deutschland' ('Rambles of an Artist through North Germany;' Sonderburg, 1822). This strange journal, which the author brought out at his own expense, is mentioned neither by Fétis nor Forkel. Probably it never became known through the usual channel of the book trade. It will be the last of the productions noticed in the present survey of literary curiosities; but, considering that it is as scarce as it is singular, an account of it more detailed than has been given of the extraordinary publications previously noticed may interest the musical reader.

Ernst Kratz was a Prussian, born during the second half of the last century. His diary commences with an account of his unsuccessful attempts, in the year 1813, to obtain a commission in the Prussian army against the French. He had then just left the University of Halle. Why he should have wished to give up his profession as a lawyer, does not transpire; perhaps his overflowing energy, and his love of adventure, made the quiet and regular life of a peaceable citizen appear to him but a miserable existence. Though of a generous disposition, he was evidently a self-willed and quarrelsome man, not likely to follow submissively the dictates of others, who perhaps might be his superiors in position, but his inferiors in talent and knowledge. Having a fine bass voice, and some skill in playing the pianoforte and the violin, it occurred to him, during a visit to a wealthy brother-in-law residing in a small town in the province of Brandenburg, to organise a concert for the benefit of the wounded soldiers disabled in the war with Napoleon I.

The zeal with which he engaged in the praiseworthy scheme secured him the co-operation of the musical dilettanti among the nobility and gentry of the town and its neighbourhood. The concert proved a decided success, and, to the gratification of all there was a good round sum of money to be handed over to the fund for the wounded soldiers.

The result of his first attempt induced Kratz to give similar concerts in different provincial towns for the same charitable purpose. The preparations caused him endless trouble, as he generally had to practise beforehand with each of the amateur singers, his or her part alone, to enable them to perform with tolerable correctness. The result was sometimes unsatisfactory, not only musically, but also financially, as the unavoidable expenses almost swallowed up the receipts. Meanwhile Kratz received from the Princess Wilhelm of Prussia, the patroness of the Society for the Relief of the Wounded Soldiers, the title of 'Kammersänger,' in acknowledgment of his benevolent exertions. The honour conferred upon him increased his fondness for a rambling life, while it was of little or no use to him in gaining the means of subsistence.

Soon he traversed large districts of Central and Northern Germany, giving concerts, with which he combined declamatory performances. Experience taught him to restrict his visits almost entirely to small towns and watering-places, where his expenses were small, and where he had no rivalry to fear. During these wanderings he occasionally met with a clergyman, a doctor, or a lawyer, with whom he had studied in Halle; and the hospitable manner in which most of his former acquaintances received him, suggests that they must have had pleasant recollections of his companionship.

He seldom omits to record in his journal the number of visitors to his concert; its proceeds and expenses; with other little business details. These memoranda he intersperses with various observations, of which the following is a specimen :—

"I may take this opportunity to confute the erroneous opinion, entertained by many, that a clever music-director can hear every false tone which occurs in the orchestra. This may be possible if there is only one instrument for each part, but not otherwise; and also not when the orchestra is playing *forte*. The music-director Türk, in Halle, known as a great theorician and as a good composer, usually had at his winter concerts the assistance of some students, as they occasioned him no expense and rendered his orchestra more complete. I offered to assist as a violin player; but, as the number of violinists was sufficient, while there was only one tenor player, he appointed me to the tenor. This I rather liked, since as the performances consisted chiefly of operatic music and oratorios, it enabled me to follow cursorily the words with the music. Without an acquaintance with the words, the music of the songs is hardly comprehensible. My colleague did the same. Not unfrequently we became so much absorbed in this pursuit that we played wrong,—nay, we lost our part,—without Türk perceiving it. On the other hand, it occurred not seldom that he cried out to us: "*Die Prätschel!*"* when we played correctly. This is easily explicable. If, for instance, five soprano singers execute in unison a passage rather rapidly, and one of them introduces a wrong tone not very loud, the best music-director will not perceive it; still less when the mistake occurs in the middle parts where the other parts cover the false tone. Of course, it is different if the tone is long sustained and sung loud."

When Kratz has made himself rather ridiculous, he can philosophize about the occurrence so that it appears to him very interesting. Take, for instance, his account of a rehearsal in which he ventured to play a violin concerto beyond his power :—

"When the orchestra had played the introductory Tutti, and I had to begin the Solo,—suddenly it becomes misty before

---

* The Tenor (Italian, *Viola di braccio*) is called in German *Bratsche*, corrupted here into *Prätschel*.

my eyes, my whole body trembles, I cannot see the notes clearly, cannot command my fingers, cannot manage the bow. We begin again, and a third time; but it is not much better, although we make some progress. By degrees I become more collected; still my playing remains a wretched attempt to the end, provoking the suppressed and loud laughter of the musicians. None of the somewhat difficult passages, which I knew by heart, could I play. I am not a *virtuoso* on the violin; but if one has attained a certain dexterity, one must be able to play those pieces which one has properly learnt. Thus this rehearsal enriched my psychology, inasmuch as it served me as an example for the proposition:— It is very difficult, if not impossible, to appear in later years before the public in a capacity in which one has not appeared in early youth. The fear for the teacher suppresses in youth the shyness for the public, and accustoms us to resist it, and not allow it to become an obstacle. The fear for the teacher is a support which later we miss, while the shyness which overcomes us is all the stronger since we have learnt the value of the opinion which formerly concentrated only in the teacher, and with which we were well acquainted beforehand. While as a singer and a declamator I feel the most at my ease when I appear before a large audience, at the rehearsal, in the presence of an orchestra only, I could not play a violin concerto, merely because the former I have done in public from early youth, and this never before."

The proceeds of his concerts he divided into two equal portions, one of which he regularly forwarded after the concert to the relief fund for the wounded soldiers, retaining the other half to defray his travelling expenses. But his concerts were often so thinly attended that they realized no proceeds to divide, and hardly sufficient means for his subsistence. He feared to come into suspicion of having appropriated to himself more than his due; and he felt vexed at the implications which he sometimes thought he detected in the remarks of strangers, intimating that the wounded soldiers were of more use to him than he to them.

Reduced to this extremity, Kratz resolved to trouble himself no further about the wounded soldiers, and henceforth to give his musical-declamatory entertainments for his own benefit. And with this step begins a new epoch in his life, in which he depicts himself in his journal as a genuine vagabond musician. After two years' rambles, he writes:—"I must mention that my purse is at present in a very low condition. This is something very common to all travelling artists with or without reputation, and does not happen now for the first time to me. In Silesia and other provinces I had already experienced the same trouble. Considering the peculiar nature of my vocation, I never expected from the very outset of my rambles that I should gain much money. That I have not suffered more frequently, is owing to my very moderate habits, and also to the circumstance that my strong physical condition enables me to brave any adversities. Whenever my endeavours to obtain an audience in a town failed, I at once submitted myself to restrictions and deprivations. I should not even now think this worth mentioning, did it not show how greatly I had to suffer on account of the musical festival at Frankenhausen. In fact, it was owing to this that I became for the first time quite destitute." This happened in 1815. The musical festival in Frankenhausen was under the management of music-director G. F. Bischoff. A new cantata by Spohr, performed in the presence of the composer, who afterwards played a violin concerto, constituted its principal attraction. It speaks much for the love of music in Kratz that, notwithstanding his miserable circumstances, he carried out his intention of attending the festival. His request for permission to assist in the orchestra, or in the chorus, met with a refusal on the pretext that it came too late, all the places being filled. Disappointed, he bent his steps to Heringen, a neighbouring small town, with the intention of giving a musical-declamatory entertainment which might help him to some food, and to the price of a ticket of admission to the concert in Frankenhausen. His struggles he faithfully records thus :—

"In Ashausen, a village three-quarters of an hour's walk from Heringen, I went into the inn for the night. It was Sunday. The room below was full. I heard music in the upper room; went up stairs, and found there was dancing going on. I watched the dancers for a long time. Then, merely for my love of music, I placed myself among the musicians and played occasionally with them. When they thus recognised me as a musician, they treated me—but, unfortunately, with spirits. However, sometimes bread and butter, and oftener cake, was handed to them, of which I was likewise asked to partake; and this suited me better. After the dancing was over, several peasants gathered round the new musician, and I played to them dance-tunes on the violin, which they liked better than the tunes of their own, band. I took up a horn, having learnt the instrument formerly, and blew them a piece or two. They now wanted to treat me with spirits, which I however felt obliged to decline, although it was fine liqueur; for I am no spirit-drinker. The cake, unhappily, was consumed. I now learnt that they were celebrating the baptism of a child. I only wished they might continue the whole night, as it would save me the expense of a bed. However, about three o'clock in the morning the last of the company departed, and I had to go down into the public room, where I threw myself on a bench to avoid paying for a bed. Nevertheless, the unreasonable host demanded that I should pay him for having slept in his house; but this I did not, because I had only two groschen* in my possession, and could not entirely divest myself of cash. I therefore paid him only a half groschen for a cup of coffee in the morning."

Arrived, on Monday, at Heringen: "In the afternoon I happen to pass the church, which is open. I enter and sit down, tarrying near to my Only Friend. There I remain alone for a long time, occupied with my reflections; for, I stand so alone in the world.—In the evening the decisive hour approaches; the concert at Frankenhausen is at stake, and— Behold! I have an audience of nineteen persons, few expenses, the host of the Town-Hall means it well with me, and Frankenhausen is safe!"

Kratz shows himself always to the greatest advantage when he is very badly off. As soon as he gains a little money, he

---

* A groschen is about an English penny.

generally becomes quarrelsome. It would only be painful to trace his ups and downs,—the former occurring but occasionally, and being but slight,—until his arrival in Cassel. In this town the manager of the theatre, perhaps in an unguarded moment of compassion, gives him hope of an engagement as singer. The music-director Guhr holds out the same encouragement, amounting almost to a promise. They afterwards find that their intention cannot possibly be carried out. Kratz, greatly disappointed, brings an action against them for breach of promise. Other persons become implicated in this formidable law-suit, which is carried on for about two years. During all the time Kratz makes constant pedestrian tours into the country, giving musical-declamatory entertainments in the small towns and villages, living on the plainest of fare and sleeping upon straw. When he has scraped together a few thalers, he returns to Cassel to hand them over to his lawyer. One cannot but admire his energy; if he had employed only half of it in a noble cause, he might have done much good. He lost his law-suit and left Cassel.

On New Year's Eve, 1816, we find him in full-dress at a ball given by a former fellow-student, now a person of high position in Quedlinburg, who has taken him for a week into his house, and has dressed him up. The next day, Kratz reflects upon the event, in his journal, thus:—

"January 1st, 1817. Every thing changes in life. The deadening winter is followed by the reviving spring; out of the moistened eye beams again the sun-ray of joy. The first day of the last year found me in the hut of a peasant, sleeping on a couch of straw, and my rest unpleasantly disturbed by the firing of volleys by the peasant lads; the first day of this year finds me awake in a brilliantly-lighted saloon, where I am surrounded by varicoloured figures moving in the brightness of light, where the sound of music floats agreeably about my ears, while I am blissfully waltzing round with the most charming girl in the room."

Unfortunately for Kratz, this blissful state was of but short duration. Soon we find him again as before in his "Rambles of an Artist," except that he now moves gradually to the North, until he reaches Hamburg, which he enters, and where we lose sight of him.

In the present survey several books have been mentioned which possess but little value. Still, they deserve a place among the fanciful, paradoxical, extravagant, and quaint publications relating to the art of music. Some more might have been cited; but the list is probably large enough to convince the lover of music that we are by no means in want of curiosities in our musical literature.

THE ENGLISH INSTRUMENTALISTS.

Towards the end of the sixteenth century, and in the beginning of the seventeenth, companies of English actors visited Germany to perform at the courts of princes, and at public festivities. The Germans called these actors 'Die englischen Comödianten' (The English Comedians); and the musicians accompanying them they called 'Die englischen Instrumentisten' (The English Instrumentalists.) Respecting the English Comedians much has already been written by Shakespearean scholars. The musical accomplishments of these strolling troupes have, however, not received sufficient attention to satisfy musicians. Although they appear not to have been remarkable, they are interesting inasmuch as they were associated with the performances of Shakespeare's dramas, and also because the English Instrumentalists have been, with few exceptions, the only English musicians who ever visited Germany with the object of gaining a livelihood in that country by displaying their skill.

Some notices of them are to be found in the historical records of the German theatres, which have been published during the present century.

What induced these actors and musicians to leave their native country?—Want of support at home. There were too many of them in England. During the sixteenth century many were in the service of English noblemen. It was a usual custom with the nobility to keep a company of instrumentalists as well as actors; and to these were not unfrequently added skilful tumblers, or acrobats, who seem to have enjoyed great popularity. Strolling troupes of the latter visited the provincial towns. W. Kelly, in his

'Notices illustrative of the Drama, and other popular amusements in Leicester, during the 16th and 17th centuries,' says: " The earliest notice we have of the visits of companies of tumblers to the town is in 1590." These personages undoubtedly also played on musical instruments. In the German records alluded to, they are called *Springer* (*i.e.* "Jumpers" or "Dancers"), and it would appear that not all the English Instrumentalists, but only the lowest class of them, combined the art of dancing and tumbling with that of music. The majority were musical actors rather than professional musicians; while others occupied themselves almost exclusively with playing on musical instruments, such as the lute, treble-viol, viola da gamba, recorder, cornet, trumpet, etc.

In a Proclamation of Queen Elizabeth, issued in the year 1571, these strolling performers are mentioned in rather disreputable company: "All Fencers Bearewardes Comon Players in Enterludes, and Minstrels, not belonging to any Baron of this Realme, or towarde any other honorable Personage of greater Degree; all Juglers Pedlers Tynkers and Petye Chapmen; wiche said Fencers Bearewardes Comon Players in Enterludes Minstrels Juglers Pedlers Tynkers and Petye Chapmen, shall wander abroade, and have not Lycense of two Justices of the Peace at the Feaste, whereof one to be of the Quorum, wher and in what Shier they shall happen to wander . . . . . shalbee taken adjudjed and deemed Roges Vacaboundes and Sturdy Beggers;" etc.*

Some interesting details concerning the nature of the performances of the English common musicians at the time when this Proclamation appeared, may be gathered from 'A Dialogue betwene Custome and Veritie, conceringe the use and abuse of Dauncinge and Mynstralsye, by Thomas Lovell, London, 1581.' The book is written in verse. Custom defends and excuses dancing and minstrelsy, which

---

* 'The English Drama and Stage, under the Tudor and Stuart Princes, 1543-1664, illustrated by a series of Documents, Treatises, and Poems. Printed for the Roxburgh Library, London, 1869.' P. 22.

Verity attacks and abuses. As regards the minstrels, Verity remarks :—

> "They are accounted vagarant roges
>   By act of Parliament,
> What reason why they should not then
>   Like Roges to Jaile be sent,
> Except they doo belong to men
>   Which are of high degree,
> As in that act by woords set downe
>   Expressly we may see.
> To such, I think, but few of these
>   Vain Pipers doo pertain :
> To men so grave a shame it were
>   Fond Fidlers to maintain.
> A great disgrace it were to them,
>   Their cloth abrode to send
> Upon the backs of them which doo
>   Their life so lewdly spend."

Respecting the performances of the minstrels, vocal as well as instrumental, Verity says :—

> "Their singing if you doo regard,
>   It is to be abhord :
> It is against the sacred woord
>   And Scripture of the Lord.
> But this doo minstrels clene forget:
>   Some godly songs they have,
> Some wicked Ballads and unmeet,
>   As companies doo crave.
> For filthies they have filthy songs,
>   For baudes lascivious rimes ;
> For honest good, for sober grave
>   Songs ; so they watch their times.
> Among the lovers of the trueth,
>   Ditties of trueth they sing;
> Among the Papists, such as of
>   Their godlesse legend spring.
> For he that cannot gibe and jest,
>   Ungodly scoff and frump,
> Is thought unmeet to play with Pipe,
>   On tabret or to thump.
> The minstrels doo with instruments,
>   With songs, or els with jest,
> Maintain them selves, but as they use,
>   Of these naught is the best."

This Dialogue, the author of which is supposed to have been a Puritan, concludes with Verity convincing and converting Custom.*

A grant under the Privy Seal of James I. for the issue of letters patent in favour of Thomas Downton and others, on transferring their services as players to the Elector Frederic, dated January 4th, 1613, contains the following names of actors and musicians: Thomas Downton, William Bird, Edward Juby, Samuell Rowle, Charles Massey, Humfrey Jeffs, Franck Grace, William Cartwright, Edward Colbrand, William Parr, William Stratford, Richard Gunnell, John Shanck, and Richard Price. These, and "the rest of their Associates" were licensed and authorised as servants of the Elector Palatine " to use and exercise the art and faculties of playing Comedies, Tragedies, Histories, Enterludes, Moralls, Pastoralls, Stage Plaies and such other like as they have already studied, or hereafter shall use or study."

In a Patent of James I., licensing the performance of plays by his Majesty's Servants at the private house in Blackfriars, as well as at the Globe, March 27th, 1620, are mentioned: John Hemings, Richard Burbadge, Henry Condall, John Lowen, Nicholas Tooley, John Underwood, Nathan Feild, Robert Benfeild, Robert Gough, William Ecclestone, Richard Robinson, and John Shancks. In a patent of Charles I., dating June 24th, 1625, which renews that of James I., we have, besides the names just mentioned, Joseph Taylor, William Rowley, John Rice, Elliart Swanston, George Birch, Richard Sharpe, and Thomas Pollard.†

The names are here given to enable the reader to compare them with the names, often arbitrarily spelt, of the English actors and instrumentalists in the German records.

The earliest account of the appearance of these foreigners

---

* 'Extracts from the Registers of the Stationers' Company of works entered for publication between the years 1570 and 1587; with notes and illustrations by J. Payne Collier.' Vol. II., London, 1849. Printed for the Shakespeare Society. P. 142.

† 'The English Drama and Stage, under the Tudor and Stuart Princes; London, 1869.' P. 50.

in Germany dates from the year 1556, when an English company of actors visited the court of the Margrave of Brandenburg. In Berlin they found a well-organized musical band belonging to the Elector Joachim II., the regulations of which, dating from the year 1570, are still extant. In a more comprehensive set of regulations issued by the Elector Johann Georg, in the year 1580, the following instruments are specified as being played by the Elector's musicians:—
Positif, Zimphonien, Geygen, Zinckenn, Qwerpfeiffen, Schalmeyenn, Krumbhörner, Dultzian, Trummeten, Posaunen, Bombarten, ("Organ, spinets, instruments played with a bow, cornets, small German flutes, shalms, cormornes, a small bassoon, trumpets, trombones, bombardos."*)

In the beginning of the seventeenth century we find in the Elector of Brandenburg's service some English musicians who had probably come to Germany with the English actors, The following are mentioned in the Prussian records, with their names more or less Germanized.

Johann Kroker (John Croker), Berlin, 1608. He must have been a rather distinguished musician; for the Elector Joachim Friedrich made him Vice-Kapellmeister, or second leader of the orchestra.

Johann Spencer. In a letter dated "Königsberg, July 14th, 1609," the Elector Johann Sigismund recommends Johann Spencer to the Elector of Saxony as an English musician who was recommended to him by the Duke Franz von Stettin, and who had been for some time in Berlin. The Elector adds that Johann Spencer's music had pleased him pretty well.† There can hardly be a doubt that this musician is the same John Spencer who was the director of a company of English Comedians travelling in Holland and in Germany.

Walter Rowe (also written Roe) Berlin, 1614. A viola-da-gamba player of some reputation. He must have been at least thirty-three years in the service of the Elector, for he

---

* 'Geschichte der Oper und des Königlichen Opernhauses in Berlin, von L. Schneider; Berlin, 1852.' Anhang, P. 15.

† 'Geschichte der Oper, etc., in Berlin, von L. Schneider; Berlin, 1852.' Anhang, P. 25.

is still mentioned as a member of the orchestra in 1647. About the year 1626 he resided for some time at the court of the Duke of Mecklenburg-Güstrow. His son, Walter Rowe, was likewise a musician in the Elector's orchestra at Berlin.

Lambert Blome (probably Bloom) is mentioned in the year 1621 as a *Clarin-Bläser* (trumpeter) in the orchestra at Berlin.

Valentin Flood was, in 1627, engaged in Berlin, as player on the Treble Viol.

John Stanley, a theorbo player, was, in the autumn of the year 1628, at the court of the Elector of Brandenburg, and in the year 1631, entered the service of the Landgrave Wilhelm of Hesse-Cassel.

Johann Boldt (probably John Bolt), Berlin, 1635. Cornetto player.

These musicians were not the only foreigners in the band of the Elector at Berlin. Several Italians are mentioned in the records, and even one or two Polish cither players. As early as in the year 1564, mention is made of an Italian virtuoso, Antonio Bontempi, who was engaged as player on the lute, theorbo, and cornetto.

Although the English comedians most probably visited the Netherlands before they made their appearance in Germany, we meet with them in Holland not earlier than in the year 1604. A company, which in 1605 performed in Leyden, had previously been in Berlin, and was provided with letters of recommendation from the Elector of Brandenburg.* Moreover, there was a company of English comedians in Denmark during the second half of the sixteenth century. Five of these, who in the old documents are mentioned as Instrumentalists, probably because they were chiefly musicians, arrived in the year 1586 at the court of Christian II., Elector of Saxony. Leaving unnoticed those who are mentioned only as actors, we find recorded in Dresden the following English instrumentalists, whose names are copied as spelt in the German documents:—

---

* 'Shakespeare in Germany, by Albert Cohn, London, 1865.' P. lxxviii.

Tomas Konigk (Thomas King), Dresden, 1586. He had previously been in Denmark.

Tomas Stephan (Thomas Stephen), Dresden, 1586.

George Bryandt (George Bryant), Dresden, 1586; also known as an actor.

Thomas Pabst (Thomas Pope), Dresden, 1586. He is supposed to have been a personal acquaintance of Shakespeare.*

Rupert Persten (probably Rupert Pierst). Dresden, 1586.

These musicians are in their appointment designated as *Geyger und Instrumentisten* ('Fiddlers and Instrumentalists') and their duties are prescribed as follows:—" They must be attentive and obedient, of good behaviour at our Court; they must follow us on our travels if we desire it. Whenever we hold a banquet, and also on other occasions, as often as they are ordered, they have to attend with their fiddles and other requisite instruments, to play music. And they must also amuse us with their art of tumbling, and other graceful things which they have learnt. They are expected to demean themselves towards us as behoves faithful and attentive servants; which they have also promised, and bound themselves to observe." †

John Price, who came to Dresden in the year 1629, was a *virtuoso* on the flute. The Elector of Saxony gave him a superior appointment in his orchestra. Mersenne ('Harmonie universelle,' Paris, 1636) mentions him as a brilliant player. The little flute which he principally used had only three finger-holes; but he is said to have been able by various expedients, or knacks, to obtain on it a compass of three octaves. He had previously an engagement at the Court of Würtemberg, in company with John Dixon, mentioned as an English instrumentalist, and with John Morell, David Morell, and two other Englishmen, who probably were comedians.

---

* 'Shakespeare in Germany, by Albert Cohn; London, 1865.' P. xxvii.

† ' Zur Geschichte der Musik und des Theaters am Hofe zu Dresden, von Moritz Fürstenau; Dresden, 1861.' Vol. I., p. 70.

In the year 1626, a company of English comedians performed in Dresden, among other pieces, Shakespeare's 'Romeo and Juliet,' 'Hamlet,' 'King Lear,' and 'Julius Cæsar.'* A troupe of English comedians, which in the year 1611 visited Königsberg, consisted of thirty-five members, nineteen of whom are designated in the records as actors, and sixteen as instrumentalists. † No doubt most of those designated as actors were also musical; but the circumstance of nearly one half of the troupe being professional musicians sufficiently shows how greatly the entertainments consisted of musical performances. Another proof of this may be found in a record stating that in Hildesheim a company of English actors gave representations in English. ‡

There were probably but few persons among the audience who understood English. It may, therefore, be surmised that music constituted the chief attraction of the entertainment. There was, however, also amusing leaping and dancing, and the funny clown,—the English Jack-Pudding, Dutch Pekelharing, German Hanswurst, French Jean Potage, Italian Signor Maccaroni. The clown derives his nickname from the favourite dish of the mob.

It is unnecessary, for the purpose of tracing the pursuits of the English actors and instrumentalists, to follow them in their visits to all the German towns which preserve records of them. Suffice it to notice their stay in Cassel, where they arrived in the year 1600. The Landgrave Moritz of Hesse Cassel took them into his service, and, in 1605, built for them a theatre in the form of a circus, to which he gave the name Ottoneum, in honour of his eldest son, Otto. The walls of this edifice were beautifully ornamented with frescoes.

However, in 1607, the Landgrave Moritz declared that he was tired of "the confounded dancers and jumpers," as he called them; and he dismissed the company from his service,

---

* 'Zur Geschichte der Musik und des Theaters am Hofe zu Dresden, von Moritz Fürstenau; Dresden, 1861.' Vol. I., p. 96.

† 'Shakespeare in Germany, by Albert Cohn; London, 1865.' P. lxxxiv.

‡ 'Shakespeare in Germany,' p. lxi.

with the exception of a few clever members, whom he retained until the year 1613. The Landgrave Moritz was a learned man, and likewise a poet and a musical composer. His opinion is therefore not without some weight. The company, after its departure from Cassel, perambulated for several years through Germany, and appears to have found everywhere a good reception,—especially at Nürnberg, where, in 1612, their "new beautiful comedies" were much admired.

Four names may here be given of English actors, who, in the year 1591, set out to go to Germany with the avowed intention of improving their impoverished circumstances. They are: Robert Brown, John Broadstreet (or Breadstreet), Thomas Sackville and Richard Jones. As in the letter of recommendation of these men, which has been discovered in the archives of the Hague, their musical accomplishments are mentioned before their other accomplishments, —it being stated that they intended to travel for the purpose "of practising their profession by performing of music, feats of agility, and games of comedies, tragedies and histories,"*— it is evident that music must have been one of their most practised arts, if not actually their original profession.

In the year 1603, Lord Spencer was sent by James I. on a special embassy to Prince Frederick, Duke of Würtemberg, to invest him with the Order of the Garter. Among Lord Spencer's retinue were four skilful musicians, who appear to have been picked English instrumentalists, to judge from the praise bestowed on them by Erhardus Cellius in his account of the visit, which was published at Tübingen in the year 1605. The following quotation is a translation, the narrative of Erhardus Cellius being originally written in Latin:—"The royal English musicians whom the illustrious royal ambassador had brought with him to enhance the magnificence of the embassy and the present ceremony [the Duke's investiture of the Order of the Garter], though few in number, were eminently well skilled in the art. For England produces many excellent musicians, comedians and tragedians most skilful in the histrionic art;

---

* 'Shakespeare in Germany,' p. xxix.

certain companies of whom, quitting their own abodes for a time, are in the habit of visiting foreign countries at particular seasons, exhibiting and representing their art principally at the courts of princes. A few years ago, some English musicians coming over to our Germany with this view, remained for some time at the courts of great princes; and their skill, both in music and in the histrionic art, procured them such favour that they returned home liberally rewarded, and loaded with gold and silver."* Erhardus Cellius was Professor of Poetry and History at Tübingen.

There remain to be noticed a few English musicians who came to Germany about the time of the visits of the English comedians, but who appear not to have been connected with any of the companies.

John Dowland, a *virtuoso* on the lute, and also a composer, visited about the year 1585 the Courts of Hesse-Cassel and of Brunswick-Wolfenbüttel. Afterwards, he was for some time lutenist in the service of the King of Denmark, where perhaps he may have associated with the English comedians. John Dowland was evidently a personal acquaintance of Shakespeare, who has immortalized him in his 'Passionate Pilgrim':—

> "If music and sweet poetry agree,
>   As they must needs, the sister and the brother,
> Then must the love be great 'twixt thee and me,
>   Because thou lov'st the one, and I the other.
> Dowland to thee is dear, whose heavenly touch
>   Upon the lute doth ravish human sense;
> Spenser to me, whose deep conceit is such
>   As passing all conceit, needs no defence.
> Thou lov'st to hear the sweet melodious sound
>   That Phœbus' lute, the queen of music, makes;
> And I in deep delight am chiefly drown'd
>   Whenas himself to singing he betakes.
> One god is god of both, as poets feign;
>   One knight loves both, and both in thee remain."

To conclude that Shakespeare must have been a practical

---

* 'England as seen by Foreigners in the days of Elizabeth and James the First, by W. B. Rye; London, 1865,' p. cvi.

musician, because he wrote beautiful poetry on the charms and power of music, would be as bold as to assume from certain passages in his dramas that he was originally a lawyer, a soldier, a tinker or a horse-dealer. Indeed, regarded as a critical opinion, his beautiful sonnet on Dowland is less valuable than the judgment of Dr. Burney, who remarks: "After being at pains of scoring several of Dowland's compositions, I have been equally disappointed and astonished at his scanty abilities in counterpoint, and the great reputation he acquired with his contemporaries, which has been courteously continued to him either by indolence or ignorance of those who have had occasion to speak of him, and who took it for granted that his title to fame, as a profound musician, was well founded."*

John Bull, another English musician of some reputation, was a virtuoso on the harpsichord and organ. Perhaps the circumstance of his playing these instruments kept him aloof from the English Comedians on the continent; otherwise his restless and unsettled life would have fitted him well for their companionship. Born in Somersetshire, about the middle of the sixteenth century, John Bull, in the year 1601, made his first journey to Holland, France and Germany, where his organ performances, and even his compositions, found admirers. Having returned to England, he went, in 1607, a second time to the continent with the object, it is recorded, of restoring his shattered health,—or perhaps, as Dr. Burney surmises, to improve his shattered financial condition. He died in Germany. Sir John Hawkins, in his 'History of Music,' gives two Riddle Canons by John Bull, written in the shape of a triangle. The anecdote about the marvellous skill of this musician, exhibited by his adding forty more parts to a song composed in forty parts,† is so absurd as hardly to provoke a smile from anyone acquainted with the theory of music. John Bull

---

* 'A General History of Music,' by C. Burney; London, 1789. Vol. III., p. 136.

† Hawkins's 'History of Music.' London, 1776. Vol. III., p. 319.

has also been praised for having composed some pieces for the Virginal so difficult that even pianists of the present day are startled by his rapid passages in thirds and sixths. But, considering how rude and unmelodious these contrivances are, he would deserve greater praise if his music were easily executable, impressive, and better suited for the instrument for which it was composed, than is the case. If R. Clark's statement, according to which John Bull was the composer of the English National Anthem, were correct, he would have a greater claim to consideration than he deserves at present. The composers of old popular tunes are seldom known; it is therefore only proper to regard the whole nation as the composer of its principal national tune, if its origin has not been definitively ascertained; and in this sense it is perhaps right to assign the composition of the English National Anthem to John Bull.

Another English musician, Thomas Cutting, went to Denmark in 1607. He was a lutenist. There is no record of his having been in Germany. John Abell, an English singer and lutenist, gave concerts in Holland, Germany, and Poland, at the time of Charles II., consequently, after the period of the English Comedians' visit to the Continent.

It is a remarkable fact that, previous to the appearance of those musicians in Germany, England had already been visited by foreign musicians, whose talents, considering the positions obtained by several of them, must have had considerable influence upon the taste of their English colleagues. There were five German musicians in the service of Richard III., in the year 1483; eighteen foreign musicians in the service of Henry VIII.; and as far as can be made out from the corrupt spelling of the names, the bands of Edward VI. and of Queen Elizabeth contained about as many foreigners as that of Henry VIII. The Dutch lutenists, Philip van Welder and Peter van Welder, held a superior position in the band of Edward VI. The former had already been engaged by Henry VIII. as teacher on the lute to the royal children. The distinguished lutenist Jacques Gaulter (or Gouter), in the service of Charles I., was a Frenchman.

The generally acknowledged superiority of the foreign musicians explains the dissatisfaction with the popular taste expressed in the works of several English musicians. Already John Dowland complains in his Prefaces of being neglected. Matthew Lock, in his 'Little Consort of three parts, containing Pavans, Ayres, Corants, and Sarabands, for Viols or Violins,' London, 1657, remarks: "For those mountebanks of wit, who think it necessary to disparage all they meet with of their own countrymen, because there have been and are some excellent things done by strangers, I shall make bold to tell them (and I hope my known experience in this science will enforce them to confess me a competent judge), that I never yet saw any foreign instrumental composition (a few French Corants excepted,) worthy an Englishman's transcribing." John Playford, in his 'Musick's Delight on the Cithren,' London, 1666, complains: "It is observed that of late years all solemn and grave musick is much laid aside, being esteemed too heavy and dull for the light heals and brains of this nimble and wanton age; nor is any musick rendered acceptable, or esteemed by many, but what is presented by foreigners: not a City Dame, though a tap-wife, but is ambitious to have her daughters taught by Monsieur La Novo Kickshawibus on the Gittar, which instrument is but a new old one, used in London in the time of Queen Mary." Again, in his 'Introduction to the Skill of Musick,' John Playford complains: "Our late and solemn musick, both vocal and instrumental, is now justl'd out of esteem by the new Corants and Jigs of foreigners, to the grief of all sober and judicious understanders of that formerly solid and good musick." This is copied from the edition published in 1683; the first edition appeared in 1655. Christopher Simpson, in his 'Compendium of Practical Musick,' London, 1667, boldly asserts: "You need not seek outlandish authors, especially for instrumental musick; no nation, in my opinion, being equal to the

English in that way; as well for their excellent, as their various and numerous Consorts of three, four, five and six parts, made properly for instruments," etc. Thus also Christopher Simpson, at the conclusion of his 'The Division Violist, or an Introduction to the Playing upon a Ground,' London, 1659, says: "And here I might mention (were it not out of the Rode of my Designe,) divers others [besides Mr. John Jenkins]; most eminent men of this our nation, who, for their excellent and various compositions, especially for instruments, have, in my opinion, far outdone those nations, so much cryed up for their excellency in Musick."

The preference given by these musicians to their own music does not, however, throw much light upon the question: Of what kind was the music played by the English instrumentalists, who accompanied the comedians on the continent?

A satisfactory answer to this question may be obtained from an examination of the secular music popular in England about three hundred years ago, and from the stage directions in the dramas performed by the strolling actors.

As regards the diffusion of musical knowledge in England at the time of Queen Elizabeth, the historical records contain contradictory statements, which however may, with some discrimination, be reconciled with each other. It is well known that England possessed at that period some estimable composers of sacred music who would probably have obtained a hearing on the continent, had they not been obscured by the excellent Flemish and Italian church composers. Some intelligent foreigners who made a trip to England, at the time of Queen Elizabeth, praise the music which they heard in the principal churches of the country. Paul Hentzner, a German scholar, who visited England in the year 1598, remarks in his journal: " The English excel in dancing and music, for they are active and lively, though of a thicker make than the French." He subsequently expresses a less favourable opinion of the musical taste of the English : " They are vastly fond of great noises that fill the ear, such as the firing of cannon, drums, and the ringing of bells."* This statement accords with a remark of Dr. Burney in his History of Music, Vol. III., p. 143; and likewise with Handel's advice to Gluck, when the latter, after the performance of his opera 'Caduta de' Giganti' in London, anno 1746, complained of want of success: "For the Englishman you must compose something which is powerful, and which acts upon his tympanum."† Music was also called noise. For instance, in Shakespeare's Henry IV., Part II., Act 2, Scene 4 :—

'And see if thou canst find Sneak's noise; Mistress Tearsheet would fain hear some music.'

It may be supposed that the popular taste for loud music was some centuries ago much the same as it is at the present day, where quantity is often more thought of than quality. But, there are some records from which it would appear that the cultivation of music was universal among the educated classes. Henry Peacham in his 'Compleat Gentleman,' London, 1634, enumerates with the many requisite accomplishments of a gentleman, some practical and theoretical knowledge of the art of music. However, he does not describe the gentleman as he finds him, but, as in his opinion he ought to be. To conclude from his description that in the seventeenth century every English gentleman was musical, would be as unwarrantable as to conclude from Lord Chesterfield's well-known advice to his son to leave violin-playing to the professional musicians, that in the eighteenth century Englishmen of education considered it derogatory to play on a musical instrument.

In Thomas Morley's 'Introduction to Practical Musick,' London, 1597, which is written in dialogue, Philomathes says to Polymathes, in the beginning of the discourse, that recently when at a party he could not join in their madrigal singing after supper "euery one began to wonder. Yea, some whispered to others, demaunding how I was brought

---

* 'England as seen by Foreigners in the days of Elizabeth and James I. By W. B. Rye; London, 1865.' P. 3.

† 'C. W. Ritter von Gluck, von Anton Schmid; Leipzig, 1854.' P. 29.

up: so that vpon shame of mine ignorance, I goe now to seeke out mine old friend master Gnorimus, to make my selfe his scholler." This statement appears, however, to be in contradiction with one made about the same time in another instruction book, entitled 'The Schoole of Mvsicke; wherein is tavght the perfect Method of trve fingering of the Lute, Pandora, Orpharion, and Viol-da-Gamba; with most infallible generall rules, both easie and delightfull. Also a Method how you may be your owne instructor for Prick-song, by the help of your Lute, without any other teacher: with lessons of all sorts for your further and better instruction. Newly composed by Thomas Robinson, Lutenist; London, 1603.' This book likewise is written in the form of a dialogue, the persons in conversation being "Knight" and "Timothevs." In the beginning of the dialogue Knight remarks : " In mine opinion I think it impossible to be a good Musitien, except a man be seene in all the seauen liberall Sciences; for I know many great clarkes in Diuinitie, Phisicke, Law, Philosophie, etc., that haue small, or no knowledge at all in Musicke, nay, some quite reject it."

No doubt, these statements of two professional musicians contradictory to each other, as to the cultivation of music by English gentlemen towards the end of the reign of Queen Elizabeth, must not be taken literally, but rather as what the authors thought an ingenious and elegant manner of proving that their works supplied a want. Thus, Thomas Morley teaching vocal music, maintains that every young gentleman is expected to be a singer; and Thomas Robinson, teaching the lute and the cither, expresses his dissatisfaction that many gentlemen know nothing about musical instruments,— indeed, nothing of music. Moreover, Thomas Robinson is a "Student in all the liberall Sciences;" we know this from his own statement on the title-page of his 'New Citharen Lessons,' London, 1609; and being a learned man, he considers it impossible to be a good musician without being versed in "all the seauen liberall Sciences."

The fact that there is no English book dating from the sixteenth, seventeenth, or eighteenth century, which contains descriptions with illustrations of the different musical instruments formerly in use in England, while a considerable number of such books were published on the continent, sufficiently proves, if other testimony were wanting, that instrumental music was not so much cultivated in England as on the continent. The English books of instruction for certain instruments were generally but poor compilations got up by the publishers themselves. The illustrations of musical instruments given in Hawkins's 'History of Music' have most of them been copied from Luscinius and Mersenne. Hawkins appears to have been unaware that these instruments, of which he gives descriptions derived from foreign sources, were formerly also in use in England. At any rate, he mentions several of them by their German names, without giving their English names.

Some English musicians who at the time of James I. visited the continent, Italianized their names, a rather unpatriotic act to which they probably would not have thought of resorting, had they not become convinced of the superiority of the continental music. John Cooper called himself Giovanni Coperario; and Peter Phillips, who lived for a time in the Netherlands, altered his name into Pietro Philippi.

As regards the national music of England at the time of the strolling instrumentalists, the inquirer may obtain reliable information by examining an old collection of popular tunes entitled 'The Dancing Master; or Directions for dancing Country Dances, with the Tunes to each Dance, for the Treble Violin.' The first edition was published by John Playford, about the middle of the sixteenth century. The work, which consisted of only one volume, became popular, and went through many editions with enlargements, until, at about the year 1700, it extended to three volumes containing nearly one thousand tunes. It may be surmised that this collection comprises nearly all the airs of the secular songs which were popular in England at the time of the Instrumentalists. It must be remembered that most of the airs of songs were also used as dance-tunes, and that comparatively but few of the dance-tunes in the earlier editions of the collection are instrumental pieces not derived from vocal music. Whether all these melodies are of English origin is another question. Some are known to be Welsh, others Irish, others Scotch; and some appear to have been derived from the continent. Some of the dances are of foreign origin, and most probably they became first known with the tunes which belonged to them when they were introduced into England. Afterwards, new tunes were composed to them, which more or less resembled the old ones. Irrespective of all those tunes in the 'Dancing Master,' which are apparently not English, there still remains a considerable number of specimens which may be accepted as genuine English tunes. They should be examined just as they are published, without modern harmony or any other arrangement which obscures their original character. Some of them are certainly odd. Take for instance the 'Cushion Dance,' with its melancholy tune, in which the dancers converse in song with the musicians.

JOAN SANDERSON, OR THE CUSHION DANCE.
AN OLD ROUND DANCE.

"*Note.*—The first strain twice; the second once; and the last as oft as is required."

" This dance is begun by a single Person (either Man or Woman) who taking a Cushion in their Hand, dances about the Room; and at the end of the Tune they stop and sing, *This Dance it will no further go.* The Musicians answer, *I pray you good Sir, why say you so?* Man, *Because Jean Sanderson will not come too.* Musician, *She must come too, and she shall come too, and she must come whether she will or no.* Then he lays down the Cushion before a Woman, on which she kneels, and he kisses her, singing, *Welcome Jean Sanderson, welcome, welcome.* Then she rises, takes up the Cushion, and both dance, singing, *Prinkum-prankum is a fine Dance, and shall we go dance it once again, once again, and once again, and shall we go dance it once again?* Then making a stop, the Woman sings as before, *The Dance*, etc. Musician, *I pray you Madam*, etc. Woman, *Because John Sanderson*, etc. Musician, *He must*, etc. And so she lays down the Cushion before a Man, who kneeling upon it salutes her, she singing, *Welcome John Sanderson*, etc. Then he taking up the Cushion, they take hands and dance round, singing, as before; and thus they do till the whole Company are taken into the Ring. And if there is Company enough, make a little Ring in the middle, and within that Ring set a Chair and lay the Cushion in it, and the first Man set in it. Then the Cushion is laid before the first Man, the Woman singing *This Dance*, etc. (as before) only instead of—*come too*, they sing—*go fro;* and instead of *Welcome John Sanderson*, etc., they sing *Farewell John Sanderson, Farewell, Farewell;* and so they go out one by one as they came in. *Note:* The Woman is kiss'd by all the Men in the Ring at her coming in and going out, and likewise the Man by all the Women."

The popular tunes of almost every European nation possess certain features of their own which the student of national music can ascertain and define. To pronounce upon the original home of any one national tune is of course often as hazardous as to pronounce upon a man's native country from his physiognomy. There are Germans who look much like Englishmen, but a number of Germans seen gathered together would not easily be mistaken for Englishmen. The same may be observed in every nation. We may occasionally meet with an Englishman who has the appearance of a Frenchman, a Chinese, or a Gipsy; but an assembly of Englishmen reveals a certain family-likeness appertaining to the English race. Thus also a collection of the popular tunes of a nation generally exhibits certain predominant peculiarities which enable us to determine whence the tunes came. Those in the 'Dancing Master,' regarded collectively, do not exhibit any family-likeness which it would be possible to indicate by words or by musical notation. They appear to have sprung from as many sources as the words of the English language. The language has, however, a strongly marked individual character from the various adopted words having become Anglicized; while the musical compositions of Englishmen bear no stamp by which they could be recognized as English.

The English instrumentalists played, of course, chiefly the popular tunes of their time. It is unnecessary to explain in detail how the music was introduced into the dramatic performances. The works of Shakespeare, with which the reader is presumably familiar, show this sufficiently. They likewise contain many instances of the admission of popular songs or ballads, — such as Desdemona's "Sing willow, willow, willow;" Ophelia's "How should I your true love know?" or the Clown's "O mistress mine where are you roaming?" in Twelfth-night. Also vocal music composed for two or more voices was occasionally introduced,—even the jocular catch, which was especially relished in England, and which Shakespeare ridicules (Twelfth-night, Act II., Scene 3) :—

'*Sir Toby Belch.*—Shall we rouse the night-owl in a catch that will draw three souls out of one weaver? shall we do that?'

After some punning, Sir Toby, Sir Andrew Aguecheek and the Clown sing together a catch.

Enter Maria.

'*Maria.*—What a caterwauling do you keep here? If my lady have not called up her steward, Malvolio, and bid him turn you out of doors, never trust me.'

In 'Hamlet,' Act III., Scene 2, strolling actors are introduced, and with them musicians playing on hautboys and recorders. In the representations of the English comedians in the Ottoneum, at Cassel, anno 1606, the instrumentalists always struck up after each act.* No doubt they played, besides their English tunes, also the most popular ones of Germany, which would ensure them a more favourable reception. Travelling musicians who perform in public, almost invariably find it to their advantage thus to meet the taste of their audience. And it appears, likewise,

---

* 'Geschichte des Theatres und der Musik in Cassel,' von W. Lynker; Cassel, 1865. P. 243.

very probable that the English Instrumentalists, on their return home, entertained their audience in England with the popular tunes, and perhaps some more elaborate pieces, with which they had become acquainted on the Continent, and which to the English public would possess the charm of novelty.

However this may be, the position of the Instrumentalists at home, after they had discontinued their continental tour, was by no means enviable, to judge from 'The Actors' Remonstrance, or Complaint for the silencing of their profession and banishment from their severall Play-houses, London, 1643,' in which the dejected actors remark: "Our Musicke that was held so delectable and precious, that they scorned to come to a Taverne under twentie shillings salary for two houres, now wander with their instruments under their cloaks, I meane such as haue any, into all houses of good fellowship, saluting every roome where there is company with, Will you haue any musike Gentlemen?"*

The English comedians in Germany generally performed in the German language. This must have been funny,—perhaps not the least so in pathetic passages, solemn admonitions, or in reflecting monologues, where even the slightest foreign pronunciation is apt to transform the sublime into the ridiculous. Here brevity must have been often desirable, and the falling in of the band may have afforded relief. Thus, the English Instrumentalists, although they have exercised no influence upon the cultivation of the art of music, are certainly interesting, inasmuch as they have assisted in the earliest representations of the dramas of Shakespeare.

---

* 'The English Drama and Stage, under the Tudor and Stuart Princes, 1543-1664, illustrated by a Series of Documents, Treatises, and Poems. Printed for the Roxburgh Library, London, 1869.' P. 263.

MUSICAL FAIRIES AND THEIR KINSFOLK.

FAIRIES notoriously possess great fondness for music. They may be seen in meadows dancing at night by moonlight; and people often find in the morning the traces in the dew, called Fairy Rings. In European countries their favourite musical instruments evidently are the harp and the fiddle. They also often excel as vocalists, and we find them reputed as enchanting singers in almost every part of the world.

Their music resembles, as might be expected, the old tunes of the country-people in the district which they inhabit. The following air of the Irish fairies is copied from T. Crofton Croker's 'Fairy Legends and Traditions of the South of Ireland:'—

This air, which, of course, is said to be of high antiquity, is commonly sung by every skilful narrator of a certain Irish fairy tale to which it belongs, to enhance the effect of the story.

THE FAIRIES OF THE MAORIES.

The fairies of New Zealand are described as a very numerous people, merry, and always singing like crickets. In appearance they are quite different from the Maories, the natives of New Zealand; they rather resemble Europeans, their hair and complexion being remarkably fair.

One day, when Te Kanawa, a chief of one of the Maori tribes, happened to fall in with a troop of fairies on a hill in the Waikato district, he heard them distinctly singing some mysterious verses, which he afterwards repeated to his friends, and which are still preserved in the poetry of the New Zealanders.

Te Kanawa had died before any Europeans arrived in New Zealand, but the details of his encounter with the fairies are not forgotten by the people. They say that he had gone out with his dogs to catch Kiwis,* when night came on and he found himself right at the top of Pukemore, a high hill. There it was where the fairies approached the brave chief, and frightened him almost to death. He lighted a fire, and therewith scared them a little. Whenever the fire blazed up brightly, off went the fairies and hid themselves, peeping out from behind stumps of trees; and when it burnt low, back they came close to it, merrily singing and dancing.

The sudden thought struck the trembling chief that he might perhaps induce the fairies to go away if he gave them the jewels he had about him; so he took off a beautiful little figure carved in green jasper, which he wore as a neck ornament; then he pulled out his jasper ear-drop finely carved, and also his earring made of the tooth of a tiger-shark. Fearing lest the fairies should touch him, he took a stick, and, fixing it into the ground, hung the precious presents upon it. Directly after the fairies had ended their song they examined the trinkets; and they took the shadow from them, which they handed about from one to another through the whole party. Suddenly they all vanished carrying with them the shadows of the jewels, but leaving behind the jewels themselves.

The verses which Te Kanawa heard the fairies sing are, as has been already said, still known, and the Maories cite them in proof that everything happened to their brave chief, Te Kanawa, as it is related.†

---

* Kiwi, or Apteryx; also called Wingless Emu. This bird is caught by torch-light.
† 'Polynesian Mythology, by Sir George Grey; London, 1855.' P. 292.

ADVENTURES IN THE HIGHLANDS.

The fairies in the Highlands of Scotland generally have their habitations in rugged precipices and rocky caverns, found in districts especially remarkable for wildness of scenery. Their favourite amusements are music and dancing, and their reels are said to last sometimes for a whole year and even longer, without intermission.

A peasant from the neighbourhood of Cairngorm, in Strathspey, who with his wife and children had settled in the forest of Glenavon, happened to send his two sons late one evening into the wood to look after some sheep which had strayed. The lads, traversing the wood in all directions, came upon a habitation of fairies from which emanated the sweetest music that one can possibly imagine,—or rather, much sweeter music than anyone can possibly imagine. The younger brother, completely fascinated by its charms, at one leap entered the abode of the fairies, from which, alas! he could not return. The elder brother, compelled to give him up as lost, ran home to his parents to tell them what had occurred.

Now, there lived in the neighbourhood a "wise man," whom they thought best to consult in the matter. This man taught the elder brother some mysterious words of disenchantment, and told him to repair to the same place where the lad had been drawn into the cliff, and to pronounce solemnly the words; but this must be done exactly a year after the occurrence of the event. The elder brother most earnestly attended to the injunction. When the year had elapsed, he stood before the cave of the fairies on the same day and precisely at the same hour at which his brother had left him. The music was still going on, and by means of the mysterious words he actually succeeded in liberating his brother, who was still dancing. The daring little boy fully believed that he had been dancing with the fairies for only half-an-hour; for, he said, he had been dancing all the while, and the first reel was not yet over. But, when he arrived at home again, his parents observed at once how much his arms, legs, and his whole body had grown during the year.

Not less remarkable is the following adventure of a village-clergyman told in the Highlands of Scotland.

A parson who enjoyed the reputation of being a very pious man, was returning home to his village one night, after having administered spiritual consolation to a dying member of his flock. The night was far advanced and he had to pass through a good deal of "uncanny" land; however, he, knowing himself to be a conscientious minister of the gospel, did not fear any spirit. On his reaching the end of the lake which stretches for some distance along the side of the road to the village, he was greatly surprised by suddenly hearing strains of music more melodious than he ever before had heard in his life. Overcome with delight, the pious minister could not refrain from sitting down to listen to the melodious sounds; besides he was very anxious to find out, if possible, the nature and source of the charming music. He had not sat listening many minutes when he could clearly perceive the gradual approach of the music; he also observed a light in the direction from whence the music proceeded, gliding across the lake towards him. Instead of taking to his heels, as any faithless wight would have done, the pious pastor, quite fearless, determined to await the issue of the singular phenomenon. As the light and music drew near, he could at length distinguish an object resembling a human being walking on the surface of the water, attended by a group of diminutive musicians, some of them bearing lights, and others, instruments of music, on which they continued to perform those melodious strains which first attracted his attention. The leader of the band dismissed his attendants, landed on the beach, and afforded the minister the amplest opportunity of examining his appearance.

He was a little primitive-looking, grey-headed man, clad in the most grotesque habit ever seen; indeed, his whole appearance was such as to lead the venerable pastor all at once to suspect his real character. He walked up to the parson, saluted him very gracefully, apologizing for the intrusion. The parson politely returned his compliment, and without further explanation invited him to sit down beside him. The invitation was complied with; upon which the minister proposed the following question:—

"Who art thou, stranger, and from whence?"

To this question, the fairy, with downcast eye, replied that he was one of those beings sometimes called 'Doane Shee,' or 'Men of Peace,' or 'Good Men,' though the reverse of this title was perhaps a more befitting appellation for them. Originally angelic in his nature and attributes, and once a sharer in the indescribable joys of the regions of light, he was seduced by Satan to join him in mad conspiracy; and as a punishment for his transgression he was cast down from those regions of bliss, and was now doomed, along with millions of fellow-sufferers, to wander through seas and mountains until the coming of the great day. What their fate would be thereafter, they could not divine.*

THE IMPORTUNATE ELVES.

An almost incredible incident is recorded in Denmark as having occurred to a youth not far from the town of Apenrade in Slesvig. The youth had sat down on a hill, called Hanbierre, and had fallen asleep. Near that hill is a grove of alders,—just the kind of place which one might expect the elves to frequent. The youth did not awaken until midnight. Presently he heard all around him most ravishing music; and looking about in astonishment, he saw two beautiful girls who were singing and dancing in the moonlight. After a little while they came near to him, and spoke to him. But he, knowing that it is dangerous to converse with elves, remained silent. They asked him many questions to induce him to speak; and when he still persisted in not answering them, they threatened him, singing—"Hearken, O youth! Wilt thou not speak to us

---

* Almost literally from 'The Popular Superstitions and Festive Amusements of the Highlanders of Scotland, by W. Grant Stewart; London, 1851.'

to-night before the cock crow, thy silver-shafted knife shall surely lay thy heart to rest!"—Again they sang strains most sweet and ravishing. He could no longer resist, and was just on the point of speaking to them, when, fortunately for him, the cock crowed, and they vanished.

From this event the hill is called Hanbierre, or Hahnenberg, which means 'Cock's Hill.'

BAD SPIRITS.

A short extract from a discussion on Spirits, written about three hundred years ago by an English inquirer into their nature and propensities, may find a place here. This description occurs in a work by Thomas Nash, Gentleman, entitled 'Pierce Penilesse his Supplication to the Deuill; Describing the ouer-spreading of Vice, and the suppression of Vertue; Pleasantly interlac'd with variable delights; and pathetically intermixt with conceipted reproofes. London, 1592.' It does not clearly appear whether the author's remarks are intended to refer especially to the Spirits of England; but this probably is the case. True, he describes them as more ill-tempered than those on the Continent are generally said to be; but this may perhaps be merely owing to the gloominess of the English climate. Howbeit, these troublesome Spirits are most likely not so bad as we find them here depicted; for, is it not a well-known fact, also mentioned by Thomas Nash, Gentleman, that they love music?

"The spirits of the earth keepe, for the most part, in forrests and woods, and doo hunters much noyance; and sometime in the broad fields, where they lead trauelers out of the right way, or fright men with deformed apparitions, or make run mad through excessiue melancholy, like Aiax Telamonious, and so proue hurtful to themselves, and dangerous to others: of this number the chiefe are Samaab and Achymael, spirits of the east, that haue no power to doo great harm, by reason of the vnconstancie of their affections. The vnder-earth spirits are such as lurk in dens and little cauernes of the earth, and hollow crevices of mountaines, that they may dyue into the bowels of the earth at their pleasures: these dig metals and watch treasures, which they continually transport from place to place that non should haue vse of them: they raise windes that vomit flames, and shake the foundation of buildins; they daunce in rounds in pleasant lawnds, and greene medowes, with noises of musick and minstralsy, and vanish away when any comes nere them: they will take vpon them any similitude but that of a woman, and terrefie men in the likeness of dead mens ghosts in the night time."

THE MUSICIAN AND THE DWARFS.

The following adventure was first related by a jolly young German, who said he was acquainted with a friend of the very person to whom it occurred.

Once upon a time, a poor musician who lived in the neighbourhood of Hildesheim, an old town in the former kingdom of Hanover, went home late at night from a lonely mill, where he had been playing dance-tunes at a christening festivity. The mill is still extant. Its name is Die Mordmühle (The Murder Mill), probably because something dreadful may have happened there years ago. His way led him past a cliff in which there was a dwarf's hole. When he cast a glance at the hole, he saw, to his amazement, sitting before it a dwarf, not more than three feet high. Scarcely had he recovered from his first fright, when suddenly he felt himself seized by invisible hands and drawn under ground many miles deep into the mountain. All this occurred in a moment's time. Immediately the poor musician found that he had been transported into a beautiful hall, illuminated with many thousand lights of various brilliant colours. The flooring of the hall was of pure silver, and the walls were all of the purest gold: the chandeliers were of emeralds and diamonds.

Presently the dwarfs desired the musician to play his best tunes. While playing, he heard quite unmistakably the little folks dancing to his music; he also heard them coughing, giggling, and laughing; but he did not see any being except the dwarf who had taken him there. After a little while the same dwarf brought in a bottle of exquisitely fine wine, and placed it before the musician. When the poor fiddler had helped himself repeatedly from the bottle, he began to feel more at his ease, and became a little talkative.

"Well, my good master," he said, "I am playing and playing here one tune after another, and hear all kinds of noises; but I see no Christian soul but yourself: could I not have just a look at the gentlefolks whom I have the honour of serving with my music?"

To this sensible request the dwarf replied: "By all means! There is no danger in that. Just take my hat and put it on thy head."

As soon as the musician had placed the dwarf's large round hat on his head, he saw the hall crowded with thousands of little pigmy ladies and gentlemen, very smartly dressed, who were promenading up and down, bowing and curtseying to each other; and with them were some little children, certainly not bigger than a thumb. After having played a country-dance to conclude the ball, the musician was dismissed, but not before the dwarf who had brought him there had filled his pockets with wood shavings, of which a large heap lay stored up just near the entrance of the hall.

"Of what use is that stuff to me!" thought the musician; and the first thing he did, when he found himself again free in the open air, was to empty his pockets and throw all the shavings into the road. Heartily tired he reached his home. On the following morning he put his hand into his coat pocket to ascertain if perchance any of the shavings remained; when, Lo! what should he draw out, but a piece of the purest gold! Directly he set off again to the road where he had disencumbered himself of the shavings the night before. But he could find nothing; all traces of the treasure had disappeared.*

---

* 'Sagen, Märchen Schwänke und Gebraüche aus Stadt und Stift Hildesheim, gesammelt von Seifart; Göttingen, 1854.' P. 30.

THE LITTLE FOLKS.

A young girl who was in service at a farm-house in the province of Schleswig in Germany, had to work daily so very hard that she became at last quite dissatisfied with her lot.

One morning when her master sent her into the field after the cows, she had to pass a hill in which people had often heard the subterranean little folks singing and dancing. The girl thought to herself how enviably happy those dear dwarfs in the hill must be, who work but leisurely and sing so cheerfully. "Alas!" she exclaimed, "could I but live with them, how gladly would I bid farewell to my present home!"

Her words were heard by one of the dwarfs, a young lad who had just been seriously contemplating how very advisable it would be for him to look out for a wife. So, when the girl returned from the field, he presented himself to her, and soon persuaded her to marry him. They are said to have lived very happily together in the hill for many years. They had also about half-a-dozen children; funnily-small dear little creatures these must have been, to be sure.

The dwarfs in that district possessed in former times a peculiar kind of cradle song, of which some fragments have been caught by the listening peasants, and are still preserved.

The music which the dwarfs produce is, as might be expected, remarkably soft and soothing. Loud and noisy music is not at all to the taste of the little folks. A peasant who one day had been to town to purchase rice, raisins, and other luxuries for the wedding festival of his daughter, which was to take place on the following morning, fell in with one of the dwarfs near an old grave-yard situated close to the road. In the course of conversation which they had together, the dwarf expressed a wish that he might be permitted to witness the festivity, and promised to bring with him for a wedding present a lump of gold as large as a man's head.

The delighted peasant said he should be most happy to welcome the generous guest; indeed, he should consider it quite an honour.

"*A propos!*" remarked the dwarf, just as they shook hands at parting, "What kind of music do you have to-morrow?"

Whereupon the rejoicing peasant rather boastingly replied: "First-rate music! We shall have trumpets and kettle-drums!"

Then the dwarf begged to be excused attending; for (he said) trumpets and kettle-drums he could not endure.*

MACRUIMEAN'S BAGPIPE.

There is in Scotland a family of hereditary bagpipers whose name is Macruimean (or M'Crimmon). Now, it is well known how it came to pass that the famous bagpiper, Macruimean, got his fine music. He was ploughing one day near a haunted hill, when one of the "Little Folks," a tiny green man, came up and invited him into the mountain. After they had entered a cave, the tiny green man gave Macruimean an exquisitely fine bagpipe, and told him that so long as any part of the instrument remained, either with him or with his offspring they would continue to be the best bagpipers in Scotland. When the lucky Macruimean had arrived with his bagpipe at his house, he found to his surprise that he could play upon it beautifully any tune which occurred to his mind. Indeed, his performance was so powerful and impressive that it astonished every one; and the people in the Highlands have still the saying, *Co ard ri Piob mhoir Mic-Chruimean*,—("*As loud as Macruimean's pipes.*")

There is also still in the Highlands a cave called *Uamh na'm Piobairean*—*i.e.*, "The Piper's Cave," into which the famous Macruimean with his children used to repair to practise the bagpipe. This cave is on the top of a brae, or rising ground, eight miles north from Dunvegan Castle. Even his daughters, people say, would occasionally steal to

---

*'Sagen, Märchen und Lieder der Herzogthümer Schleswig, Holstein und Lauenburg, herausgegeben von Karl Müllenhoff; Kiel, 1845.' Pp. 189, 300, 310.

the cave, if they could lay hold on their father's favourite set of pipes, and indulge in a vigorous practice for an hour or so. Moreover, at what time the Macruimean family was first established as the hereditary bagpipers of the Lairds of MacLeod, no one can say now; for it was so very long ago.*

THE GYGUR FAMILY.

As regards giants, there are now-a-days only very few remaining in European countries. Formerly, it would appear, they were abundant, and many traces of their habitations and doings are still pointed out by the people. However, respecting the capacity of the giants for music, but little is recorded. Jacob Grimm alludes to the charming musical powers of Gygur, a Scandinavian giantess and sorceress, and he thinks it likely that an old German name for the violin, which is *Geige*, was derived from Gygur. † If this be so, the French *Gigue* and the English *Jig* may be supposed likewise to have their origin from the name of that mysterious monster. There was evidently in olden time a whole Gygur family; but it is very doubtful whether any of its members are still extant. If there are yet any to be found, it must be up in the North, perhaps in Norway, Sweden, or Iceland; at any rate, the people in these countries still speak occasionally of their old giants, or trolls as they are also called.

LINUS, THE KING'S SON.

This story is current in Iceland. It was told to a German traveller in that out-of-the-way part of the world by a poor joiner,—evidently a true-born Icelander, well versed in the folk-lore of his country, but a somewhat prosy narrator.

---

* 'The White Wife, with other Stories;' collected by Cuthbert Bede; London, 1865; p. 220. 'A Collection of Ancient Piobaireachd,' by Angus Mackay; Edinburgh, 1838.

† 'Kinder und Hausmärchen, gesammelt durch die Brüder Grimm;' Göttingen, 1856. Vol. III. p. 192.

The story is here given in a condensed form. True, there is not much said in it about music; but its chief incidents are brought about by the agency of magic songs. The singing of the swans lulls the king's son into a death-like slumber, and it is by means of music that the sweet foster-sister of Linus, when she finds him reposing on the couch,—but all this the reader will see in the story itself, and to tell it first in a preamble, and then a second time, would be even worse than the prolixity of the honest Icelandic joiner. So let us proceed to the story.

There was once a king and a queen who had a son whose name was Linus. Every one in the whole kingdom admired the young prince for his fine person and his many accomplishments.

Now it happened that when Linus, the king's son, had attained the age of twenty years, he suddenly disappeared, and no one could say what had become of him.

Not far from the king's palace lived with her parents in a little hut a young girl who was the prince's foster-sister; and he had always been extremely fond of her. No wonder that he liked her so much, for she was as beautiful as she was amiable.

"Mother," said the girl, "pray, now let me go, that I may seek for him until I find him again!"

When the mother heard her speaking thus, she became convinced that all dissuasion would be useless, and she permitted her daughter to go. However, she gave her a magic ball of thread, and taught her how to throw it before her as a guide to the hidden abode of the king's son; for the old lady was not altogether inexperienced in the mysteries of sorcery. The girl took the ball of thread and let it run before her; and it rolled and rolled many miles over mountains and through valleys, until it suddenly stopped near a precipitous cliff.

"Here he must be!" ejaculated the girl, and anxiously looked about whether there was not somewhere an entrance into the cliff. But all she could find, after a careful search was a narrow crevice, somewhat hidden by a projecting rock, scarcely wide enough for her to squeeze herself through.

When she had succeeded in entering the cliff, she found herself in a large cavern, the walls of which were smoothly planed, and suspended on them were all kinds of odd implements. Surveying the cavern with a curiosity not unmixed with fear, she discovered on one side a short passage leading into another cavern not quite so large as the first, but handsomer in appearance. Having entered the second cavern, she observed a splendid bed standing in the middle of the room. Trembling with hope and fear, she drew nearer to the bed, and lo! there she found him lying asleep, the beloved Linus, the king's son!

Her first thought was to awaken him as quickly as possible, that he might fly with her out of the mountain. But all her exertions to arouse him had no effect, although she tried various means which ought, it might be supposed, certainly to have awakened him. While considering what she should do, she was suddenly terrified by a rumbling sound like that of distant thunder, which gradually became louder and louder, until it appeared to be quite near the entrance to the cavern. She had just time to hide herself behind some furniture in the corner, when the cliff opened widely, and in came a giantess, seated on a chariot of ivory, inlaid with gold, and having a golden whip in her hand.

As soon as the giantess, who was also a great sorceress, had entered the cavern, the opening in the cliff closed again. Presently she went to the bed on which the king's son was reposing, and summoning two swans from the end of the cavern, she recited the spell:—

"Sing, sing ye my swans,
To awake Linus, the king's son!"

Immediately the swans began to sing a song, charming beyond all description; and as they sang the youth awoke. Then the horrid giantess sat down by the side of the king's son, and told him how very fond she was of him; and that she should never be happy until he was her husband. But, Linus, the king's son, smiled without answering her; and, turning his head aside, he thought of his foster-sister in the little hut not far from his father's palace. How little did he suspect that the dear girl was near to him, hidden in the cavern!

However, the giantess perceiving that she was talking in vain, at last determined to await a more propitious time. So she again called her swans, and recited the spell:—

"Sing, sing ye my swans,
To charm the king's son to sleep!"

Immediately the swans sang a song inexpressibly soothing, and the king's son fell asleep again. Thinking the youth safely secured, the giantess took up her golden whip, and seating herself in the chariot of ivory, inlaid with gold, she recited the spell:—

"Run, run my precious chariot,
And carry me to the Lifsteinn!"

As soon as she had said these words the cliff opened, and the chariot flew off like a flash of lightning. Now, when the watchful girl heard the thundering sound gradually diminishing into a feeble murmur, she knew that she might venture out of her hiding-place. The first thing she did was to command the swans:—

"Sing, sing ye my swans,
To awake Linus, the king's son!"

Immediately the swans began to sing most charmingly, and the beloved Linus awoke. Oh! how unspeakably happy he was when he beheld his dear foster-sister standing before him! For a time the cavern was to them a paradise;—but soon the anxious question arose how to escape from the clutches of the giantess.

Then the quick-witted girl suggested a plan which Linus hopefully adopted; and having summoned the swans to lull the youth to sleep again, she withdrew into her hiding-place; for the increasing rumbling of the chariot warned her of the approaching danger.

The giantess had not long returned to the cavern when she determined on making another attempt to gain the affection of the king's son. So she commanded the swans to sing him awake. The prince arose, appeared much more compliant than before, and expressed his willingness to marry her on the following day, if it were not otherwise destined.

Then the enamoured giantess, in answer to his inquiries, revealed to him various secrets as to her magic powers; and when he asked her to tell him candidly whither she went so often in her chariot, she replied:—

"Ah, my dear boy, there is no cause for jealousy! The fact is, I have a brother who is a great giant, and we both, my brother and I, have but one life, and that is bound up in a Lifsteinn ('Stone of Life'). Now, you must know, the Lifsteinn is very brittle, and if it should be broken our death would be certain. Daily I visit my brother, who lives far off in a valley near a deep spring under three high trees. We then fetch up our Lifsteinn, which lies in the deep spring, and carefully examine it; for, nothing affords us greater satisfaction than to find our Lifsteinn uninjured."

This valuable information was listened to with breathless attention by the young girl in her hiding-place; and when the giantess, having previously ordered the swans to sing the king's son to sleep, had taken her departure in the chariot, the girl lost no time in hastening from the cavern; and, rolling the ball of thread before her, she followed it over mountains and through valleys until she had reached the deep spring under the three high trees. The great giant, whose mere breathing made all the leaves of the trees tremble, was just placing the Lifsteinn in the lap of the giantess,—when the courageous girl sprang out from behind the trees, and snatching it up threw it on the ground and shattered it to fragments. In a moment both the giant and the giantess fell down dead.

Now the girl ascended the ivory-golden chariot, took up the golden whip, and smacking it, recited the spell—

"Run, run my precious chariot,
And take me to Linus the king's son!'

When the chariot had entered the cavern, she at once commanded the swans to awaken the king's son; and this they did in strains of music so melodiously beautiful that no mortal had ever heard the like. Linus and his dear foster-sister, having provided themselves with as many jewels and as much gold and silver from the cavern as they could carry, took their seats in the chariot and commanded it to take them straight to the king's palace. Oh! how they all rejoiced throughout the whole kingdom! There was no end of festivities!

But the most glorious festival was that when they celebrated the marriage of Linus, the king's son, with his sweet foster-sister. On that day the old king, in his happiness, resigned the crown in favour of his dear son. Of course, king Linus and his beloved queen were quite happy then and ever after.*

NECKS.

The Necks, or water-spirits, are renowned for their love and talent for music. There exist, people say, various kinds of these interesting creatures. The Swedes relate wonderful stories respecting the marvellous harp-playing of a Neck called Strömkarl, who generally prefers the vicinity of water-mills and cascades for his abode. In olden times, before the introduction of Christianity into Sweden, the people used to sacrifice a black lamb to the Strömkarl, who, in return, taught them his charming music. Also the Norwegians sacrificed formerly to a similar Neck, called Fossegrim. He taught his enchanting harp-playing to anyone who on a Thursday evening would throw a young white ram into a river flowing northwards, meanwhile averting his face.†

The Neck, or Nicker, has become quite a stranger in England. Some Englishmen, however, take care to preserve his name, applying it to a spirit of another element than water, and everyone knows at once whom they mean when they speak of "Old Nick."

It is said that there are still to be found in Sweden minstrels who have learnt their music from the Necks. A certain farm in Smaland, called Neckaryd, has, according to popular tradition, derived its name from having been inhabited in olden time by a family of minstrels whose name was Neckar, and who learnt their music from a Neck. The last survivors of this remarkable family are still remembered by the people. They were four brothers who used to

---

* 'Isländische Volkssagen der Gegenwart, gesammelt von Konrad Maurer;' Leipzig, 1860, p. 277.

† 'Deutsche Mythologie, von Jacob Grimm;' Göttingen, 1854. Vol. I. p. 461.

play at weddings and on other festive occasions. Their grandfather is said to have first played the following Necken-Polska, which is still a favourite national dance in Sweden.

In some districts of Sweden this tune is played with C-natural, instead of C-sharp, in the first bar. The former is the older form, and may therefore be regarded as exhibiting more accurately the tune as originally derived from the Neck, than the present notation with C-sharp, which is, however, now almost universally adopted. Another tune, which is likewise said to have been caught from hearing it played by a Neck, and which is certainly a very old favourite of the people, is as follows:—

This tune exhibits less the characteristics of the old Swedish dance-tunes than the former, which, like most of them, is in the Minor Key.

THE CHRISTIAN NECK.

The musical performances of the Neck are not any longer confined to secular music. The country people, in some parts of Sweden, assert that they have heard him occasionally playing sacred tunes on his golden harp. Thus we are told of a Neck near the Hornborga bridge, who used to play and to sing with a sweet voice: "I know, I know, I know that my Redeemer liveth!"

Some boys who happened to hear him, called out to him: "What good is it for you to be thus singing and playing? you will never enjoy eternal happiness!"

Then the poor Neck began to cry bitterly, and hid himself beneath the water.

A clergyman in Sweden, riding one evening over a bridge, heard most delightful sounds of some stringed instrument. He looked about, and saw on the surface of the water a youth wearing a little red cap, and with golden hair, long and wavy, which streamed over his shoulders. In his hand he held a golden harp. The clergyman knew at once that this must be a Neck; he, therefore, in his zeal, called out to him:—

"How canst thou play so cheerfully on thy harp? As likely is this dry staff, which I am carrying in my hand, to bud and blossom, as that thou shouldst inherit eternal life!"

The unhappy Neck sorrowfully threw his golden harp into the stream, and sat down on the water weeping most piteously.

The clergyman spurred his horse and continued on his way. But he had not proceeded far, when to his great surprise he saw that his old walking-staff began to put forth leaves; and soon there appeared between them flowers more beautiful than he had ever seen. This he understood to be a sign from Heaven that he should teach the consoling doctrine of reconciliation in a more liberal spirit than he had hitherto done. So he hastened directly back to the Neck, who was still sitting on the water sorrowfully complaining; and showing him the green staff, he said :—

"Dost thou see now my old staff is budding and blossoming, like a young plant in a garden of roses? thus also blossoms hope in the hearts of all created beings, for their Redeemer liveth!"

Consoled, the Neck took up again his golden harp, and heavenly sounds of joy resounded far over the water the whole night long, and many people heard them along the banks of the stream.

MAURICE CONNOR.

Like the Siren, so does the female Neck enchant youths with sweet music, and draw them down into the water. Thus also Hylas, a king's son, is commemorated in Greek Mythology as having been drawn into the water by nymphs enamoured of the beautiful youth.

The Irish relate a somewhat similar story of a famous bagpiper, whose name was Maurice Connor, and who had the reputation of being the best piper in the whole province of Munster. One day, when he played on the sea coast, at a lonely place in the county of Kerry, a beautiful lady with green hair came up from the sea, singing and dancing most charmingly; and when she invited him to go with her, and to marry her, he could not resist. Thus Maurice Connor became the husband of the green-haired lady deep in the sea. The union evidently proved happy. For several years afterwards the sea-faring people often heard, on a still night, the sounds of a bagpipe off the coast, and some say they are quite sure that it was Maurice Connor's music which they heard.*

---

* 'Fairy Legends and Traditions of the South of Ireland. By T. Crofton Croker.' London, 1862; p. 215.

WATER LILIES.

The Water Lily (*Nymphæa*) is by the Germanic nations regarded as the flower of the Nixes, or Water Nymphs. These charming beings, it is said, are so fond of music and dancing that they occasionally come up from the water to the villages lying near their abode, especially at the celebration of a wake, to join in the festivity. But, if they tarry too long at these visits, and fail to return home before the crowing of the cock, they must forfeit their life, and on the glassy surface of the water, into which they have again descended, may be seen a tinge of blood.

One evening in the autumn, after the vintage was finished, the young folks of Jupille, in Belgium, were cheerfully dancing on the village-green, when three beautiful maidens suddenly approached from the banks of the Meuse, and joined the merrymakers. They were dressed in dazzling white garments; and on their blond, wavy hair, they wore wreaths of water-lilies just unfolded. Whether they walked or merely floated over the earth nobody could tell; but certainly never had the youths of Jupille had such aërial partners.

After dancing, all the company sat down in a circle, and the three maidens began to sing with voices so lovely that everyone listened with fixed attention, unconscious how fast the time was passing. However, as soon as the clock struck twelve, the three maidens whispered some words to each other, greeted all around, and vanished out of sight.

On the following evening, just as the moon had arisen, they came again. The youths directly hastened forward to invite them to dance. As the air was sultry, one of them drew off her gloves, and her partner took care of them for her. This evening, the dancing was carried on with even greater spirit than before, and they were still engaged in it when the clock struck twelve. Startled by the sound, the three maidens ceased dancing, and one of them asked hurriedly: " Where are my gloves?"

But the youth wished to retain the gloves as a token of love, and the maiden was compelled to leave them and to hasten away with her companions. The youth followed the three maidens quickly; for he wished above all things to know where his beautiful partner lived. He pursued them further and further, until they reached the river Meuse. The three maidens threw themselves into the stream and vanished.

When, on the following morning the love-sick youth returned to the river where he had lost sight of his partner, he found the water at that place blood-red; and the three maidens have never appeared again.*

IGNIS FATUUS.

As regards the 'Will-o'-the-Wisp,' or 'Jack-in-a-Lanthorn,' there are various opinions prevailing in folk-lore. The Germanic races generally regard these fiery phenomena as wandering souls which, for some culpable cause, have not become partakers of the heavenly rest. Among these are especially classed the souls of covetous husbandmen, who in tilling their fields encroached upon the property of their neighbours; and also the souls of unbaptized children. A Dutch parson, happening to go home to his village late one evening, fell in with three Will-o'-the-Wisps. Remembering them to be the souls of unbaptized children, he solemnly stretched out his hand, and pronounced the words of baptism over them. But, what was the consequence? A thousand and more of these apparitions suddenly made their appearance, evidently all wanting to be baptized. They frightened the good man so terribly, that he took to his heels, and made for home as fast as he could.†

On the ridge of the high Rhön, near Bischofsheim, where there are now two morasses, known as the red and the black morass, there stood formerly two villages, which sunk

---

* 'Niederländische Sagen, herausgegeben von J. W. Wolf;' Leipzig, 1843, p. 611.
† 'Niederländische Sagen, herausgegeben von J. W. Wolf;' Leipzig, 1843, p. 617.

into the earth on account of the dissolute life led by the inhabitants. There appear on those morasses at night maidens in the shape of dazzling apparitions of light. They float and flutter over the site of their former home; but they are now less frequently seen than in the olden time. A good many years ago, two or three of these fiery maidens came occasionally to the village of Wüstersachsen, and mingled with the dancers at wakes. They sang with inexpressible sweetness; but they never remained beyond midnight. When their allowed time had elapsed, there always came flying a white dove, which they followed. Then they went to the mountain, singing, and soon vanished out of sight of the people who followed, watching them with curiosity.*

THE FAIRY MUSIC OF OUR COMPOSERS.

Ancient myths and miracles have always been favourite subjects for operas, and the lover of music does not need to be told that several of our dramatic composers have admirably succeeded in producing music of the fairies and of other aërial conceptions of the fancy. It is, however, not only in their great operatic works, but even in ballads with the accompaniment of the pianoforte, that we meet with exquisitely enchanting strains of fairy music. Take, for instance, Franz Schubert's 'Erl-King,' or Carl Lœwe's 'Herr Oluf.' Nor have some composers been less happy in music of this description entirely instrumental. Mendelssohn's overture to 'A Midsummer Night's Dream,' his first orchestral work of importance, and perhaps his best, seems to depict the fairies dancing in a ring on a moonlight night. But, probably no composer has written instrumental pieces which might be classed with the fairy music, so beautifully as has Beethoven. The *Largo assai* in his pianoforte

* 'Beitrag zur deutschen Mythologie, von F. Panzer;' München, 1848, p. 184.

Trio in D major, Op. 70, is a remarkable instance. Beethoven does not head this movement with words intimating that he intends to tell a fairy-tale in tones. Very possibly he did not even think of the fairies when he composed that wonderful music. Be this as it may, its tremulous chords with their tenderly-vibrating passages, descending the scale *pianissimo*, occasionally swelling to loudness and then subduing again into their former soft Æolian murmur—and, above all, its mysterious and unhomely modulations—convey an impression more analogous to the effect produced by some of our best fairy-tales than is the case with many musical compositions which avowedly were suggested by such stories.

SACRED SONGS OF CHRISTIAN SECTS.

A collection of specimens of the sacred songs, with the tunes, used by the different Christian sects, would be very interesting, and might be instructive to the musician if it were compiled according to the following plan.

The collection should contain the most characteristic and favourite songs used at the present day in public worship and in family devotion. Probably at least a dozen specimens would be required from each sect, to exhibit clearly the characteristics of the common songs. But, besides these, specimens of the songs performed at religious festivals and such-like extraordinary occasions, should be given.

The tunes should be rendered in notation exactly as they are usually sung. If the people sing them in unison, they should not be harmonized; and if they sing them in harmony, the several parts should be faithfully written down, however they may be, without any attempt at improvement, and without unwarranted additions.

If instrumental accompaniment is used, it should not be arranged for any other instrument than that on which it is usually played; its original peculiarities should be strictly preserved.

There exist not unfrequently different readings of the same tune. Wherever this is the case, the most common reading should be given first; and, of the deviations or varieties of the tune, which may chance to be preferred by some congregations, the most usual ones ought to be indicated in small notes after the notation of the tune as it is most commonly sung.

Many of the tunes belonging to the songs are very old, and several of them have been derived from secular songs. Some historical account of these songs would greatly enhance the value of the collection. The alterations which they have undergone in the course of time might, where they are traceable, be shown in notation referring to different centuries or periods; and if the secular melody from which the sacred tune has been derived is still extant, it might likewise be given.

The specimens of songs appertaining to a sect should be prefaced by some account of the doctrines and religious ceremonies peculiar to the sect, and especially by a lucid explanation of the prevailing manner in which the music is executed.

Furthermore, the value of the collection would be increased by admitting also examples of the most popular instrumental pieces used in divine worship; or, at any rate, by giving a description of them, should they be too long for insertion. The field for research and selection of materials for the preparation of such a work is so extensive that much discernment would be required, in order to exhibit clearly the distinctive features of the music of each sect without enlarging the work to a size which would be inconvenient.

The immense number of hymn-books for congregational use, published with or without musical notation, which have appeared since the time of the Reformation, is almost overwhelming to the student, and rather increases than facilitates the labour of selecting the most noteworthy examples for a work like that in question. Here, however, valuable assistance might be obtained by a careful reference to certain works on hymnology by C. von Winterfeld, G. von Tucher, Hoffmann von Fallersleben, P. Wackernagel, and others.

Although congregational singing has been especially cultivated since the time of the Reformation, it is not foreign to the Roman Catholic Church; indeed, a very interesting collection might be made of old songs with the music occasionally performed by Roman Catholic congregations. With their spiritual songs and hymns in Latin, which were composed during the Middle Ages, they had sacred songs in their vernacular language dating from a period anterior to the Reformation. After having flourished, especially in Germany during the seventeenth century, the congregational singing of the Roman Catholic Church fell gradually more and more into disuse until the present century, when attempts to revive it have been made in some of the dioceses. The oldest known Roman Catholic hymn-book in German dates from the year 1517, and was compiled by Michael Vehe. It contains seventy-four tunes, some of which were especially composed for the book; the others were old and well-known tunes. However, the most comprehensive of the old collections of sacred songs for popular use dates from the year 1625, and was compiled by the Abbot David Gregorius Corner. Among the books of this description subsequently published are several which contain songs in the German language intended to be sung by the people at the principal church festivals, in processions, pilgrimages, and also at Holy Mass. On the last-mentioned occasion a hymn was sometimes introduced after the Transubstantiation. It was also not unusual on high festivals for the priest to sing in Latin, and the people to respond in German. The musical student would do well to acquaint himself with the modern publications of Roman Catholic songs, as for instance, 'Cantica Spiritualia,' Augsburg, 1825; 'Kirchen und religiöse Lieder aus dem 12 ten bis 15 ten Jahrhundert,' by J. Kehrein, Paderborn, 1853; the sacred songs collected by Freiherr von Ditfurth, Leipzig, 1855, and others.

Examples of elaborate vocal compositions, with or without instrumental accompaniment, generally performed by an appointed choir of singers and by professional musicians, would probably demand too much space in a compendium like that which has been suggested above; but, at all events, some account might be given of such compositions. Those belonging to the Roman Catholic Church are especially important. The most popular specimens should be pointed out. They are in many instances easily obtainable. True, the most popular ones are by no means generally also the best; but it would be desirable to ascertain accurately the popular taste of the present day.

As regards the Chorales of the Lutheran Church, it would be necessary to trace the alterations which they have undergone in the course of time. For this purpose the best Chorale books published in Germany during the 16th and 17th centuries would require especial attention; as for instance, those by Spangenberg, 1545; Prætorius, 1604; Hassler, 1607; Schein, 1627; Schütz, 1628; Crüger, 1640, and others. The division of Germany into many little principalities may be the chief cause of the enormous number of published collections of songs for congregational use, since every petty sovereign liked to have in his dominion something exclusive, and the people liked it too. Thus, there is no hymn-book which is universally adopted in the Lutheran Church of Germany, and many publications of the kind are but poor compilations,—at any rate, as far as the music is concerned. The noble Chorale of the time of Luther has gradually lost, by tamperings with its harmony and its rhythmical flow, much of its original dignity and impressiveness. It has suffered especially by the objectionable interludes which the organists introduced, and still introduce, not only between the verses, but also at every line which terminates with a pause in the musical notation. These interludes, which not unfrequently are extempore effusions of the organist, may afford him an opportunity to display his skill in counterpoint, and perhaps his manual dexterity; but they are for this reason all the more out of place in a Chorale. Still, as they constitute one of the characteristics of certain congregational musical performances of the present day, some examples of them should be given in the work.

Likewise the notation of a Chorale with a figured bass should not be omitted. A considerable number of Chorale books containing only the tunes with the bass, the harmony produced by the tenor and alto being indicated by figures, have been published chiefly for the use of organists, who of course may be supposed to be familiar with thorough-bass. In the year 1730, Georg Philip Telemann, in Hamburg, published his 'Fast allgemeines Evangelisch-Musicalisches Lieder-Buch,' which contains 433 Chorales; the different readings of the same tune, in use at that time, are indicated by small notes, and the tunes have a figured bass, with some instruction at the end of the book for inexperienced thorough-bass players.

The Chorales of the Hussites are especially deserving of investigation. Luther appreciated them highly, and several of them were adopted by the Protestants at the time of the Reformation. The Enchiridion, anno 1524, which has already been mentioned in another place,* contains two from this source. The earliest published collections of the Chorales of the Hussites, in which the poetry is in the Czech language, are: Jona Husa, Cantional, 1564; Girjka Streyce, Chorales with Goudimel's harmony, 1593; D. K. Karlsperka, Chorales, 1618. Noteworthy are likewise the songs of the Hussites collected and published by K. J. Erben, Prague, 1847. Also the following in German: A Chorale book of the Bohemian and Moravian Brethren, edited by Michael Weiss, 1531. The same enlarged by Johann Horn, 1596. A Chorale book of the Herrnhut Brethren, edited by Christian Gregor, 1784. Gregor, who was organist as well as bishop in Herrnhut, is the inventor, or originator, of the peculiar construction of the organ generally adopted by his sect, in which the player is seated so as to face the congregation. His publication, which contains 467 Chorales with figured basses, was the first work of its kind printed for the Herrnhut Brethren, and constituted the musical portion of their song-book printed in 1778.

Turning to the sacred poetry of the Reformed Church in Switzerland and France, we find a famous collection of metrical psalms in French, written at the request of Calvin by Clément Marot and Théodore de Bèze, to which tunes were composed or adapted, by Bourgeois, in 1547, and by Goudimel, in 1565. Some musical historians assert that

---

* Above, p. 15.

Bourgeois and Goudimel derived their tunes from a German collection by Wilhelm Franck, published in Strassburg in the year 1545, so that their merit consists only in having set them in four-part harmony. It would certainly be desirable to have the tunes properly traced to their original source.

Several of these old Chorales were gradually adopted by various denominations in different countries. A collection with the poetry in the Czech tongue, edited by G. Streyce in 1593, which has already been alluded to, corresponds exactly with a French edition published in Paris in the year 1567, which bears the title 'Les CL. Pseaumes de David, mis en rime Francoise par Clément Marot et Théodore de Bèze,' and in which the syllables of the Solmisation are printed with the notation of the tunes. On Marot's poetry with Goudimel's music is also founded the German Cantional entitled 'Psalter des Königlichen Propheten David,' by Ambrosius Lobwasser, Leipzig, 1574, a publication which was highly thought of in Germany, Switzerland, and Holland, and which retained its popularity until the eighteenth century.

Also the Italian Chorale book, entitled 'Sessanta Salmi di David, tradotti in rime volgari italiene, etc. De la stampa di Giovanni Battista,' Pinerolo, 1566, contains, besides a number of new tunes, several which have evidently been borrowed from the French work.

Again, the first edition of metrical psalms with musical notation for the Church of England, by Sternhold and Hopkins, London, 1562, contains several tunes derived from the Calvinists and Lutherans on the Continent. This edition has merely the melodies without any harmonious accompaniment, not even a bass. They were intended, as the title-page informs us, "to be sung in churches of the people together, before and after evening prayer, as also before and after sermon; and moreover in private houses, for their godly solace and comfort, laying apart all ungodly songs and ballads, which tend only to the nourishment of vice and corrupting of youth." In an edition dating from the year 1607 the syllables of the Solmisation are annexed to the musical notation, as we find it in Marot's version with Goudimel's music. This was intended as an assistance to unmusical singers; or, as the English publisher says, "that thou maiest the more easily, by the viewing of these letters, come to the knowledge of perfect solfayeng whereby thou mayest sing the psalms the more speedilie and easilie." Even the tablature of the lute is used in combination with the notation, in a curious English book entitled 'Sacred Hymns, consisting of fifty select Psalms of David and others, paraphrastically turned into English Verse, and by Robert Tailovr set to be sung in five parts, as also on the Viole and Lute or Orpharion. Published for the vse of such as delight in the exercise of Mvsic in hir original honour,' London, 1615.

The 'Chorale Book for England,' edited by W. S. Bennett and O. Goldschmidt, London, 1865, contains in a Supplement some tunes of English composers of the seventeenth and eighteenth centuries; while the great majority of the tunes of which the work is compiled have been taken from the famous old Chorale books of the Lutheran Church. It rather shows how, in the opinion of the compilers, the congregational music of the Church of England ought to be, than how it actually is at the present day. At all events, it cannot be regarded as a repository of the most favourite tunes of the majority of the congregations. The tunes preferred are often without originality, rather morbidly-sentimental, not unlike modern secular airs of a low kind. The collection of the tunes used by a congregation is not unfrequently a compilation by the organist. Many of the organists are but superficial musicians, while the clergymen generally know nothing about music. Performances of elaborate compositions are attempted, which would tax the power of well-trained professional musicians, and which the congregations would not think of attempting if they possessed musical knowledge. In fact, the only vocal music which a congregation is competent to perform in an edifying manner is a simple tune in a small compass, like the old Chorales, sung in unison, —or, more strictly speaking, sung by male and female voices in octaves,—while the organ accompanies in four-part harmony. To execute a tune well even thus, is more difficult than many imagine; but, if it is accomplished by the whole congregation, the effect is very solemn and impressive. The inquirer ought, of course, to examine the most popular collections of the present day, such as 'Hymns Ancient and Modern;' 'Church Hymns with Tunes,' edited by A. Sullivan, published under the direction of the Tract Committee of the Society for Promoting Christian Knowledge; and the comprehensive 'Hymnary' edited by J. Barnby. Moreover, regard should be taken to the preference given to certain kinds of musical performances by the several congregations of worshippers belonging to the Anglican Church, such as the High, the Low, the Broad Church-men.

The admission of secular tunes into the hymnology, which in the Anglican Church finds advocates even in the present century, has caused the publication of several curious collections of sacred poetry set to melodies taken from secular compositions of Haydn, Mozart, Beethoven, and other celebrated musicians, and often painfully distorted to adapt them to the metre of the verses. True, the adaptation of secular melodies for sacred songs is not a new expedient. It was resorted to by our estimable composers of chorales and promoters of congregational singing at the time of the Reformation. The old secular songs from which some of the chorales have been derived are still known, and it appears probable that several chorales, the origin of which is obscure, likewise emanated from this source. The secular origin of such old tunes does not detract from their suitableness for devotional service, since their secular ancestors are no longer popular, and also because three hundred years ago there was not the difference between the style of sacred and secular music which exists in our day. It is a very different thing to apply to sacred words a modern secular tune the secular words of which are well known.

Still, something similar was done by the Netherlandish composers of church music even long before chorales were constructed from secular tunes. These composers introduced the airs of popular songs into their Masses, to render their labours in counterpoint more attractive to the multitude.

About the middle of the sixteenth century, some noteworthy metrical versions of the psalms in Dutch were published in Antwerp. All the tunes of these psalms, given in notation, are derived from secular popular Dutch songs. Of this description is Symon Cock's publication, entitled 'Souter Liedekens ghemaect ter eeren Gods op alle die psalmen van David,' anno 1540. The most important work of the kind, however, was brought out by Tielman Susato. It probably comprises most of the secular airs and dance-tunes which were popular in the Netherlands during the sixteenth century. Tielman is supposed to have been a native of Soest, a town in Westphalia, Germany, which the citizens called in Latin *Susatum;* hence his adopted name Susato. His work consists of six small volumes, in oblong octavo, containing in all 245 tunes. The first volume is entitled: 'Het ierste musyck boexken mit vier Partyen daer inne begrepen zyn XXVIII. nieuue amoreuse liedekens in onser neder duytscher talen, gecomponeert by diuersche componisten, zeer lustig om singen en spelen op alle musicale Instrumenten. Ghedruckt Tantuuerpen by Tielman Susato vuonende uoer die nieuue vuaghe Inden Cromhorn. Cum Gratia et Privilegio. Anno MCCCCCLI.' ("The first Music Book, in four parts, wherein are contained 28 new lovely songs in our Low Dutch language, composed by different composers, very pleasant to sing and to play upon all kinds of musical instruments. Printed at Antwerp by Tielman Susato, dwelling in the Cromhorn over against the new Weighing house, anno 1551.") The Cromhorn (German, *Krummhorn;* Italian, *Cormorne*), an old wind-instrument of the bassoon family, was evidently used by Tielman Susato as a sign for his office, just as we find with the English music-sellers some centuries ago the sign of the "Base Viol," the "Golden Viol," &c. Volume II. contains likewise secular songs in four-part harmony. Volume III. contains a collection of dance tunes, called on the title-page "Basse dansen, Ronden, Allemaingien, Pauanen, Gaillarden," etc., and appeared with the preceding ones in the year 1551. The old Dutch dances were generally walked, or trodden, and the dancers sang at the same time.

Volume IV. bears the title: 'Sovter Liedekens, I. Het vierde musyck boexken mit dry Parthien, waer inne begrepen syn die Ierste XLI. psalmen van Dauid, Gecomponeert by Jacobus Clement non papa, den Tenor altyt houdende die voise van gemeyne bekende liedekens; Seer lustich om singen ter eeren Gods. Gedruckt Tantwerpen by Tielman Susato wonende voer die Nyeuwe waghe Inden Cromhorn. Anno 1556.' ("Sweet Songs, I. The fourth music book, in three parts, wherein are contained the first 41 Psalms of David, composed by Jacobus Clement non papa, the Tenor always having the air of commonly-known songs; very pleasant to sing to the honour of God. Printed at Antwerp, by Tielman Susato, dwelling in the Cromhorn over against the New Weighing house, anno 1556.") The other volumes likewise contain psalms with secular tunes arranged in the same way. Clement was a celebrated musical composer, who obtained the addition of *non papa* to his name, to guard against the possibility of his being mistaken for Pope Clement VII. his contemporary. The secular song from the air of which the three-part music has been constructed, is always indicated in the heading, by the first line of the secular song. For instance: 'Den eersten Psalm, *Beatus vir qui non*, etc; Nae die wyse, *Het was een clercxken dat ginck ter scholen.*' ("To the air: He was a little scholar who went to school.") 'Den XVIII. Psalm; Nae die wyse, *Ick had een ghestadich minneken.*' ("To the air: I had a stately sweetheart.")

Moreover, not only secular music, but also sometimes the poetry of a popular secular song, was altered for sacred use. H. Knaust published, in the year 1571, in Frankfurt: 'Gassenhawer, Reuter vnd Berglidlin Christlich moraliter vnnd sittlich verendert,' etc. ("Low Street Songs, Soldiers' and Miners' Songs, altered into Christian and moral Songs.")

No sect probably has been more extraordinary in the adoption of secular tunes than the Muggletonians in England. Lodowicke Muggleton and John Reeve founded this sect, in the year 1651. Macaulay, in his History of England, (London, 1854, Vol. I., Chap. 2) notices the former in terms by no means complimentary. He says: "A mad tailor, named Lodowicke Muggleton, wandered from pothouse to pothouse, tippling ale, and denouncing eternal torments against those who refused to believe, on his testimony, that the Supreme Being was only six feet high, and that the sun was just four miles from the earth." In the year 1829 Joseph and Isaac Frost published in London 'Divine Songs of the Muggletonians, in grateful praise to the Only True God the Lord Jesus Christ.' Many of the hymns are written to secular tunes, such as—*By a prattling stream on a midsummer's eve;—When I spent all my money I gained in the wars;—Cupid, god of soft persuasions;—Dear Cloe, come give me sweet kisses;* etc. The following commencements of a few of the hymns will suffice to show their character:—

                SONG VI.
Happy Muggletonians, who only
True faith have to receive;
Revelation ever new
Gave to great Muggleton and Reeve.

                SONG IX.
Hail! hail! two prophets great,
Whose message does relate
To the state of Adam's seed, etc.

                SONG CXXXIII.
I do believe in God alone,
Likewise in Reeve and Muggleton, etc.

In a work illustrating the musical performances of the various denominations even small and eccentric ones must not be omitted.

As regards the Protestant Church of the Scandinavians, the following remarks may perhaps serve as a guide for research:—Schiörring published in the year 1783 a Danish Chorale book, of which an improved edition, with figured basses, by P. E. Bach, appeared in 1794. An account of the old Swedish psalm-books of Swedberg, and others, is to be found in 'Den Nya Swenska Psalmboken framställd uti Försök till Swensk Psalmhistoria, af Johan Wilhelm Beckman,' Stockholm, 1845. A Lutheran hymn-book was printed in Skalholt, Iceland, in 1594, and went through many editions.

In the Baltic Provinces of Russia, J. L. E. Punschel published in Dorpat, in the year 1839, a Chorale book containing 364 different melodies in four-part harmony. A second edition appeared in 1843, and a third in 1850. Its title is—' Evangelisches Choralbuch, zunächst in Bezug auf die deutschen, lettischen, und esthnischen Gesangbücher der russischen Ostsee-Provinzen, auf den Wunsch Livländischen Provinzial-Synode bearbeitet und angefertigt.' The preface contains some interesting notices of the old hymnbooks formerly in use in Livonia, Esthonia and Courland.

The Greek Church of Russia obtained its music originally from Greece. The performances are entirely vocal, without instrumental accompaniment. Although the original music has in the course of time undergone several reforms, it is still very antique, characteristic, and beautiful. Among the works which have been written on the music of the Greek Church may be mentioned the following, which are more easily accessible to most musical inquirers in Western Europe than are the works written in the Russian language: Prince N. Youssoupoff published in the year 1862, in Paris, the first part of 'Histoire de la Musique en Russe,' which treats on 'Musique sacrée, suivi d'un choix de morceaux de Chants d'Eglise anciens et modernes.' Chaviara and Randhartinger published in 1859, at Vienna, a complete collection of the liturgical songs of the Greek Church, with the Greek words. Another work, being an 'Introduction to the Theory and Praxis of the Greek Church Music,' by Chrysanthos, written in Greek, was printed at Paris in 1821.

In Poland we have, besides the usual compositions of the Roman Catholic Church, some old books of metrical psalms with the music. The most noteworthy publication of this kind is by Nicolas Gomolka, dating from the year 1580. Gomolka was a celebrated Polish musician, who himself composed the psalms translated into his native language. A selection of them was published by Joseph Cichocki, Warsaw, 1838. Attention must also be drawn to a work by Ephraim Oloff, written in German, and entitled ' Liedergeschichte von Polnischen Kirchen-Gesängen,' etc., Danzig, 1744, which contains an account of the old Polish hymn-books. Furthermore, the Abbé Michel-Martin Mioduszewski published at Cracow, in 1838, a collection of ancient and modern songs used in the Roman Catholic

Church of Poland. To this work supplements have more recently been issued. He likewise published at Cracow, in 1843, a collection of Polish Christmas Carols with the tunes. It may be remarked here that Christmas Carols of high antiquity and originality are to be found among several European nations. Interesting collections of them have been published in France and in England.

Turning to America, in the United States we meet with a remarkable variety of hymn-books for the use of different sects, many of which are but poor compilations, musically as well as poetically. A little treatise by George Hood, entitled 'A History of Music in New England, with biographical sketches of Reformers and Psalmists,' Boston, 1846, is the earliest and most noteworthy publication containing an account of the hymn-books popular in the United States during the seventeenth and eighteenth centuries. The student ought likewise to consult 'Church Music in America, comprising its history and its peculiarities at different periods, with cursory remarks on its legitimate use and its abuse; with notices of the Schools, Composers, Teachers and Societies; by N. D. Gould,' Boston, 1853. There is also a circumstantial account of American psalmody in J. W. Moore's 'Encyclopædia of Music,' Boston, 1854. The first psalm-book used in New England was a small edition of Henry Ainsworth's version of the psalms, which the Puritans brought with them when they came to this country in the year 1620. It was published in England in 1618, and had tunes resembling the German Chorale, printed over the psalms, without harmony. The notation was in the lozenge or diamond shape, and without bars. The first book of metrical psalms published in America was compiled by thirty ministers, and appeared at Cambridge in the year 1640. It was, in fact, the first book printed in the English Colonies of America. It passed through many editions. G. Hood says: "The history of music in New England for the first two centuries is the history of Psalmody alone," and this accounts for his calling his little publication before mentioned a "History of Music," although it treats exclusively of psalmody. But, if a history of the music of

America should be written, it might commence with an account of the music, sacred and secular, of the aborigines, which, at any rate in Mexico, Central America, and Peru, had made some progress long before the arrival of the Puritans; and which, although it has not exercised any influence upon the cultivation of the music introduced into America from Europe, is well worthy of examination, inasmuch as it illustrates several curious questions relating to ethnology and national music. As in South and Central America the Indians, soon after the discovery of their countries, were appealed to by the Roman Catholic priests who made use of the help of sacred music, thus also in the United States the Protestant missionary, John Elliot, translated the psalms into Indian verse, and had them printed at Cambridge in 1661. The converted natives sung them with much fervour. Indeed, it is recorded that many of the Indians excelled as vocalists in the performance of the European tunes which had been taught them by the missionaries.

Among the enthusiastic promoters of congregational singing in that country, during the eighteenth century, deserves to be mentioned, William Billings, who, in 1770, published at Boston, 'The New England Psalm-Singer, or American Chorister; containing a Number of Psalm-tunes, Anthems and Canons, in four and five parts; never before published.' W. Billings, whose publications are recorded to have "opened a new era in the history of psalmody in the colonies," was in his youth a tanner by trade, and knew but little of the theory of music; nor did he care about it, although he composed sacred songs harmonized for different voices. The popularity which his productions obtained reveals the uncultivated taste of his contemporary countrymen. In his address "To all Musical Practitioners," he says: "Nature is the best dictator; for all the hard, dry, studied rules that ever were prescribed will not enable any person to form an air. . . . . For mine own part, as I do not think myself confined to any rules for composition laid down by any that went before me, neither should I think, were I to pretend to lay down rules, that any who came after me were any ways obliged to adhere to them any further than they should think proper. So, in fact, I think it best for every composer to be his own carver." And as to the effect of the music of his own "carving," he exclaims: "It has more than twenty times the power of the old slow tunes; each part straining for mastery and victory, the audience entertained and delighted, their minds surpassingly agitated and extremely fluctuated, sometimes declaring for one part and sometimes for another. Now, the solemn bass demands their attention—next, the manly tenor; now, the lofty counter—now, the volatile treble. Now here—now there —now here again. O, ecstatic! Rush on, ye sons of Harmony!"

In order to ascertain exactly the present condition of Church music in the United States, it is as necessary to refer to some of the tasteless publications of hymns, as to examine the valuable collections. The former are, however, only deserving of attention if they are very popular, or if they tend to illustrate the peculiarities of certain religious sects. The character of the following books is sufficiently indicated by their lengthy titles:—

'The Southern Harmony, and Musical Companion; containing a choice collection of Tunes, Hymns, Psalms, Odes, and Anthems, selected from the most eminent authors in the United States; together with nearly one hundred New Tunes which have never before been published; suited to most of the Metres contained in Watts's Hymns and Psalms, Mercer's Cluster, Dossey's Choice, Dover Selection, Methodist Hymn Book, and Baptist Harmony; and an easy Introduction to the Grounds of Music, and plain rules for Beginners. By William Walker. New Edition, thoroughly revised and greatly improved. Philadelphia, 1854.'

'The Golden Censer; A Musical offering to the Sabbath Schools, or Children's Hosannas to the Son of David; by W. B. Bradbury, author of the Golden Chain, Golden Shower, Oriola, Jubilee, Key-Note, etc., etc. New York, 1864.'

'Chapel Gems for Sunday Schools, selected from the Snow Bird, Robin, Red Bird, Dove and Blue Bird, by G. F. Root and B. R. Hanby; and from the Linnet, by F. W. Root and J. R. Murray. With additional pieces by D. P. Horton of Brooklyn, N. Y. Chicago, 1868.'

Publications of sacred songs for children, which are taught in school, especially deserve attention, inasmuch as they affect the musical taste of the people, and ensure the popularity of certain hymns.

Furthermore, the dances of the Shakers should be noticed, with examples of the songs to which they are performed. Sacred dancing was practised by the Hebrews at the time of King David, and is still one of the ceremonies observed by the Roman Catholic priests in the Cathedral of Seville, by the Dervishes of the Mohammedans, and by several pagan nations. It would be desirable to ascertain exactly the reason, or biblical warrant, which induces Christian sects to advocate its practice.

An interesting collection of Negro songs, mostly sacred, entitled 'Slave Songs of the United States,' was published at New York in the year 1867. The songs, which are from different districts of the United States, contain the musical notation with the words, and were collected by W. F. Allen, C. P. Ware, and L. M. Garrison. This curious publication supplies us with some information respecting the religious vocal performances of the American negroes, and the intense fervour which is displayed by the worshippers while they are singing. Moreover, they have also a kind of sacred dance, called "The Shout," which consists in shuffling round, one after the other, in a ring, with a jerking, hitching motion, which agitates the entire shouter, while they sing in chorus a "Spiritual." These performances are especially in favour with the Baptist negroes. The tunes, some of which exhibit traces of an African origin, are extremely interesting.

The Negro Baptists at Richmond, in Virginia, have in their church a choir consisting of about forty singers. An Englishman, who attended their service, records: "The voices were exquisitely sweet, well deserving the praise which I heard accorded to them. The hymn selected concluded with these words and direction :—

> 'Give the hand of friendship ere we part,
> May heaven now embalm it in each heart!'

> (*Rise, and clasp hands.*)

"Acting on this the large congregation, for the church was full, rose and clasped each other's hands."*

From the reports of missionaries in different parts of the world it would appear that the converted pagans not unfrequently prove excellent psalm-singers. Sometimes their own tunes have with good result been adapted to the sacred poetry translated for them into their native language. This, for instance, has been done in the 'Hindustani Choral Book, or Swar Sangrah; containing the Tunes to those Hymns in the Gi't Sangrah which are in Native Metres; compiled by John Parsons;' Benares, 1861. This book contains ninety Hindu tunes, most of which are evidently of secular origin. We therefore find here an expedient resorted to somewhat similar to that which we have observed with the Dutch more than three centuries ago.

Again, to render the survey more complete, it would be requisite to incorporate into it some specimens of church music of the Christian Abyssinians, Copts, Armenians, and other Eastern sects who possess peculiar liturgies, and notations of their sacred songs or chants.

The value of the collection might be further increased by an introductory essay surveying the sacred musical performances of non-Christian religions. Here the synagogical songs of the Jews, the chants of the Mohammedans, and the musical performances in the temples of the Buddhists and the Brahmins, would require special consideration: but the music used in the ceremonies of the pagan religions of the least civilized races should not be left unnoticed.

END OF VOL. I.

---

* 'A Vacation Tour in the United States and Canada,' by C. R. Weld; London, 1855, p. 295.

www.ingramcontent.com/pod-product-compliance
Lightning Source LLC
Chambersburg PA
CBHW021819230426
43669CB00008B/805